Working with Vulnerable Families

Working with Vulnerable Families embodies the universal edict – that for societies to flourish we must enhance the opportunities for our children to reach their physical, intellectual, emotional and social potential. For families facing issues of marginalisation, poverty, domestic violence, drug and alcohol dependence or mental illness, such ideals can seem particularly daunting. In a thoroughly candid and engaging style, this groundbreaking text transcends narrow professional boundaries to demonstrate how those working in diverse health, education and social welfare settings can work collaboratively with one another and with parents to protect, nurture and support young children from birth to eight years.

The book draws together a broad range of research-based theory, practice wisdom and successful real-world exemplars to explicate the core values, knowledge and skills required when working with families with multiple and complex needs. A range of pedagogy is employed, including reflective questions and activities to encourage analysis, inspire ideas, and prompt both student and experienced service provider to engage with best practice to protect young children within a family-centred milieu.

Dr Fiona Arney is Deputy Director and Senior Research Fellow at the Australian Centre for Child Protection at the University of South Australia.

Professor Dorothy Scott is the Foundation Chair of Child Protection and Director of the Australian Centre for Child Protection at the University of South Australia.

Working with Vulnerable Families

A partnership approach

Edited by
Fiona Arney and Dorothy Scott

CAMBRIDGE
UNIVERSITY PRESS

CAMBRIDGE UNIVERSITY PRESS
Cambridge, New York, Melbourne, Madrid, Cape Town, Singapore,
São Paulo, Delhi, Dubai, Tokyo

Cambridge University Press
477 Williamstown Road, Port Melbourne, VIC 3207, Australia

Published in the United States of America by Cambridge University Press, New York

www.cambridge.org
Information on this title: www.cambridge.org/9780521744461

First published 2010

Cover design by Liz Nicholson/DesignBite
Typeset by Aptara Corp.
Printed in China by C&C Offset Printing CO., Ltd

A catalogue record for this publication is available from the British Library

National Library of Australia Cataloguing in Publication data

> Scott, Dorothy.
> Working with vulnerable families : a partnership approach / editors, Fiona Arney,
> Dorothy Scott.
> 9780521744461 (pbk.)
> Includes index.
> Family services.
> Poor families–Services for.
> Child welfare.
> Arney, Fiona (Fiona Marie)
> Scott, Dorothy.
> 362.828

ISBN 978-0-521-74446-1 paperback

This book is dedicated to our partners, Kenneth Wilson and Alan Clayton.

Foreword

Nelson Mandela suggested that the soul of a nation was reflected in how well it treated its most vulnerable; Hilary Clinton used an old African saying for the title of a book 'it takes a village to raise a child'. Both quotes are pertinent to this book.

We live in a world of pressures – to earn lots of money, to be smart, to be successful, to look like a film star, to have a big house, to cook like a TV hostess, to eat like a king, to work long hours, to have lots of stuff – where are our children in all of this frenetic activity? How can we be parents as well as workers? Where are our role models? How valued are the carers of our children? How much do we value children for themselves? What if my child does not look or behave like the one on the back of the Farex packet smiling sweetly at dinnertime? Does anyone care? The authors of this book do and they have taken a determined and well-researched path to help us to understand and help vulnerable families in today's challenging society.

I feel honoured to have been asked to write the foreword for this wonderful book which is so very timely for Australian parents, children and those who work in the range of services aimed at helping them grow through the most vulnerable times of their lives. The book has emerged from the Australian Centre for Child Protection at the University of South Australia and under the wise and kind 'head, heart and hands' of Dorothy Scott and her very able colleagues. Dorothy was the first (and still only) Professor of Child Protection in Australia and her work and that of her Centre has been a wonderful blend of research, advocacy, practitioner training and support.

The public health approach to child abuse and neglect suggested here is a sensible and urgent one; to continue to observe the increases in child abuse substantiations and to only respond to the crisis end in punitive ways is both illogical and inhumane. Approaches that attempt to prevent families reaching such crisis situations and that harness all possible ways to enhance family functioning in this challenging 21st century are clearly the way that child abuse and neglect will be reduced. A public health approach to child maltreatment means that we need to know the causes, to intervene in effective ways along the various pathways and to build the capacity of practitioners to do so.

I appreciate the ways in which the book relates the understandings of how children and parents interact and develop and how for so many families the challenges of parenting make the family vulnerable due to a variety of different scenarios. Understanding these contexts is essential if we are to deliver the services that will really help. I have just become a grandmother, which is a joy beyond imagination and this little one is surrounded by love and care, easily accessing his child health nurse, having a good GP and already planning his nursery placement. I often imagine the circumstances of other children not so blessed and feel anguished for them and their families.

From the various chapters emerge a holistic, sensible, caring and evidence-based set of approaches to help vulnerable families with many real life examples of what works best. Although this has an Australian focus (good for us that we have at last some great home-grown examples!), this book is relevant for all children, all families and communities everywhere. The principles apply wherever children are being born and nurtured.

Professor Fiona Stanley AC
Director, Telethon Institute for Child Health Research
Professor, School of Paediatrics and Child Health,
The University of Western Australia

Contents

Figures, tables and boxes

Figures

Tables

Boxes

Contributors

Fiona Arney

Dr Fiona Arney is the Deputy Director of the Australian Centre for Child Protection at the University of South Australia. Fiona is a member of research teams examining the factors affecting the use of research in policy and practice and the organisational and individual preconditions required for the adoption and adaptation of promising practices. She has over 12 years' experience as a researcher in the areas of parenting support, child protection and child and adolescent mental health and well-being.

Dorothy Scott

Professor Dorothy Scott is the Foundation Chair of Child Protection and the inaugural Director of the Australian Centre for Child Protection at the University of South Australia. Her clinical practice has been in the fields of child welfare, sexual assault and mental health. Her research has also been in these areas as well as in the fields of maternal and child health, and child protection policy reform. She has been an advisor to national and state governments, and for her services to the community she was awarded the Medal of the Order of Australia and the Centenary Medal.

Sylvia Asay

Dr Sylvia Asay is a lecturer of marriage and family relationships and cross-cultural family patterns at the University of Nebraska at Kearney. She has co-authored and co-edited two books and several articles and book chapters using the family strengths perspective.

Maria Barredo

Maria Barredo is the Managing Director of Barredo Holland, which offers migration advice, settlement and cross-cultural training, and is a cross-cultural facilitator and cultural competency trainer with over 20 years of experience working with migrant and refugee communities. She was a member of the South Australian Multicultural and Ethnic Affairs Commission (from 2003–08) and a national chair of women's policy with the Federation of Ethnic Communities Council of Australia for four years.

Kerrie Bowering

Kerrie Bowering is the Director of the Child and Family Health Service (CaFHS), a community-based division of the Children, Youth and Women's Health Service in South Australia offering the Family Home Visiting Program. Kerrie has a health and management background, and experience in service delivery, planning and development.

Leah Bromfield

Dr Leah Bromfield is the Manager of the National Child Protection Clearinghouse at the Australian Institute of Family Studies. She has broad research interests and experience in the fields of child abuse prevention, child protection and out-of-home care. Her areas of specialty are child protection systems, chronic maltreatment and cumulative harm, and research into policy/practice.

Alwin Chong

Alwin Chong, Wakamin descendent from North Queensland, is Senior Research and Ethics Officer for the Aboriginal Health Council of South Australia. He is responsible for the development and implementation of a research agenda that identifies Aboriginal and Torres Strait Islander communities' research topics rather than academically driven research topics. Alwin manages the Aboriginal Health Research Ethics Committee and is a member of the National Health and Medical Research Council (NHMRC) HoMER Indigenous Working Group.

Marie Connolly

Dr Marie Connolly is the Chief Social Worker within the New Zealand Government. She has published extensively in her area of scholarship, including eight books, most recently *Child Death by Maltreatment* (2007), *Morals, Rights and Practice in the Human Services* (2008), and *Social Work: Contexts and Practice* (2009). She has a particular interest in the development of rights-based practices in the context of child and family welfare.

John DeFrain

Dr John DeFrain is Professor of Family Science at the University of Nebraska at Lincoln, holds an Honorary Appointment as Conjoint Professor of Family Studies at the University of Newcastle, Australia and serves as a Research Scientist in the Center for Family Studies, Shanghai Academy of Social Sciences, People's Republic of China. John has co-authored and co-edited 24 books from a strengths-based perspective and his research on families has also been published in more than 100 professional articles in books, journals and extension publications.

Edwina Farrall

Dr Edwina Farrall recently gained a PhD in developmental psychology from the University of Adelaide, focusing on examining theories and methodologies to explicate children's optimism. She has a strong research interest in the use of social marketing as a means of preventing child maltreatment and has undertaken research exploring the degree to which psychology students' tertiary training equips them to work effectively in the field of child protection.

Richard Fletcher

Dr Richard Fletcher is Leader of the Fathers and Families Research Program at the Family Action Centre, Faculty of Health, University of Newcastle, New South Wales. He pioneered domestic violence prevention within health promotion and initiated men's and boys' health as areas of study in Australia.

Judi Geggie

Judi Geggie is Director of the Family Action Centre (FAC) at the University of Newcastle. During her 22 years at the FAC, Judi has developed and managed a diverse range of family and community programs for groups and individuals in the community who experience marginalisation or invisibility. As Director of the FAC, Judi has strengthened the Centre's capacity to provide training and support to community service organisations in research and evaluation in order to enhance practice.

Christine Gibson

Christine Gibson is a Research Fellow at the Australian Centre for Child Protection at the University of South Australia. Her practice has been in the fields of child and family welfare, out-of-home care, domestic violence, tenancy and immigration. As well as substantial experience with both the conduct and oversight of studies evaluating service interventions, she has conducted research on out-of-home care and the application of diffusion of innovation theory to child welfare.

Virginia Healy

Virginia Healy is currently the Program Manager for Service Development and Strategic Support at Nunkuwarrin Yunti, the Aboriginal community control-led health service for metropolitan Adelaide. Virginia has worked closely with the Aboriginal cultural consultants and other key management and service delivery staff to ensure cultural appropriateness of the design and establish-ment of the Family Home Visiting Program for Aboriginal families.

Prue Holzer

Prue Holzer is a Senior Research Analyst at the Productivity Commission. She has conducted research, published and presented on a range of child and fam-ily social policy issues, including: trends in child protection data and child and family welfare policy across Australia; research use in the Australian child and family welfare sector; evaluating the effectiveness of child abuse prevention programs; and triggers for on-going conflict after separation and divorce.

Ruth Lange

Ruth Lange works in a clinical and project position as a mental health nurse in Families SA, South Australia's statutory child protection service. She is a registered general nurse and mental health nurse with 30 years' experience in nursing.

Kerry Lewig

Kerry Lewig is the Research Coordinator at the Australian Centre for Child Protection, University of South Australia. Her research interests include work satisfaction, engagement, work stress and burnout in the services and volunteer sectors, research informed policy and practice, and the role of organisational change in this process.

Helen McLaren

Dr Helen McLaren is Senior Social Worker with Child Protection Services at the Women's and Children's Hospital, South Australia. Helen's key research interests have centred on oppression, exclusion, disadvantage, inequity, shame, blame and silencing. She has utilised her clinical experience with victims of childhood sexual abuse and domestic violence in her research in this area.

Mary Salveron

Mary Salveron is undertaking her PhD in Psychology at the University of South Australia. Mary's research interests include barriers and facilitators to parental contact and visitation, evaluating programs for parents whose children are in care, supporting parenting in refugee communities, and examining the literature on the 'diffusion of innovations'.

Graham Vimpani

Professor Graham Vimpani is Professor and Head of the Discipline of Paediatrics and Child Health at the University of Newcastle; Clinical Chair of Kaleidoscope: Hunter Children's Health Network within the Hunter New England Area Health Service; and Medical Director of the Child Protection Team of the John Hunter Children's Hospital in Newcastle. He is a community paediatrician with a long-standing interest in promoting child health and development through a range of early intervention strategies that address the support needs of families with infants and young children. He is co-chair of the Children's and Young People's Health Priority Task Force in New South Wales; a member of the Health Care Advisory Council; and is Chair of the Board of NIFTeY Australia (the National Investment for the Early Years) – a cross-sectoral advocacy body established in 1999 to promote greater awareness of the importance of the early years of life.

Bob Volkmer

Bob Volkmer is currently the Strategic Manager, Service Improvement for Children, Youth and Women's Health Service, South Australia. He has published numerous peer-reviewed articles across a range of child health issues ranging from child injury prevention to childhood asthma and childhood obesity, and has a strong interest in evidence-based planning and in the translation of research into policy and practice.

Carole Zufferey

Dr Carole Zufferey is a lecturer at the School of Psychology, Social Work and Social Policy, University of South Australia. She has been employed as a social work practitioner, researcher and educator over the past 20 years. She has experience in diverse practice areas such as child protection, aged care, disability, mental health, domestic violence, women's employment and homelessness.

Acknowledgements

We would like to thank the following people for their contributions to the book:

The families, practitioners, policy makers and researchers who have given so much towards our efforts. By participating in our research, by sharing their wisdom and knowledge and by collaborating with us in our endeavours, they have made a great contribution to the lives of vulnerable children and their families.

Our colleagues at the Australian Centre for Child Protection for their assistance in preparing the manuscript and particularly to Elizabeth Oram for coordinating our efforts and compiling the final draft.

Our friends and families for their valuable support and patience during our writing efforts.

We would also like to acknowledge the following funding sources for their contributions to the research presented in specific chapters of this book:

The Australian Research Alliance for Children and Youth (ARACY) Australian Research Council (ARC)/National Health and Medical Research Council (NHMRC) 'Future Generation' Research Network Encouragement Grant that in part funded work towards the literature review in Chapter 6.

The South Australian Department for Families and Communities for their funding of the Working with Refugee Families Project described in Chapter 8 and the evaluation of the Mental Health Liaison Project outlined in Chapter 9.

Good Beginnings Australia for funding the evaluation of the Parents Plus Playgroups Program presented in Chapter 11.

The Australian Research Council for supporting the research examining the diffusion of innovations across Australia reported in Chapter 13. This research was supported under the Australian Research Council's Linkage Projects funding scheme (project number LP0669297).

Fiona Arney and Dorothy Scott

Introduction

Fiona Arney and Dorothy Scott

The challenge of ending child abuse is the challenge of breaking the link between adults' problems and children's pain.

(UNICEF, A League Table of Child Maltreatment Deaths in Rich Nations, September 2003)

This book is about working with vulnerable parents so that we might prevent child abuse and neglect and enhance the well-being of our children.

Who are 'vulnerable families'? In this book, when we refer to families we are talking about children and the adults who care for them, be they mothers, fathers, grandmothers, grandfathers or other extended family members. If we are honest, all parents will acknowledge times when they have felt very vulnerable and their feelings of vulnerability have impacted upon family life. The birth of a child is a joyous event but brings with it a time of significant change and disruption to families as well as the need for adjustment which some parents may find overwhelming. Parents can also experience vulnerability when facing natural disasters such as fire or flood; stressful life events such as marital breakdown; the illness or death of a family member or friend; the loss of a job or eviction and so on. Life challenges such as these can overwhelm a family's ability to cope, but for some, it may also provide opportunities for growth and positive change.

All families differ in their ability to manage difficult challenges and have different internal and external resources to draw upon. Internal resources such as good family attachments, cohesion and communication, and external resources such as good social support and financial security have all been shown to help families manage difficult times. Some parents are doubly blessed. Those having grown up in stable and nurturing families are more likely to have a supportive extended family to help as they embark on raising their own children. Other parents are not so lucky. Many have not had a childhood grounded in a stable and nurturing family and this may be compounded by having to raise their own children in the absence of a supportive extended family. History, as we know, is not destiny and many parents who have suffered deprivation in their childhood do make strong supportive 'kin-like' relationships with friends and neighbours who provide support to both them and their children.

There are some situations in which a family's needs cannot be met from within their own resources or their kith and kinship networks and where services can make a valuable contribution to child and family well-being. In this book we explore some of the knowledge, skills and strategies that service providers need in order to work successfully with parents and families, including those with multiple and complex needs who are trying to nurture young children in the face of adversity.

The knowledge and skills required for this work rest on a foundation of values. The values we bring to our work and those of the wider society are fundamental in determining the level of respect and compassion shown to families. Embedded in many of the interventions we look at in this book you will find the principles of 'relationship-based practice' that are founded on empathy, respect, genuineness and optimism.

The opening chapters of the book provide a broad overview of some of the key ideas and conceptual frameworks that inform our practice with families. These include selected dimensions from bodies of knowledge on: child well-being and resilience; cross-cultural understandings of family strengths; and organisational and inter-organisational processes. Some readers will already be familiar with some of this content while for others this may be new.

In Chapter 1, Dorothy Scott, Fiona Arney and Graham Vimpani investigate the importance of considering the child, their family and community strengths and supports in working with vulnerable families. They explore the bio-psychosocial impacts upon children's development and well-being and describe the relevance of ecological and family-centred frameworks to practice with children and their families.

John DeFrain, Sylvia Asay and Judi Geggie expand the focus on the family using a strengths-based approach in Chapter 2. The chapter highlights the importance of identifying and developing family, community and cultural strengths when working with vulnerable families. Several examples from Australia and overseas are given of family strengths-based approaches.

Chapter 3 examines a related framework for relationship-based practice with children and families – resilience-based practice. In this chapter, Edwina Farrall and Fiona Arney examine models of resilience developed internationally and through the voice of practitioners examine the utility of one such model in practice with Australian families.

In Chapter 4, Dorothy Scott describes the way in which the 'think child, think family, think community' approach to working with families with complex needs requires enhanced practitioner skills and knowledge as well as mechanisms for building bridges between services. In the latter half of the chapter, she identifies the potential conflicts (and suggested strategies) that can occur between and within organisations, between professions, and between and within individuals when working with families with multiple and complex needs.

Building on the conceptual foundation of the first four chapters, we then explore a broad range of promising approaches aimed at assisting vulnerable families. Most of these are programs which the Australian Centre for Child Protection has been involved in evaluating. Others, such as those on family group conferencing and working with fathers, have been written by invited authors with special expertise in these areas.

These chapters are presented such that those that are more preventive in their orientation and based in universal services come first and those that are more specialist and remedial in their orientation follow. The range of interventions examined in the book covers the spectrum of primary, secondary and tertiary prevention. These terms come from the field of public health. Primary prevention services are usually 'universal' or accessible to all families. For example, local child and family health services, pre-schools and primary schools are ideal settings to reach all families. Secondary prevention services are offered to families who may be at greater risk or who already show signs of struggling – by intervening early it is hoped that a service might help to prevent the situation deteriorating. These can be offered from the 'platform' of universal services or from a more specialised service setting. Tertiary prevention services respond to the needs of families once there is already an established problem and typically involve specialist or statutory services, where the objective is to reduce the harm it has caused and to prevent its recurrence.

While we do not want to suggest that social problems, such as child neglect, should be thought of as diseases, we think that a public health approach is useful for three reasons. One, it draws our attention to the environment as well as the individual. Two, it emphasises prevention as well as remediation. And three, wherever possible, it is based on evidence.

In Chapter 5, Dorothy Scott describes the important role of early childhood services in working with vulnerable families to give children the best start to life. This chapter presents a range of innovative exemplars of working with families in early childhood settings.

Another example of such an initiative is described in more detail in Chapter 6 wherein Fiona Arney, Kerrie Bowering, Alwin Chong, Virginia Healy and Bob Volkmer examine the ways in which the Family Home Visiting Program has been able to provide culturally appropriate support and assistance to Aboriginal families with a newborn in metropolitan South Australia.

Richard Fletcher presents the rationale for working with fathers in vulnerable families in Chapter 7, including the unique contribution they can make to their children's development and well-being. In this chapter he describes strategies and programs for working with fathers in a range of settings including home-based programs for fathers whose partners have post-natal depression and a program to end violent and abusive behaviours.

In Chapter 8 Kerry Lewig, Fiona Arney, Mary Salveron and Maria Barredo describe the contextual and cultural challenges in relation to parenting in a new culture for families from refugee backgrounds. They describe the results of qualitative research with child protection practitioners and members of eight community groups with refugee experiences, examining the role of the government in parenting, the need for culturally sensitive and family-inclusive practice in child and family services and strategies to support parents from refugee and migrant backgrounds in Australia.

Chapter 9 shifts the focus towards secondary and tertiary prevention strategies, with Fiona Arney, Ruth Lange and Carole Zufferey describing the need for intersectoral approaches for families with complex needs involved with the child protection system. The Mental Health Liaison Project is used as a program exemplar to illustrate the ways in which child protection and adult mental health services can work together with the aim of improving outcomes for children and their families who come to the attention of child protection services and where there are concerns about parental mental health.

Marie Connolly also explores the engagement and involvement of families in decision making when child protection concerns have been identified. In Chapter 10 she examines the role of the New Zealand Family Group Conferencing model in empowering families (including extended family members) to make and enact decisions about the safety and well-being of children.

Chapter 11 focuses on strategies for supporting parents to have a role in their children's lives after children have been removed from their care. Mary Salveron, Kerry Lewig and Fiona Arney particularly focus on the role of groups in supporting parents who have had their children removed and present the findings from the evaluation of one such initiative in South Australia – the Good Beginnings Australia Parents Plus Playgroups.

The last part of the book considers three key issues relating to the sustainability and wider impact of promising programs: how to utilise research in our practice and programs and how to facilitate the spread of innovative ideas and approaches such as those we investigate in this book.

In the current context of moves towards evidence-based policy and practice, in Chapter 12 Fiona Arney, Kerry Lewig, Leah Bromfield and Prue Holzer describe the implications of this for those working in the Australian child and family services sector. The potential use and misuse of research in practice and policy is highlighted and the chapter presents a range of strategies to support practitioners to critique and incorporate knowledge from a range of sources with the aim of improving outcomes for their clients.

In the final chapter, Kerry Lewig, Fiona Arney, Mary Salveron, Helen McLaren, Christine Gibson and Dorothy Scott highlight the challenges and opportunities for the adoption and adaptation of the innovative practices and programs presented throughout the book. Specific examples are given of programs that have spread, contrasted with those that have remained largely in their original sites. The role of evidence, champions, funding, networks and luck are examined as key features of elements of program adoption, replication and sustainability.

The book has been written with a diverse range of readers in mind – for students and practitioners from different disciplines and fields of service, health, education and social services, and encompassing both traditionally 'child-focused' and 'adult-focused' sectors, who are interested in family-focused, child-sensitive practice. We also hope that the book will be of interest to supervisors, team leaders and managers of services, as well as policy makers and professional educators.

All contributors to this book bring research to bear on the challenges of working with vulnerable families whilst appreciating that working with families requires a special synthesis of head, heart and hands. We hope we have captured something of our deep respect for this complex and creative work, and for the compassion and commitment of those who work with and walk alongside parents who struggle in the face of adversity to nurture their children.

Think child, think family, think community

Dorothy Scott, Fiona Arney and Graham Vimpani

Learning goals

This chapter will enable you to:

1. Be aware of some of the bio-psychosocial factors and conceptual frameworks which affect child well-being and the capacity of families to nurture young children
2. 'Think child, think family and think community' in the way you might work
3. Appreciate the centrality of 'relationship-based practice'
4. Identify the values, knowledge and skills you bring to working with vulnerable families, and reflect on areas in which you may have gaps.

Introduction

Promoting child development, well-being and safety relies upon the ability to 'think child, think family and think community'. Our knowledge about how biological, psychological and social factors interact to influence the development and well-being of children has never been greater. In a growing number of countries, this knowledge has led to intense interest in early childhood, motivated both by social justice concerns as well as an increasing awareness that the economic future of a society depends on the degree to which its children are healthy, educated and well-adjusted.

Some children are exposed to a volatile mix of poverty, violence, parental mental illness and substance dependence that can erode the capacity of families to nurture their children, causing intense suffering and long-term harm. There are a number of conceptual frameworks and ideas that enable us to understand this, including an ecological model of human development.

Family-centred practice is based on four elements: the centrality of the family as the unit of attention; maximising families' choices; a strengths rather than a deficits perspective; and cultural sensitivity. The quality of the worker–family relationship is the cornerstone of family-centred practice. The key practitioner qualities of empathy, respect, genuineness and optimism are vital to working with vulnerable families.

We each bring a unique combination of personal qualities and values, knowledge and skills to our work. It is important for us to identify our strengths as well as the areas in which further professional development or the expertise of others may be required if we are to serve families and their children well.

Descriptive knowledge

We now know a lot about the long-term consequences of different forms of childhood adversity (including child abuse and neglect, witnessing domestic violence, parental mental illness and parental substance dependence) on adult physical and mental health (Middlebrooks & Audage, 2007). And it takes only a little imagination and the willingness to listen to those who were, or are still, exposed to such adversity, to understand the intensity of suffering that children in such situations can experience.

We also know quite a lot about the factors associated with the resilience of some children to such adversity. This is discussed in Chapter 3, along with some of the implications for practice.

The breadth of the knowledge which helps us to understand the many influences on children's development and well-being is nicely captured in the title of the book *From Neurons to Neighborhoods* (Shonkoff & Phillips, 2000), auspiced by the US National Research Council and Institute of Medicine of the National Academies. Based on the work of 17 experts from a broad range of disciplines, the key conclusions of this publication are worth stating:

- The nature–nurture debate is obsolete
- Early intervention can improve the odds for vulnerable children
- How young children feel is as important as how they think
- Nurturing and dependable relationships are crucial
- Culture influences development via childrearing beliefs and practices
- There is little evidence that 'special stimulation' leads to 'advanced brain development' in infancy.

Reflective questions

Do you know more about the biological, psychological or social factors influencing child and family well-being? What might be the advantages and disadvantages of your particular knowledge base? How might you address any major knowledge gaps you can identify?

Genetic influences

There is growing evidence that many of the long-term consequences of childhood adversity are, at least in part, a result of interactions between environmental experience and our genetic make-up. For example, Caspi et al. (2003) found that the risks of later depression in children who had been abused were greater in those who had two copies of the short variant of a gene involved in serotonin transmission (5-HTT). Those with two copies of the long variant of the gene had no increased risk of depression, whilst those with one of each had intermediate risks.

   More recently, McGowan and colleagues (2009) found that individuals who suicided as adults following a history of childhood abuse had differences in a neuron-specific glucocorticoid receptor promoter that is associated with the functioning of one of the major stress response systems (HPA), compared with those who suicided without a history of childhood abuse or died from accidental causes. Specifically, they found that hippocampal NR3C1 gene expression was reduced in suicide victims who had been abused as children compared with victims who had not been abused, or those who had died from accidental causes. The effect of this is to increase activation of the HPA stress response system.

Parent–child attachment

The human attachment system is said to work when children behave in ways that enable them to stay close to adult caregivers who can give a secure base from which to explore the world. Children are said to build 'internal working models' of their own self-worth from how they experience and see their caregivers' abilities and readiness to provide security and protection. In this way children can build different types of attachment relationships with different caregivers. Children who are not provided with sensitive and responsive caregiving are unable to build working models that will result in secure attachment behaviours and will experience less adaptive forms of attachment to their caregiver/s. These are likely to influence not only their relationships with their caregivers but also subsequent relationships with significant others. Attachment patterns in the early years while associated with later outcomes are not necessarily deterministic. Research has shown that children can still develop positively despite receiving early caregiving that is deficient, as long as subsequent caregiving experiences are warm and loving and provide a secure base (Bacon & Richardson, 2001).

For a long time there has been abundant evidence on the importance of parent–child attachment, which is itself influenced by complex biological, psychological and social factors. From the early work of John Bowlby in the 1950s on attachment and separation anxiety in infants and young children (Bowlby, 1953), to recent work on breastfeeding as a protective factor in relation to maternal neglect (Strathearn et al., 2009), researchers have helped to identify the factors which enhance or impair parent–child attachment. As Daniel Siegel says:

> *Human infants have an inborn, genetically determined motivational system that drives them to become attached to their caregivers. Although infants become attached to their caregivers whether or not those caregivers are sensitive and responsive, attachment thrives especially on predictable, sensitive, attuned communication in which a parent shows an interest in, and aligns states of mind with those of a child…Early attachment experiences directly affect the development of the brain (Kraemer, 1992)…Human connections create neuronal connections…Caregivers are the architects of the way in which experience influences the unfolding of genetically pre-programmed but experience-dependent brain development…These salient emotional relationships have a direct effect on the development of the domains of mental functioning that serve as our conceptual anchor points: memory, narrative, emotion, representations and states of mind. In this way, attachment relationships may serve to create the central foundation from which the mind develops. Insecure attachment may serve as a significant risk factor in the development of psychopathology (Jones, Main & Del Carman, 1996). Secure attachment, in contrast, appears to confer a form of emotional resilience (Rutter, 1997).*

> *(Siegel, 1999, pp. 93–4)*

Some of the implications of attachment theory and research for working with vulnerable families and children, where there is impaired attachment, have been identified (Howe et al., 1999). The preventive implications of this knowledge are also gaining greater interest. For example, Boukydis (2006) has outlined how health professionals can use ultrasound consultation to enhance the attachment of mothers to their unborn babies, decrease maternal anxiety and increase positive attitudes toward health during pregnancy.

Following birth, the Circle of Security Model, a video-based intervention aimed at strengthening parental capacity to observe and respond to their infants (www.circleofsecurity.org), is gaining currency. The Circle of Security Model is an early intervention approach which can be taught to a broad range of practitioners in health, early childhood education and social service settings. Chapter 6 outlines parental responses to a nurse home-visiting service that uses the principles of the Circle of Security Model when working with Aboriginal families and their infants.

Experience-based brain development

There have been great advances in our understanding of the way in which children's early experiences of their world continuously interact with genetic predispositions to shape the architecture and function of the brain. These experiences begin before birth and, if healthy and stimulating, can help establish brain architecture that 'operates at full genetic potential'. Conversely adverse experience leads to 'weak brain architecture with impaired capabilities' (National Scientific Council on the Developing Child, 2007, p. 3).

Brain growth following birth is rapid and is made up of the establishment of myriads of connections between brain cells and supportive tissue. With the exception of brain cells in the hippocampus, a part of the brain involved in memory, new cells are not added after birth. As young children get older, the pathways between cells are pruned down on a 'use it or lose it' principle.

It is important to recognise that the parts of our brain that are responsible for different sets of functions (e.g. language, memory of recent events, memory of facial expressions, planning and emotional responsiveness) mature at different times. Thus sensitive periods occur at different ages for different parts of the brain (Gogtay et al., 2004). Further, the pathways involved in processing lower levels of information mature earlier than those processing higher level information (Burkhalter, Bernardo & Charles, 1993). The performance of higher level pathways in turn builds on the functionality of lower level pathways. Experiences encountered by young children need to be age appropriate as children's abilities to interpret what they experience change over time as their pathways are built. For example, looking at pictures and not focusing on written words is important for a toddler.

The nature of the relationships in the child's world and the level of stress experienced have important roles in fine-tuning brain architecture. Adverse early experiences can have damaging effects on the way the brain develops (Nelson, 2007; Rice & Barone Jr, 2000; Siegel, 1999). Too much unpredictable and uncontrollable stress during the sensitive period when the stress response system is maturing in early life is likely to lead to the development of a dysregulated stress response system (Perry, 1997). This in turn affects the way children are able to self-regulate their impulses and behaviour and their ability to learn.

Excessive stress experienced by children recalibrates the stress response system, such that children's feelings may progress rapidly from calmness to anxiety and terror when confronted with threat – moods that affect learning capacity and interpersonal behaviour. This is one of the reasons why abuse may affect young children so profoundly, well before they are able to verbally express their feelings about the abuse, increasing their risks of behavioural, health and learning problems and the early onset of health problems in adult life (Anda et al., 2006). This is one reason why studies of children entering out-of-home care show that these children as a group are amongst the least healthy in our community (American Academy of Pediatrics, 2002).

Nevertheless it is important to recognise that brain plasticity continues throughout life, even though the degree of adaptability diminishes with age (Karmarkar & Dan, 2006). For example, whilst the best time to become fluent in hearing, understanding and speaking multiple languages is early in life, people can still learn foreign languages across the lifespan. But it does need to be recognised that whilst 'the residual capacity for plasticity in mature neural circuits allows for some recovery of brain capabilities' when subjected to new experiences, these must be 'tailored to activate the relevant neural circuits and the individual's attention engaged in the task'. The task will inevitably be 'harder, more expensive in terms of societal and individual effort and potentially less extensive and durable' (National Scientific Council on the Developing Child, 2007, p. 8).

Reflective question

Imagine you are a teacher in a primary school and one of your students repeatedly hits out at other children when they get too close to him physically. You know this child is in foster care because of earlier emotional and physical abuse. How might an understanding of the influence of earlier experiences in a stressful environment on brain development and stress response systems help to explain this boy's behaviour?

Parenting adaptability

Parent–child attachment and positive child development depend upon a parent's ability to meet their child's needs in a consistent and effective way. Parents do this by demonstrating adaptability in their parenting – being able to constantly adjust their responses to meet a child's changing needs. Parenting that shows adaptability has three components:

- Perceptiveness: being 'tuned in' to the child, the situation and the parent's own responses; picking up and accurately interpreting the child's signals
- Responsiveness: having the capacity to stay 'in sync' with the child; being able to continually change and adjust, responding in light of cues being given by the child or by the context
- Flexibility: the behavioural capacity of the parent; having a broad behavioural repertoire (Centre for Community Child Health, 2004, pp. 80–1).

Children's needs for parental adaptability will vary over the child's development (e.g., the needs of an infant are different to those of a pre-schooler), in different contexts (e.g., a child living in a high-risk neighbourhood will have different needs compared with a child living in a neighbourhood with high social capital), in response to characteristics of the child (e.g., whether the child has an easygoing or a more active temperament; whether the child has a disability) and as a result of day-to-day variation (e.g., the needs of a child when tired or sick are likely to be higher than when alert or healthy). In the same way that children's needs for adaptable parenting are variable and determined by many factors so too are levels of parenting adaptability multiply influenced. How effectively a parent can respond to their child's needs might be determined by their own experiences of being parented, their mental health and use of drugs and alcohol, their financial resources, their experiences of parenting other children and whether they are adequately supported by friends, families and where needed, services (Centre for Community Child Health, 2004). The chapters of this book explore many features that relate to supporting parents to meet the needs of their children in adaptable ways. The following sections of this chapter describe a range of frameworks that can be used to support parents and communities in raising children in effective and adaptable ways.

Family theory

There are many conceptual frameworks relating to family structure and interaction (Handel & Whitchurch, 1994), derived mainly from the disciplines of anthropology and sociology. Family systems theory, which forms the main conceptual underpinning of family therapy, incorporates individual, family and social perspectives, and has been applied in general ways to understand families across the family life cycle, as well as in counselling and therapy settings (Carter & McGoldrick, 1999).

Synthesising psychodynamic and family systems concepts and drawing on the ideas of British social worker and psychoanalyst Clare Winnicott, Gillian Schofield (1998) offers three guiding principles for understanding the worlds of the family – inner, outer, past and present.

- Inner worlds express themselves and have an impact on outer worlds (e.g., chronic maternal depression often exhibits itself in self-neglect and the neglect of children)
- Outer worlds affect inner worlds (e.g., depressing environments induce despair and violent environments induce fear)
- Past worlds affect present worlds (e.g., experiences in the parent's childhood may affect the way they parent their own children, and the way they perceive and give meaning to events).

Practitioners in child and family services, especially those in socially disadvantaged communities, often encounter parents who carry within them the pain of past worlds which can greatly impair their capacity to nurture their child. When this coexists with an outer world that is characterised by the fear of violence or the despair of poverty, then there is a double layer of difficulty in nurturing their children.

Reflective questions

Apply ideas about inner, outer, past and present worlds to a parent you know who may be struggling to nurture their child or children. What insight does this give you into why patterns of behaviour may be resistant to change? How do such insights affect your attitudes and feelings toward the parent?

An ecological perspective

In the 1970s Urie Bronfenbrenner, Director of the College of Human Ecology at Cornell University, began to emphasise the importance of understanding the development of the child in the context of the family, social network, community and wider society. His ecological model of human development highlights the importance of different contexts in which the child is embedded:

- The various 'microsystems' of which a child is a part, such as the family, the immediate neighbourhood, the early childhood centre or the classroom
- The mesosystem – the interrelationships between two or more of these systems and the extent to which experiences are reinforcing or conflictual (a system of microsystems)
- The exosystem comprising settings of which the child is not a member, but of which others who influence the child – such as parents or siblings – are significant members, for example the parents' workplaces or siblings' peer groups, or health and educational services
- The macrosystem or the overarching cultural blueprint of a society (individualist or collectivist; secular or religious; patriarchal or matriarchal; violent or peaceful).

Bronfenbrenner (1979) has likened these systems to 'a nest of Russian dolls'. Those who work in child and family services may, under some circumstances, become important figures in the lives of children and their parents, and thus become one of the family's microsystems, or more remotely influence the child as part of the mesosystem. The organisations through which such services are delivered are part of the exosystem, and the values transmitted through social policies and services reflect core macrosystem values such as the status of children and families or the importance of social equality.

James Garbarino extended the work of Urie Bronfenbrenner, describing the family as the 'headquarters of human development' and applying an ecological model to the specific problem of child abuse and neglect (Garbarino, 1982). He later coined the evocative phrase 'socially toxic societies' to describe social environments of low social cohesion, adversity and violence, which are strongly correlated with child abuse, juvenile crime, and adolescent substance dependence (Garbarino, 1999).

These problems all have very similar 'causal pathways' to other closely associated problems such as low birthweight, conduct disorders, teenage pregnancy, poor academic achievement and adolescent mental health problems. This means these problems all share similar risk and protective factors (Durlak, 1998). Preventive strategies that are broadly based and tackle the common risk and protective factors rather than target a specific problem in isolation such as low birthweight, have been found to be most effective (Durlak, 1998). Common risk factors include poor parent–child attachment, low peer connectedness, social isolation and poverty.

Reflective questions

Think about some of the differences in values between primary schools run by mainstream service providers (e.g., state education authorities) and families from minority cultures who use them. Would this be different if schools were run by communities or minority cultures?

Using three different generations in your own family, think about how the wider social and historical context has influenced childrearing in each of these generations.

Social networks

It has been long known that social support is a major protective factor in relation to individual well-being (Brown & Harris, 1978; d'Abbs, 1982; Gottlieb, 1981; Henderson, Byrne & Duncan-Jones, 1981). The social networks or webs of kith and kin relationships into which we are born, and which we build across the lifespan, can buffer us from stressful life events and provide access to a broad range of resources. Social networks also make demands on us, exerting pressures on individuals to conform to their norms and creating a system of mutual obligations.

At times of key transitions in the life course, social support is especially important. For example, social support is a protective factor in relation to maternal depression (Brown et al., 1994). Social networks may change markedly during transitions such as marital separation, and the impact of such stressful life events on relationships with family and friends may lead to diminished rather than greater social support at the time it is most needed (Webber & Boromeo, 2005).

There is a significant body of research on the relationship between a lack of social support and poor quality childrearing, and child abuse and neglect (Crittenden, 1985; Quittner, Glueckouff & Jackson, 1990) although this is not a simple one-way relationship. An understanding of the 'natural help-ing networks' in a neighbourhood is vital in both community development work and in working with individual families (Collins & Pancoast, 1976). For 'socially excluded families' with an inter-generational history of child neglect and who have very truncated social networks, carefully matched and very well supported volunteer families may be able to act as functional sub-stitutes for kith and kin (Mitchell, 1995).

Activity

Draw a map of your own social network, placing yourself as a circle in the centre and then representing each family member, friend, neighbour, colleague etc. with whom you are in contact as separate circles around you. Draw a line between all individuals and others in your social network with whom they have contact. Can you see separate clusters in the pattern (e.g., indicating the different sub-groups to which you belong)? To what degree are the people in your social network directly connected with others? What are the implications of this for you in rela-tion to the flow of information, obligations, practical assistance and personal autonomy?

Reflective questions

Think about the factors which might shape an individual's ability to receive assistance from family and friends if they urgently needed someone to take care of their child if they were hospitalised.

To whom would you first turn if you needed practical support such as money or accommodation? To whom would you first turn if you needed emotional support? Are they the same people? Who might turn to you for such support? What would happen if the support you needed was not available?

Communities and social capital

Old wisdom supports much of our new knowledge, as indicated by the proverb that 'it takes a village to raise a child'. The next question therefore is 'and what might it take to rebuild the village?' The work of Robert Putnam, popularised in books such as *Bowling Alone* (Putnam, 2000), has highlighted the importance of 'social capital', or the trust and reciprocity which transcends kith, kin and clan, and which is the social glue that holds communities, and ultimately societies, together.

Putnam differentiates 'bonding social capital' based on the affiliations which exist within homogeneous groupings (people of a similar religion, age group, ethnicity, social class etc.) and 'bridging social capital', those webs of relationships which create linkages between such different groups in a society. Services for children and families can be delivered in ways that enhance both bonding and bridging social capital in the communities they serve. For example, maternal and child health centres, kindergartens and schools can serve as 'the village well' or the nucleus in social networks for families with young children.

Alternatively, services can mitigate against the establishment of bridging social capital, for example, where schools that reflect the values of the dominant culture may be antithetical to the values of the sub-culture of the child, and make some families feel unwelcome.

There is an impressive history of community work which long precedes the recent literature on social capital. Some child and family welfare services have embraced community development as part of their mission and have pioneered new approaches to rebuilding community (Beilharz, 2002).

Activity

Observe the neighbourhood in which you live over a period of one week and note the indicators of 'social capital' (trust and reciprocity). Compare this with another neighbourhood where you may have lived or with which you are familiar. How might you explain the similarities or differences? What might it be like to live in a community which is low on social capital?

Prescriptive knowledge

It is one thing to know about a phenomenon (descriptive knowledge) and another thing to know how to intervene in relation to the phenomenon (prescriptive knowledge). Knowing about anatomy is different from knowing how to do surgery; just as knowing how children learn is different from knowing how to teach them. In relation to working with vulnerable families, some would say that it is more of a craft than a science. Nevertheless, there is a growing research base to guide practitioners working with troubled families and the potential for 'evidence-informed practice' is continually increasing. How practitioners might best use research is explored in Chapter 12.

Our descriptive knowledge is still much greater than our prescriptive knowledge. For example, while quite a lot is now known about the effects on a child of exposure to alcohol *in utero*, as well as the effects on the mother and the child of exposure to domestic violence, a practitioner needs to know more than this. 'How should I respond to a depressed pregnant woman with a drinking problem who shows signs of being physically assaulted by her partner?' is a very different type of question from 'what are the effects of exposure to alcohol and domestic violence?'

Similarly we know about the effects of 'low warmth–high criticism' parenting styles but this does not give a practitioner an answer to the question: 'How do I respond when I see a stressed single father with a childhood history of physical abuse and who is facing eviction and serious financial pressures, speaking to his four year old son in a harsh and punitive way?'

In relation to such practice questions, 'evidence-informed' rather than 'evidence-based' practice is a more realistic goal, as evidence is often not available or if it is, it is not applicable to a specific situation. There may be no 'right answer' to such practice questions, as what may be appropriate and effective will depend on the context. Practitioner judgement and 'practice wisdom' thus need to complement research as sources of 'knowledge for practice'.

The 'how to' questions in practice are very dependent not only on a practitioner's values, knowledge and skills, but also on the nature of the practitioner's relationship with the family, the professional role, the organisational setting, and the policy and legal context in which practitioners work.

Activity

Think of a 'knowledge about' question which relates to risk and protective factors for child development and well-being. Using appropriate 'key words', search the internet to explore this question and critically assess the quality of the information you can find.

Now consider a 'knowledge how' question that might face a practitioner trying to reduce these risk factors and strengthen the protective factors. How would you go about finding answers to this question?

Family-centred practice

Just as an ecological perspective can give an overarching conceptual framework for understanding human development, so a family-centred perspective can give an overarching conceptual framework for working with vulnerable families, regardless of specific practitioner roles, settings and services. A literature review commissioned by the Social Exclusion Taskforce in the UK has provided an excellent overview of family-centred approaches in a broad range of fields including mental health, disability and child welfare (www. cabinetoffice.gov.uk/social_exclusion_task_force/families_at_risk.aspx).

They have classified the approaches as follows:

- Category 1: services that work with the family to strengthen the ability of the family to offer support to an individual member
- Category 2: services that identify and respond to the specific needs of members of the primary client's family members in order to enhance the support to the primary client
- Category 3: services and policies that work with the whole family as a unit.

The term family-centred practice encompasses many approaches to working with families. Allen and Petr (1998) have argued that there are four core elements of family-centred practice:

- The centrality of the family as the unit of attention
- An emphasis on maximising families' choices
- A strengths rather than a deficits perspective
- Cultural sensitivity.

Family-centred practice with vulnerable families requires a practitioner to have not only the appropriate knowledge and skills, but also appropriate values and personal qualities. Values based on compassion, respect, integrity and self-determination are the foundation, while personal qualities include a high level of emotional intelligence, interpersonal skills and self-awareness.

There are many challenges in family-centred practice. Sometimes what is described as family-centred practice is really mother-centred practice. This can ignore the significance of fathers and place an undue burden of responsibility on mothers. In Chapter 7 we explore father-inclusive practice. Sometimes what is described as family-centred practice is nuclear family-centred practice, ignoring the role of extended family members, especially relatives such as grandparents who may be very significant in the lives of children.

Sometimes what is described as family-centred practice is really parent-centred practice. This renders children invisible and inaudible. Sometimes what is described as family-centred practice is really child-centred practice, and this may reinforce parental feelings of failure and shame, exacerbating problems such as depression or substance use and posing greater risk to children. There will therefore be many dilemmas for practitioners committed to family-centred practice.

Similarly, while family-centred practice is 'strengths based' (See Chapter 2), in some situations deficits will need to be clearly identified if children are to be safe and to have their needs met. In these situations the challenge is to find ways of engaging with and advocating for children while working collaboratively with parents and the extended family. In Chapter 10 we explore family group conferencing as one approach to working with, and tapping the resources of, whole families.

A commitment to the self-determination of families underpins efforts to maximise their choices. The ethos is one of 'power with', not 'power over'. Even when the scope for choice is very circumscribed, there is usually still some room to give children and parents some control. For example, even when a child in care is separated from his or her parents, and the level of access is determined by a court, how and where to meet may still be something over which the child and parent can exercise choice.

As explored in Chapter 8, practitioners need to be culturally sensitive and competent if they are to work effectively with families from diverse cultural backgrounds. Childrearing is heavily shaped by cultural norms and contexts – for example, the age at which it is appropriate for a child to be left alone or in the care of an older child or adolescent, may vary greatly. At the same time practitioners need to be aware of the risk of over-attributing childrearing practices to cultural differences. This requires knowledge of and respect for cultural differences.

In some Aboriginal communities there are painful historical legacies related to the removal of children that make it much more difficult for families to trust services. Cultural consultants can play a vital role in assisting workers to become 'culturally competent' when working with families from different backgrounds than their own (see Chapter 6 for an example of this).

Reflective questions

Think about the diversity of childrearing attitudes and behaviours in your community and across different communities. What might be the 'grey' area between what is seen as 'family business' and what is seen as an obligation by the State to intervene on behalf of vulnerable children?

What experiences and attitudes do you bring from your own family background that might pose challenges for you in working respectfully with vulnerable families with young children from different socio-economic or cultural backgrounds?

Relationship-based practice

At the heart of family-centred practice is the quality of the working relationship with families. Most of the research in this area has been on 'therapeutic relationships' in counselling and psychotherapy but there is a growing body of research on working relationships across the human services. This includes how working relationships may be different for workers and families in rural settings, and in organisational settings such as child protection, where clients are not voluntary.

Asay and Lambert (1999) have drawn on a broad range of studies on the factors responsible for positive outcomes in psychotherapy, including the meta-analysis by Lambert (1992) which identified the degree to which positive outcomes can be attributed to different factors:

- 40%: client factors and environmental factors such as social support
- 30%: qualities of the therapeutic relationship
- 15%: hope and expectancy of positive outcome
- 15%: specific intervention techniques.

We do not have a similar body of research which specifically relates to family-centred practice with vulnerable families. However, these are the very same elements emphasised in intensive family-based services – environmental interventions, a therapeutic relationship based on rapport, nurturing hope and using evidence-based techniques (Whittaker et al., 1990). In any service responding to vulnerable families with young children, a supportive relationship with a parent can be valuable as an end in itself, as well as being a vehicle for specific intervention, enhancing social support or reducing situational stressors.

Scott and colleagues (2007) have pulled together some of the research on the importance of practitioner qualities in engaging families and have coined the acronym ERGO for the combination of empathy, respect, genuineness and optimism.

ERGO

Empathy

Empathy is the worker's ability to understand what the client is saying and feeling, and is expressed through warmth, active listening and through affirming and helping behaviours.

Respect

Workers show respect in practical ways such as arriving for a home visit on time, as well as by being non-judgemental and treating people as unique rather than as 'cases' or numbers.

Genuineness

Practitioners who can show humanity, humour and humility come across as individuals who are 'real' rather than in a 'role' even though they are 'in role'.

Optimism

Practitioners who can feel and convey optimism will be more able to nurture hope in families.

Family Partnership training is a model of care that enhances the provision of family-centred services (Davis, Day, & Bidmead, 2002). It facilitates the development of respect, empathy and partnership amongst practitioners working with families. It turns the concept of expert-driven interventions on its head in emphasising the importance of parent-initiated and practitioner supported changes that will be beneficial to family and child functioning.

In relation to child abuse risk situations, the research of Trotter (2002) suggests that it is also important to encourage pro-social behaviours directly and to have very clear roles and issues on which to focus.

Developing and sustaining relationships based on empathy, respect, genuineness and optimism under such challenging situations is not easy. Factors relating to the practitioner, the family, the service setting and the social environment are all important.

The practitioner

Each of us has a unique personality and our values, personal experiences and educational background shape how we relate with others. There are times when workers struggle to feel and therefore to express empathy, respect, genuineness and optimism. None of us is immune from common mental health problems such as anxiety or depression. For example, high levels of depression in low paid North American child care workers has been identified as a serious concern (Whitebook et al., 2004). Practitioners who are in close contact with children and who identify strongly with their suffering may understandably struggle to feel empathy for or convey respect to the parents.

The family

Each member of a family will influence the practitioner's capacity to offer and sustain a positive relationship. For example, parents whose own early history makes it hard for them to trust may take a lot longer to engage. Parents who have an insecure or conflictual relationship with their child may feel uneasy when they witness their child responding positively to a carer. The triangle of the worker–parent–child relationship can be a complex one and children may be very mindful of the tension in the working relationship.

Service setting

Service settings shape the working relationship. The physical nature and emotional climate of the service gives strong cues about whether it is welcoming to children and adults, while the nature of the organisation powerfully shapes the relationship by defining the worker's role and mandate. Resources are also a vital factor and high workloads make it harder to establish rapport as building good relationships takes time.

Social environment

The social environment shapes our working relationships too. Green, Gregory and Mason (2006) have used the metaphor of 'stretching the professional elastic' to describe rural working relationships on the continuum from 'professional, objective expert' to 'helpful friend'. This notion challenges traditional ideas of professional ethics, values and rules about professional boundaries as they relate to the development and maintenance of the working relationship. In rural and remote settings, the tyranny of distance also poses very practical challenges.

Activity

Use Figure 1.1 to identify factors which might affect positively or negatively the potential to develop and sustain positive partnerships with parents.

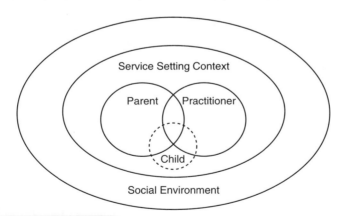

Figure 1.1: The worker–parent relationship in context (based on Scott et al., 2007)

Conclusion

There is a large and growing body of knowledge which relates to working with vulnerable families with young children. This chapter has touched on some of the research, ideas and conceptual frameworks that can help us understand and respond to families struggling with their childrearing roles. It is easy to be daunted by the level of knowledge which is available and by what we don't know. Just as we work best with families by building on their strengths, it is important to identify what we know and what we can offer. Being able to tap into the expertise of others to address gaps in one's own knowledge is an important skill. Perhaps the greatest gift we can offer families is ourselves – a working relationship based on empathy, respect, genuineness and hope, and a willingness to ask them what might help.

Useful websites

Australian Research Alliance for Children and Youth: www.aracy.org.au
Bernard van Leer Foundation: www.bernardvanleer.org
Circle of Security: www.circleofsecurity.org
The Family Action Centre: www.newcastle.edu.au/research-centre/fac
Raising Children Network: The Australian Parenting Website: http://raisingchildren.net.au
St Luke's: www.stlukes.org.au
St Luke's Innovative Resources: www.innovativeresources.com.au
ThinkFamily: www.cabinetoffice.gov.uk/social_exclusion_task_force/families_at_risk.aspx
What Works for Children?: www.whatworksforchildren.org.uk
Wilfrid Laurier University: www.wlu.ca/index.php

References

Allen, R. & Petr, C. (1998). Rethinking family centred practice. *American Journal of Orthopsychiatry*, 68 (1), 4–16.

American Academy of Pediatrics (2002). Health care of young children in foster care. *Pediatrics*, 100 (3), 536–41.

Anda, R. F., Felitti, V. J., Walker, J., Whitfield, C. L., Bremner, J. D., Perry, B. D. et al. (2006). The enduring effects of abuse and related adverse experiences in childhood: A convergence of evidence from neurobiology and epidemiology. *European Archives of Psychiatry and Clinical Neurosciences*, 56 (3), 174–86.

Asay, T. & Lambert, M. (1999). The empirical case for the common factors in therapy – quantitative findings. In M. Hubble, B. Duncan & S. Miller (eds) *The Heart & Soul of Change: What Works in Therapy*, 33–56. American Psychological Association, Washington, DC.

Bacon, H. & Richardson, S. (2001). Attachment theory and child abuse: An overview of the literature for practitioners. *Child Abuse Review*, 10 (7), 377–97.

Beilharz, L. (2002). *Building Community – the Shared Action Experience*. Solutions Press, Bendigo, Victoria.

Boukydis, Z. (2006). Ultrasound consultation to reduce risk and increase resilience in pregnancy. *Annals of the New York Academy of Sciences*, (1094), 268–71.

Bowlby, J. (1953). *Child Care and the Growth of Love*. Penguin, London.

Bronfenbrenner, U. (1979). *The Ecology of Human Development: Experiments by Nature and Design*. Harvard University Press, Cambridge, MA.

Brown, G. & Harris, T. (1978). *Social Origins of Depression*. Tavistock, London.

Brown, S., Lumley, J., Small, R. & Astbury, J. (1994). *Missing Voices: The Experience of Motherhood*. Oxford University Press, Melbourne.

Burkhalter, A., Bernardo, K. L. & Charles, V. (1993). Development of local circuits in the visual cortex. *Journal of Neuroscience*, 13 (5), 1916–31.

Carter, B. & McGoldrick, M. (eds) (1999). *The Expanded Family Life Cycle* (3rd edn). Allyn & Bacon, Boston.

Caspi, A., Sugden, K., Moffitt, T. E., Taylor, A., Craig, I. W., Harrington, H. et al. (2003). Influence of life stress on depression: Moderation by a polymorphism in the 5-HTT gene. *Science*, 301 (5631), 386–9.

Centre for Community Child Health (2004). *Parenting Information Project. Volume One: Main Report*. Commonwealth of Australia, Canberra.

Collins, A. & Pancoast, D. (1976). *Natural Helping Networks. A Strategy for Prevention.* National Association of Social Workers, Washington, DC.

Crittenden, P. (1985). Social networks, quality of childrearing and child development. *Child Development,* 5 (56), 1299–313.

d'Abbs, P. (1982). *Social Support Networks.* Australian Institute of Family Studies, Melbourne.

Davis, H., Day, C. & Bidmead, C. (2002). *Working in Partnership with Parents: The Parent Adviser Model.* Harcourt Assessment, London.

Durlak, J. A. (1998). Common risk and protective factors in successful programs. *American Journal of Orthopsychiatry,* 68 (4), 512–20.

Garbarino, J. (1982). *Children and Families in the Social Environment.* Aldine Publishing Co., New York.

Garbarino, J. (1999). *Raising Children in a Socially Toxic Environment.* Jossey-Bass, San Francisco.

Gogtay, N., Giedd, J. N., Lusk, L., Hayashi, K. M., Greenstein, D. & Vaituzis, A. C. (2004). Dynamic mapping of human cortical development during childhood through early adulthood. *Proceedings of the National Academy of Sciences USA,* (101), 8174–9.

Gottlieb, B. (1981). *Social Networks and Social Support.* Sage, Beverly Hills.

Green, R., Gregory, R. & Mason, R. (2006). Professional distance and social work: Stretching the elastic? *Australian Social Work,* (59), 449–661.

Handel, G. & Whitchurch, G. (1994). *The Psychosocial Interior of the Family* (4th edn). Aldine de Gruyter, New York.

Henderson, S., Byrne, D. & Duncan-Jones, P. (1981). *Neurosis and the Social Environment.* Academic Press, Sydney.

Howe, D., Brandon, M., Hinings, D. & Schofield, G. (1999). *Attachment Theory, Child Maltreatment and Family Support.* Lawrence Erlbaum Associates, Mahwah, NJ.

Karmarkar, U. R. & Dan, Y. (2006). Experience-dependent plasticity in adult visual cortex. *Neuron,* 52, 577–85.

Lambert, M. J. (1992). Implications of outcome research for psychotherapy integration. In J. C. Norcross & M. R. Goldfried (eds), *Handbook of Psychotherapy Integration,* 94–129. Basic Books, New York.

McGowan, P. O., Sasaki, A., D'Alessio, A. C., Dymov, S., Labonté, B., Szyf, M. et al. (2009). Epigenetic regulation of the glucocorticoid receptor in human brain associates with childhood abuse. *Nature Neuroscience,* 12 (3), 342–8.

Middlebrooks, J. S. & Audage, N. C. (2007). *The Effects of Childhood Stress on Health Across the Lifespan.* Centers for Disease Control and Prevention, National Center for Injury Prevention and Control, Atlanta, GA.

Mitchell, G. (1995). *Child Welfare Families: Elaborating an Understanding.* University of Melbourne, Melbourne.

National Scientific Council on the Developing Child (2007). 'The timing and quality of early experiences combine to shape brain architecture: Council Working Paper #5'. Available online at: developingchild.harvard.edu/library/reports_and_working_papers/wp5/

Nelson, C. A. (2007). A neurobiological perspective on early human deprivation. *Child Development,* (1), 13–18.

Perry, B. D. (1997). Incubated in terror: Neurodevelopmental factors in the 'cycle of violence'. In J. D. Ofosky (ed.), *Children in a Violent Society,* 124–49. Guilford Press, New York.

Putnam, R. D. (2000). *Bowling Alone*. Simon & Schuster, New York.

Quittner, A., Glueckouff, R. & Jackson, D. (1990). Chronic parenting stress: Moderating versus mediating effects of social support. *Journal of Personal Psychology*, 59 (6), 1266–78.

Rice, D. & Barone Jr, S. (2000). Critical periods of vulnerability for the developing nervous system: Evidence from humans and animal models. *Environmental Health Perspectives*, 108 (Suppl. 3), 511–33.

Schofield, G. (1998). Inner and outer worlds: A psychosocial framework for child and family social work. *Child and Family Social Work*, (3), 57–68.

Scott, D., Salveron, M., Reimer, E., Nichols, S., Sivak, L. & Arney, F. (2007). 'Positive partnerships with parents of young children', Topical Paper 9: Australian Research Alliance for Children and Youth. Available online at: www.aracy.org.au/publicationDocuments/TOP_Positive_Partnerships_with_Parents_of_Young_Children_2007.pdf

Shonkoff, J. & Phillips, D. (eds) (2000). *From Neurons to Neighbourhoods: The Science of Early Childhood Development*. National Academy Press, Washington, DC.

Siegel, D. (1999). *The Developing Mind: Toward a Neurobiology of Interpersonal Experience*. Guilford Press, New York.

Strathearn, L., Mamum, A., Najman, J. & O'Callaghan, M. (2009). Does breastfeeding protect against substantiated child abuse and neglect? A 15-year cohort study. *Pediatrics*, 123, 483–93.

Trotter, C. (2002). Worker skill and client outcome in child protection. *Child Abuse Review*, 11, 38–50.

Webber, R. & Boromeo, D. (2005). The sole parent family: Family and support networks. *Australian Journal of Social Issues*, 40 (2), 269–83.

Whitebook, M., Phillips, D., Bellm, D. & Almaraz, M. (2004). *Two Years in Early Care and Education: A Community Portrait of Quality and Workforce Stability*. University of California, Berkeley.

Whittaker, J., Kinney, J., Tracy, E. & Booth, C. (1990). *Reaching High-Risk Families: Intensive Family Preservation in Human Services*. Aldine de Gruyter, New York.

Family strengths: an international perspective

John DeFrain, Sylvia Asay and Judi Geggie

Learning goals

This chapter will enable you to:

1. Understand the key propositions derived by family strengths researchers around the world over the past four decades and see how these ideas can be used to help strengthen families at times of vulnerability
2. Learn about the major qualities of strong families: appreciation and affection, commitment, positive communication, enjoyable time together, spiritual well-being, and the ability to manage stress and crisis effectively
3. See how family strengths, community strengths and cultural strengths interrelate from a global perspective, and how these resources can be used to support vulnerable families in positive ways
4. Find a realistic answer to parents who ask: 'Is there hope for me and my kids? I did not grow up in a strong family, but a terribly troubled family. Will I be able to parent my children successfully?'
5. Understand how research on family strengths, community strengths and cultural strengths can be applied directly in the lives of individuals and families.

Introduction

Considerable effort around the world over the past four decades has gone into the study of strong families. Motivated by a rising tide of divorce and family disruption in the US in the 1960s and 1970s, researchers began focusing on the broad question of why families fail:

- Why do relationships that begin in love end in divorce?
- Why do parents abuse their children?
- Why do spouses abuse their partner?
- Why do people abuse alcohol and other drugs, and what damage is caused in families because of this?

These and countless other similar questions captured the interest of Western societies, and many researchers and other investigators searched for answers. Though most of the research energy expended during this period focused on the study of failure and breakdown in families, another thread of interest and research was also growing. The search intensified during this time to find answers to the broad question of how families succeed:

- What is a strong family?
- Does it make sense to define strong families in terms of their structure or type, i.e., two-parent, single-parent, extended family, gay and lesbian, and so forth?
- Or, should we think more about family strengths in terms of family functions, such as communication and conflict resolution, appreciation and affection, commitment, and so forth?
- How are family strengths similar and different from culture to culture around the world?
- How can these ideas be used to help strengthen couple and family relationships?

Investigators looking at problems and focusing on the question of why families fail have learned a tremendous amount about these subjects. This is undeniable. However, it is also beyond question that learning about *what does not work* in families does not tell you much about *what does work*. This is the logic behind the wave of interest in couple and family strengths research we see today.

Unfortunately, as outlined in Chapter 1, there is still a knowledge gap between what researchers know about the qualities of strong families and how to help strengthen families who face considerable challenges in life. The research on family strengths worldwide is well-grounded. The new frontier in regard to the understanding of family strengths focuses on the question, how can these ideas be applied in the daily lives of couples and families, and professionals working with couples and families? This chapter begins to close this knowledge–practice gap and brings the world of the researcher and the world of the practitioner closer together.

What family strengths research has taught us

We work with a worldwide network of researchers, clinicians and community development workers who are interested in helping to strengthen families. From these efforts a series of beliefs or guiding principles have evolved that can be quite useful to professionals and families with young children:

- Families, in all their remarkable diversity, are the basic foundation of human cultures. Strong families are critical to the development of strong communities and cultures, and strong communities and cultures promote and nurture strong families.
- Not all families are strong, but all families have strengths. Many families are on their way to becoming strong. Families can be especially vulnerable in the beginning, for example, when relatively youthful partners are adjusting to each other and when the children are young. It is important to remember, however, that even those families facing considerable challenges in life have many strengths that need to be recognised and encouraged.
- It's not about structure, it's about function. Many people make the mistake of thinking that the type of family is somehow especially important. Think about a sole or single-parent family, for example. When someone focuses only on family structure, a single-parent family theoretically may not look as strong as a two-parent family. But in reality, there are many strong single-parent families, just as there are many very troubled two-parent families. Focusing only on family structure can cause one to miss the point: that how a family functions – how family members demonstrate love and care for each other – is more important than who the family members are or what type of family they represent.
- Everything that happens to you happens to me. Family strengths research has roots in family systems theories, which argue that family members are inextricably connected with each other (see Chapter 1). That is to say, when something happens to one member of the family, it has effects on the other members of the family. In strong couples and families, each member takes these intimate connections very seriously by celebrating the success of each member of the family when something positive has happened, and by banding together to help when one of the family is having difficulty in life. This one-for-all and all-for-one approach can make even the most vulnerable family stronger.
- Strong couple relationships are at the centre of many strong families. The couple relationship is an important source of strength in many families with children who are doing well. Parents need to find ways to nurture a positive couple relationship for the good of everyone in

the family. Professionals working with families need to encourage and support the couple relationship in those cases in which the partners are mutually beneficial for each other.

- If you grew up in a strong family as a child, it will probably be easier for you to create a strong family of your own as an adult. But it's also quite possible to do so if you weren't so lucky and grew up in a seriously troubled family. This fact can give considerable hope to many people who are trying to rise above their past (Skogrand et al., 2007).

- The relationship between money and family strengths is tenuous. Once a family has adequate financial resources to meet basic needs, the relentless quest for more is not likely to increase the family's quality of life, happiness together, or the strengths of their relationships with each other. Struggling families can be rich or poor. Poverty adds to the stress on families and can make it more difficult for them to have happy family relationships, but the inner strengths and cohesion of some poor families and communities enable them to be strong even in the face of poverty.

- Strengths develop over time. When couples start out in life together, they sometimes have considerable difficulty adjusting to each other, and these difficulties are quite predictable. Adjusting to each other is not an easy task. Many couples who are unstable at first end up creating a healthy, happy family.

- Strengths are often developed in response to challenges. A couple's and family's strengths are tested by life's everyday stressors and also by the significant crises that all of us face sooner or later. The difficulties many families face today can teach them how to prevent stress and survive crisis later in their life together. For example, the majority of families in an Australian family strengths project told researchers that they became aware of their strength after enduring challenges as a family. It was during these crises that the families needed to *pull together* and support each other. Though adversity may strain the relationship initially, it is in hindsight that families acknowledge how the crisis has strengthened their bond (Geggie et al., 2000).

- Strong families don't tend to think much about their strengths, they just live them. Likewise, families with fewer family, community and cultural resources at their fingertips are also unlikely to think about their strengths, but it can be very useful for them to carefully examine their strengths and discuss precisely how family members use their strengths to great advantage.

- Strong families, like people, are not perfect. Even in the strongest of families we can sometimes be like porcupines: prickly, disagreeable, eager and ready to enjoy conflict with each other. But, like porcupines, we also have a considerable need to cuddle up with each other for warmth and support when the night is cold. A strong family is a work of art always in the process of growing and changing, and a family today can put down the roots they need to become a strong family in the not-too-distant future.

- When seeking to unite groups of people, communities, and even nations, uniting around the cause of strengthening families – a cause we can all sanction – can be a powerful strategy. This is why family professionals and activists in many countries around the world have begun talking about strengthening families in recent decades. Vulnerable families are not jumbles of pathology in need of fixing, but collections of human beings with considerable potential for growth and achievement. By reframing how we talk about families, we begin to think differently about these families and soon we are freed from our stereotypes and can act differently toward them.

- Using the glass half full approach. Believing that all individuals, families and communities have strengths is also the central feature of the asset-based community development approach. This approach focuses on the gifts and skills of the individual, the family and the assets of the community in order to tackle the issues that impact upon their lives. The glass is both half full and half empty (ABCD Institute Chicago, 2009; Asia Pacific ABCD Network, 2009).

- Human beings have the right and responsibility to feel safe, comfortable, happy and loved. With support from the greater community, many families have the capability to grow in positive directions.

Family strengths

Research on strong families and family strengths can be traced back to 1930 with C. G. Woodhouse's study of 250 successful families in the US during the Great Depression. The vast majority of research on families in the 20th century, however, tended to accentuate the negative by focusing on the question of why families fail rather than the more useful question of how families succeed. Why this is the case has never been adequately answered, though human beings seem by nature to be problem focused and seek solutions to difficulties they are having. However, in the case of family research, a strong family is simply not the flip side of a troubled family. Success is much more than the opposite of failure and the study of strong families uncovers a great deal of information that can be invaluable to those interested in creating strengths in their own intimate relationships.

Herbert Otto's work on strong families and family strengths in the 1960s (Gabler & Otto, 1964; Otto, 1962, 1963) laid the foundation for Nick Stinnett and his colleagues at Oklahoma State University in the early

1970s and subsequently beginning at the University of Nebraska-Lincoln in the late 1970s. Researchers at the University of Nebraska led by John DeFrain; at the University of Alabama led by Stinnett; at the University of Minnesota-St. Paul led by David H. Olson; at Kyung Hee University in Seoul, Republic of Korea led by Yoo Young Ju; at the Shanghai Academy of Social Sciences in the People's Republic of China led by Xu Anqi; at the University of Newcastle, NSW led by Judi Geggie, plus affiliated institutions in the US and around the world, have studied families from a strengths-based perspective. More than 26 000 family members have participated in studies in 38 countries in all of the seven major geocultural areas of the globe.

The similarities that are found among research with families globally point to a set of qualities that describe the characteristics of strong families. When people from country to country and culture to culture talk about what makes their family strong, these are some of the traits they commonly identify.

Table 2.1: Characteristics of strong families

Appreciation and affection	Commitment
Caring for each other	Trust
Friendship	Honesty
Respect for individuality	Dependability
Playfulness	Faithfulness
Humour	Sharing
Positive communication	**Enjoyable time together**
Giving compliments	Quality time in great quantity
Sharing feelings	Good things take time
Avoiding blame	Enjoying each other's company
Being able to compromise	Simple good times
Agreeing to disagree	Sharing fun times
Spiritual well-being	**The ability to manage stress and crisis effectively**
Hope	Adaptability
Faith	Seeing crises as both challenges and opportunities
Compassion	Growing through crises together
Shared ethical values	Openness to change
Oneness with humankind	Resilience

Australian Family Strengths Research Project

In 1999 the Family Action Centre at the University of Newcastle conducted the Australian Family Strengths Research Project, which involved 600 parents who considered their families to be strong. These families participated in a survey designed to ascertain:

- The characteristics of their families that they considered to be their strengths, and
- The language they use to describe their strengths.

Eight themes emerged from the families' perceptions:

Table 2.2: Family strengths

Resilience	Communication
Ability to withstand and rebound from crises and diversity	Open, positive and honest communication
Aware of family's strengths when faced with serious challenges	
Togetherness	**Sharing activities**
Providing a sense of belonging	Sharing sports, hobbies, games, reading stories
Sharing of values, beliefs and morals	Going camping or on holidays together, socialising
Affection	**Support**
Regular expressions of love, care, concern and interest through hugs, cuddles and thoughtfulness	Assisting, encouraging, reassuring and 'looking out for each other'
Acceptance	**Commitment**
Reflected in respect, appreciation and understanding of each other's individuality	Dedication and loyalty toward the family as a whole to co-parental relationships, parent–child relationships, sibling relationships, extended family and community
Tolerance of differences	

(Geggie et al., 2007)

Activity

Fill out Box 2.1, below, to understand some things that strong families do when facing stress or dealing with a crisis.

Box 2.1: How strong families manage stress and crisis effectively

Research on strong families across the country and around the world reveals useful approaches to dealing in a positive manner with stress and crisis in one's life. Tick the approaches your family uses:

- *We look for something positive* and focus on that positive element in a difficult situation.
- *We pull together rather than apart.* We don't see the problem as an individual's problem, but as a challenge for the whole family.
- *We get help outside the nuclear family when we need it.* Help from extended family members, supportive friends, neighbours, colleagues, members of our religious community, professionals in the community. 'It takes a whole village to resolve a crisis.'
- *We create open channels of communication.* Challenges are not met when communication shuts down.
- *We keep things in perspective*: 'These things, too, shall pass.'
- *We adopt new roles in a flexible manner.* Crises often demand that individuals learn new approaches to life and take on different responsibilities.
- *We focus on what is most important and minimise fragmentation.* Without focus on the essentials, the details can make us edgy, even hysterical.
- *We give up on worrying or put our cares in a box.* Worrying usually causes people more misery than the actual event they are worrying about. Sometimes it's best to stuff the worry down, or resolve to worry 10 minutes a day and then forget it. The mind simply has to rest.
- *We eat well, exercise, love each other and get adequate sleep.* Often human beings forget that they are biological beings not unlike kindergarteners. We all need a good lunch and we need to play. We need to have our hair stroked and we need a good nap.
- *We create a life full of meaning and purpose.* All people face severe crises in life. We will not be able to avoid these challenges. Rather, our aim can be to live a useful life of service to our community. This brings a richness and dignity to our lives, in spite of the troubles we endure.
- *We actively meet our challenges, head on.* Disaster in life does not go away when we look in another direction. But, it is also helpful sometimes to withdraw for a time and replenish ourselves.
- *We go with the flow to some degree.* Sometimes we are relatively powerless in the face of crisis. At this point it can be useful to simply 'let it go and see what happens'.
- *We are prepared in advance for the challenges in life.* Healthy family relationships are like an ample bank balance: if we have kept

our relational accounts in order, we will be able to weather life's most difficult storms. Together.

- *We know how to laugh and we know how to cry,* for both are essential if we are to maintain an emotional balance in life.
- *We do not blame others for our fate,* but work with others to build a more satisfying world for all.
- *We take life's challenges one day at a time.* In especially tight situations, we sometimes need to take things one hour at a time, or perhaps one minute at a time.
- *We realise that suffering can be a catalyst for positive growth.* Crisis, by definition, is a difficult time in our lives. But it can also be a turning point, planting the seeds for a satisfying and successful future. This is hard to internalise, but useful to remember.
- *We identify spiritually with the grand procession of life.* Through good times and bad times we as individuals come and go, but life from whence we all spring is eternal. There is something satisfying and soothing about that thought.

In the space below, please add other useful approaches for managing stress and crisis that you have found helpful in your family:

1. _____
   _____
2. _____
   _____
3. _____
   _____
4. _____
   _____

Adapted from the Nebraska-Lincoln Extension Guide, *Creating a Strong Family: Effective Management of Stress and Crisis* by John DeFrain, Jeanette Friesen, Dianne Swanson and Gail Brand, 2008.

Community strengths

Strong families contribute to the well-being of communities, and strong communities enhance the development of strong families. A number of important community strengths were identified through qualitative research on family strengths in 18 countries in all seven of the major geocultural areas of the world (DeFrain & Asay, 2007). These community strengths include:

- A supportive environment that genuinely values families, and a general willingness and natural generosity infused in the culture to help when families are in need. The contributions of the community to the family are undeniable. It is this connection to other individuals and families that serves as a safety net for many families experiencing considerable difficulty in life. Vulnerable families, almost by definition, cannot go it alone. At least for a time, they need the greater community to help them gain the skills, attitudes and behaviours which will make success as a relatively independent family possible in the future. For example, the Caravan Project in the Lower Hunter Region of New South Wales works with low income, marginalised families who live in caravan parks and manufactured home villages. This project assists residents in improving their quality of life: providing on-site support for families; creating strengths-based programs in collaboration with residents; encouraging and supporting residents to achieve personal goals; and promoting leadership and a sense of community (Geggie, 2006).

- An effective educational delivery system. This important function is usually created and maintained by the community, sometimes in formal educational institutions and other times in more informal settings. Either way, education is vital for the survival and strength of families whether it occurs in a classroom in England or under the shade of a bush in Somalia with village elders sharing their wisdom for the benefit of assembled village children. One creative approach in Australia is called the Rainbow Readers. This is a group of volunteers who initially trained as home-visiting volunteers. They identified a community interest in increasing young children's literacy through making reading fun. They use the model of doorstep reading, setting out in pairs across an estate for two hours of reading on the doorsteps of any interested families who have children aged up to five years. Children are given library bags, and if they would like to, they can borrow a book or two for the week. A fortnightly event in the estate brings neighbours together to share food, have a laugh and play games (Family Action Centre, 2008).

- Family service programs developed by government and non-government organisations for families. Social services provided by communities also play an important role in family life. In some countries, family policy is well-defined and provides services to families in communities, helping to ensure the proper development of children. These programs can be invaluable to struggling families. For example, 'Brothers Inside' is a program that works with Indigenous men whilst they are in correctional centres in Australia and provides them with support and information on their roles and rights as fathers whilst inside. A male Indigenous facilitator delivers a four full day program covering topics such as strengths of dads, keeping kids safe, domestic violence, connecting with kids and partner, and our role as dads (Stuart & Hammond, 2006). Chapter 7 provides more examples of engaging fathers in practice.

- A safe, secure and healthy environment. From a global perspective, the community usually takes on the responsibility for protecting individuals and families. A safe environment is necessary if a family is to carry out its basic functions effectively. In countries ravaged by terrorism, war and natural disaster, families can be stressed to breaking point.
- Religious communities for families seeking this kind of support. The religious community may play an important role in enhancing spiritual well-being for many families by providing sanctuary and positive social contact. It can also support families in a variety of other ways, including the provision of food and shelter in hard times, as a social regulator for marriage customs and the passing on of other important values in a community through religious education.

Cultural strengths

A third set of strengths was identified during the qualitative study of family strengths and challenges in 18 countries around the world (DeFrain & Asay, 2007). This set of strengths can be called *cultural strengths*. Challenges to and initiatives that may support cultural strengths for Aboriginal families and families from refugee backgrounds, respectively, are examined in Chapters 6 and 8. Cultural strengths include:

- A rich cultural history. The heritage and historical legacy of each country contributes to the strengths of families, giving them meaning, direction and inspiration for dealing with life's challenges. As you read the history of any country, you realise the bequest given by the people who have come before – the creation of a culture unlike any other in the world. This gift gives future generations a foundation from which to build and a purpose for living.
- Shared cultural meanings. Strong families also share understandings about the world that are built into their culture. Many countries have words of wisdom or maxims that are localised to a particular country. Many of these cultural meanings defy simple translation because they are tied to unique aspects of life in the country, embedded in the fabric of people's daily lives in a way that only people living in the culture can really understand their meaning and importance. Examples include the ideas of botho in Botswana, the mauri in New Zealand, Ubuntu in South Africa, fair go in Australia and the oikos in Greece. Even the more well-known concepts of filial piety in China and Korea are difficult for people in other countries to grasp without explanation of their philosophical and historical context.
- A stable political process. The political environment of a country affects families in countless ways, and vulnerable families often living at the

bottom of the social ladder have fewer financial and social resources to defend themselves during tumultuous times. A stable government provides an atmosphere in which families do not need to expend precious energy worrying about the future, for the government is able to maintain order, providing and protecting in a consistent manner that can be trusted. On the other hand, in countries such as Somalia, for example, mass killings, starvation, destruction of resources and the separation of families have resulted from civil war that has divided the country.

- A viable economy. A stable and functioning economic system contributes to a family's ability to provide for themselves and gather resources to sustain life. All families use resources to carry out their daily activities and when a country's economy is failing, the families in the country are forced to adapt or suffer the consequences. In Mexico, for example, economic troubles have forced families to adapt by putting more family members into the workforce, particularly women. This solution to economic crisis leads to a change in the basic structure and function of many families (Esteinou, 2007). Political instability and economic problems in many countries force many families to emigrate; other families separate in response to these difficulties with some family members staying in the home country while their relatives emigrate to find work and send money home to help those left behind. Many immigrant families are especially vulnerable and in need of social support (Dalla et al., 2008).

- An understanding of the global society. Families benefit from learning about other cultures. Each culture in the world develops creative ways for dealing with the many challenges that life inevitably brings, and families can be strengthened by international and intercultural experiences which can bring meaning, stability and joy to the family wise enough to look for these experiences. Globalisation impacts families around the world in many ways, for better and worse. Globalisation can contribute to the erosion of traditions such as familism and patriarchal structures as well as causing resistance to change in family structure. Globalisation can also increase information and awareness of the world outside, providing a new perception of how one fits into the world and giving a sense of the human interconnectedness with all people around the globe. Increased cultural understanding may reduce misunderstanding and fear.

Two models for conceptualising family, community and cultural strengths

The easiest way to understand how family strengths, community strengths and cultural strengths are interconnected is a visual representation. In Figure 2.1 you can see how the strengths interact with each other from dimension to

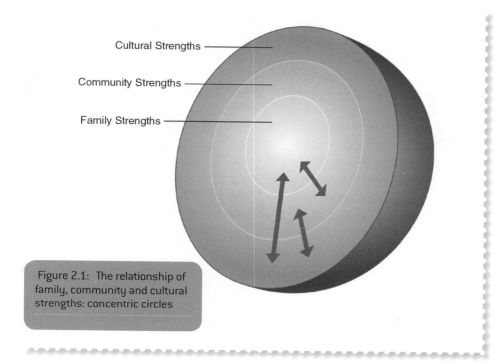

Cultural Strengths

Community Strengths

Family Strengths

Figure 2.1: The relationship of family, community and cultural strengths: concentric circles

dimension, and from level to level on each dimension. Families who are strong and doing well in life contribute to the strength of the community in which they live and the cultural values that impact on their life. Struggling families, on the other hand, have fewer resources to invest in their communities and less energy to contribute to positive cultural values because their lives are so tenuous. In this model, the three areas of strengths move out and away from the single-family unit to the broader cultural context, related to each other in a concentric fashion. The three areas not only interact from dimension to dimension but also have depth, thus interacting on various levels.

In Figure 2.2 you can see how family strengths, community strengths and cultural strengths can intersect with each other. The point at which all three areas of strengths intersect is a very beneficial place for families to be: they benefit from the strengths of a healthy family; the strengths of a viable community; and cultural strengths that bring meaning, purpose and understanding to life. Of course, families can still be strong when living in communities and cultures that are in disarray because of economic, political or environmental troubles. But the task of living well and happily is much more difficult. In this model, the family, community and cultural strengths intersect. Although this intersection represents the strong family, when one or more areas are lacking, a state of equilibrium may be reached and a strong family is still possible.

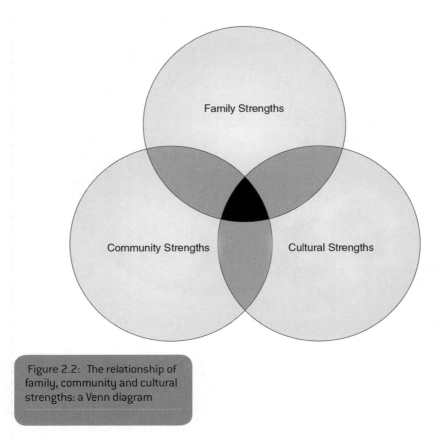

Figure 2.2: The relationship of family, community and cultural strengths: a Venn diagram

To illustrate these conceptual models, consider the research of Healy and Hillman, who explored how relocation from a metropolitan to a non-metropolitan area affects young families' vulnerability to social exclusion, particularly low income families or families with complex needs. The study found that social and economic factors, and a lack of access to services and infrastructure increased young families' vulnerability to social exclusion (The Benevolent Society, 2008). One recommendation from the study was that an important role that government and non-government agencies could play was in developing initiatives aimed at promoting inclusion of new arrivals. Home-Start in the East Lake Macquarie area of New South Wales has operated for 20 years and has found the most significant reason for referral of families was social isolation. Many families had moved into the area and had little knowledge of the local community and were lacking a network of family and friends to assist them. Immigrant families in the community are even more isolated as the cultural values, beliefs and practices can be significantly different from those of their country of origin.

Home-Start has developed a specific training program for volunteers who will be linked with immigrant families. The ability of volunteers and professional services to assist immigrant families in their transition into the community and to translate the cultural beliefs and values for these families is of vital importance for maximising the development of children. Chapter 8 also explores the challenges and strategies reported by parents from refugee backgrounds encountering new cultural beliefs and values regarding childrearing.

Transcending a traumatic childhood

Countless observers have noted how family problems can be passed from one generation to the next. This phenomenon has been labelled inter-generational transmission and we are often asked the question, 'Is there hope for me and my kids? I did not grow up in a strong family, but a terribly troubled family. Will I be able to parent my children successfully?' The answer is, 'Yes, of course but it will not be easy.' For this reason, it is extremely important to prevent family problems before they occur, because the wounds inflicted upon young children heal slowly and our strengths-based research on how individuals survive and rise above the traumas they endured in childhood, demonstrates that it is quite possible to heal but the process is long and difficult (Skogrand et al., 2007).

Vulnerable families are at risk for the abuse and neglect of children. Children who are abused, for example, have a greater chance of growing up and being abusive toward their own children (Dixon, Browne & Hamilton-Giachritsis, 2009). As our research found, many people are capable of transcending the misery of their past and not inflicting it on the next generation. Two factors in our research on people's perceptions that seem to stand out among those who transcend their past is that they make a personal decision to be different from those who abused them as a child, and they find individuals in life who are supportive and serve as role models for a better way of living. The abused child or young person may have an abusive parent or parents, but other people in their life are good, loving and supportive and these people are beacons of shining light on a better path (Skogrand et al., 2007). Collishaw and others (2007) point out that it is difficult to really know how many adults have overcome this type of crisis given that researchers have had a difficult time in defining resilience because of the diversity used to explain life trajectories such as heredity, individual characteristics and experiences. However, McGloin and Widom (2001) found that about half of those who experienced abuse or neglect do not meet criteria for psychiatric disorders and that about one quarter could be classified as 'resilient'.

Conclusion

Many years of research on family strengths has uncovered a wealth of ideas. Though these ideas need to be disseminated more widely, many researchers, practitioners and laypersons saw the value of them very quickly and began creating ways to use strengths-based approaches in real life.

Understanding family strengths can have considerable benefits for families themselves. Couples and families can assess relationship strengths to see how family members perceive their strengths as a group. Families also have the opportunity to use those strengths to build upon and become a stronger family. The American Family Strengths Inventory© (AFSI) that is presented in the activity below is a good example of how couples and families can assess their strengths. Once a family is able to identify their strengths, they can talk about how they can use those strengths to become even stronger. In addition, they can discuss areas that show a need for growth that the family can work on together. As a result, a goal can be developed to build on each strength as well as each potential growth area.

People in many different professional fields have begun using strengths-based approaches in their work with children and families.

Family therapists have begun thinking about their work from a strengths-based perspective, focusing on the gifts that families possess in the context of their culture and using these strengths to help tell a new family story with a more positive outcome (Coombs, 2005). The blending of family strengths research, which began in the US and narrative therapy, which began in Australia, for example, is an excellent example of how synergy can be developed between cultures: one plus one can often equal much more than two (DeFrain, Cook & Gonzalez-Kruger, 2005; White & Morgan, 2006).

Community development workers take a strengths-based approach when they focus on the inherent good in families, communities and cultures. This idea is exemplified by the work of the Multicultural Council of the Northern Territory (2008) in Australia. In a DVD entitled *Strong Families Sharing Cultural Parenting Knowledge*, the Multicultural Council based in Darwin focuses on four immigrant families telling their stories. Each family, sitting around a table in their kitchen or on the verandah, tells the story of why they came to Australia; what drew them to a new country and the difficulties they felt they needed to leave behind in their old country. The DVD does a magnificent job of depicting the strength and determination of these families in the face of terrible odds and tragic difficulties in their home country, and makes it clear to the viewer that these families bring considerable gifts to their new homeland, Australia.

Policy makers at local, state, regional, national and international levels can help strengthen families by realising that families – in all their rich and fascinating diversity – are the basic social unit of every known culture on earth, and that work to strengthen families also serves to strengthen every other aspect of the culture. David H. Olson has observed that, 'All the problems in the world either begin in families or end up in families' (Olson, DeFrain & Skogrand, 2008). What Olson means is that sometimes families create their own problems and sometimes the world imposes problems upon families. Either way, all the world's problems in the final analysis end up on the door of the family and the family is faced with dealing with these problems. For example, families do not start wars, but families, ultimately, have to deal with the devastation caused by these wars. For this reason, families need our attention and must be seen as critical stakeholders in the forefront of every major policy issue. Families, like every other social institution, are part of the problem and part of the solution. What better place could there be to begin our task of strengthening families and creating a better world than by working with vulnerable families with young children?

As a result of the Australian Family Strengths Research Project, a Family Strengths Kit was developed as a tool for practitioners and families, communities and organisations. 'Our Scrapbook of Strengths: Strong Families, Strong Community' merged matching key concepts from the research with appropriate graphic images or visual metaphors. This tool serves as conversational prompts for exploring strengths with families and groups of children, parents and also community groups. A similar tool has been developed for Indigenous families and communities. This comprises photographic images acting as stimuli for individuals and groups to reflect on the strengths of their families and community (available online at St Luke's, Bendigo: www. innovativeresources.org). Also, the Asset-Based Community Development approach described by the publications of the Asset-Based Community Development (ABCD) Institute, Chicago (www.abcdinstitute.org), provides professionals with tools for mapping individual and community strengths/assets. Many other resources have also been developed in Australia.

Reflective questions

What are the strengths of your family? How have these strengths helped make you the person you are today? How will you personally help to maintain the strengths of your family in the future?

What are the strengths of the community in which you live? How do you contribute to the healthy development of your community?

What are the cultural strengths that you have inherited from generations past? What kind of cultural legacy will you leave at the end of your life? What will you have given back to the world that has nurtured you?

How can you use these ideas about family strengths, community strengths and cultural strengths in the work that you are doing with families as a professional or volunteer today?

Activities

Families benefit from understanding family strengths. To best see how this works, visit the University of Nebraska-Lincoln website and find the AFSI. Print out copies of the AFSI and follow the simple directions for filling it out. In 10 or 12 minutes you will have an excellent idea of the strengths of your couple or family relationships from your perspective. If you have a partner, adolescent or young adult children, they could also fill out separate inventories and then you could share your perceptions with each other. Remember: no couple or family relationship is perfect and each individual has her or his own unique perception about how the relationship is functioning. Using what you have learned from the AFSI, you can discuss ways to strengthen your relationships by enhancing various strengths. The website includes in-depth discussions of the various family strengths and tips on how couples and families can achieve these strengths. You may have to adapt some of the questions, designed for the North American context, to fit the culture in which you live. A similar activity can also be completed with the Family Strengths Kit and ABCD resources described above.

Useful websites

American Family Strengths Inventory (AFSI): www.ianrpubs.unl.edu/epublic/
   live/g1881/build/g1881.pdf
Asia Pacific Asset-Based Community Development (ABCD) Network:
   www.newcastle.edu.au/research-centre/fac/workshops
Asset-Based Community Development (ABCD) Institute, Chicago:
   www.abcdinstitute.org
The Benevolent Society: www.bensoc.org.au/uploads/documents/
   TBSresearchsnapshot-vol3-aug2008.pdf
The Family Action Centre, University of Newcastle: www.newcastle.edu.au/
   research-centre/fac
Kansas State University at Manhattan: www.oznet.ksu.edu/DesktopDefault.
   aspx?tabid=22
The National Council on Family Relations: www.ncfr.org
St Luke's Innovative Resources: www.innovativeresources.com.au
University of Missouri at Columbia Extension: www.extension.missouri.
   edu/main/family/index.shtml
University of Nebraska-Lincoln Extension: www.ianrpubs.unl.edu/epublic/
   pages/index.jsp

References

ABCD Institute, Chicago (2009). Available online at: www.abcdinstitute.org

Asset-Based Community Development: Asia Pacific Network (2009). Available online at: www.newcastle.edu.au/research-centre/fac/workshopsabcd

The Benevolent Society (2008). 'Research Snapshot: A Summary of Research and Evaluation Findings'. Available online at: www.bensoc.org.au/uploads/documents/ TBSresearchsnapshot-vol3-aug2008.pdf

Collishaw, S., Pickles, A., Messer, J., Rutter, M., Shearer, C. & Maughan, B. (2007). Resilience to adult psychopathology following childhood maltreatment: Evidence from a community sample. *Child Abuse and Neglect*, 31, 211–29.

Coombs, R. J. (ed.) (2005). *Family Therapy Review*, 3–20. Lawrence Erlbaum Associates, Mahwah, NJ.

Dalla, R. L., DeFrain, J., Johnson, J. & Abbott, D. A. (2008). *Strengths and Challenges of New Immigrant Families: Implications for Research, Education, Policy, and Service*. Lexington Books/Rowman & Littlefield, Lanham, MD.

DeFrain, J. & Asay, S. M. (eds) (2007). *Strong Families Around the World: Strengths-based Research and Perspectives*. Routledge, Taylor & Francis Group, London.

DeFrain, J., Cook, R. & Gonzalez-Kruger, G. (2005). Family health and dysfunction. In R. J. Coombs (ed.), *Family Therapy Review*, 3–20. Lawrence Erlbaum Associates, Mahwah, NJ.

Dixon, L., Browne, K. & Hamilton-Giachritsis, C. (2009). Patterns of risk and protective factors in the intergenerational cycle of maltreatment. *Journal of Family Violence*, 24, 111–22.

The Engaging Fathers Project (nd). *Indigenous Men as Mentors Project*. Family Action Centre, University of Newcastle, Callaghan, Australia.

Esteinou, R. (2007). Strengths and challenges of Mexican families in the 21st century. In J. DeFrain & S. M. Asay (eds), *Strong Families Around the World: Strengths-based Research and Practice*, 309–34. Routledge, Taylor & Francis Group, London.

Family Action Centre (2008). *2007–2008 Home-Start Annual Performance Report to NSW Department of Community Services*. University of Newcastle, Newcastle, NSW.

Gabler, J. & Otto, H. (1964). Conceptualization of family strengths in the family life and other professional literature. *Journal of Marriage and the Family*, 26, 221–3.

Geggie, J. (2006). Australian practices in family education. *In Urban Transition and Family Education*, 219–33. Shanghai Culture Publishing House, Shanghai.

Geggie, J., DeFrain, J., Hitchcock, S. & Silberberg, S. (2000). *Family Strengths Research Project*, 55. Family Action Centre, University of Newcastle, Newcastle, NSW.

Geggie, J., Weston, R., Hayes, A. & Silberberg, S. (2007). The shaping of strengths and challenges of Australian families: Implications for policy and practice. In J. DeFrain & S. M. Asay (eds), *Strong Families Around the World: Strengths-based Research and Practice*, 217–420. Routledge, Taylor & Francis Group, London.

McGloin, J. M. & Widom, C. S. (2001). Resilience among abused and neglected children grown up. *Development and Psychopathology*, 13, 1021–38.

Multicultural Council of the Northern Territory (2008). *Strong Families Sharing Cultural Parenting Knowledge* (DVD). Northern Territory Government of Australia, Darwin.

Olson, D. H., DeFrain, J. & Skogrand, L. (2008). *Marriages and Families: Intimacy, Diversity and Strengths* (6th edn). McGraw Hill Higher Education, New York.

Otto, H. A. (1962). What is a strong family? *Marriage and Family Living*, 24, 77–81.

Otto, H. A. (1963). Criteria for assessing family strength. *Family Process*, 2, 329–39.

Skogrand, L., DeFrain, N., DeFrain, J. & Jones, J. E. (2007). *Surviving and Transcending a Traumatic Childhood: The Dark Thread*. Routledge, Taylor & Francis Group, London.

Stuart, G. & Brooks, D. (2008). *Stepping Stones: Supporting Students in a Caravan Park*. Family Action Centre, University of Newcastle, Callaghan, Australia.

Stuart, G. & Hammond, C. (2006). *Brothers Inside: Reflections on Fathering Workshops with Indigenous Prisoners*. Family Action Centre, University of Newcastle, Callaghan, Australia.

White, M. & Morgan, A. (2006). *Narrative Therapy with Children and Their Families*. Dulwich Centre Publishers, Adelaide.

Harnessing 'resilience' when working with children and families

Edwina Farrall and Fiona Arney

Learning goals

This chapter will enable you to:

1. Recognise how 'resilience' can highlight pathways and outcomes for vulnerable children and families
2. Consider how resilience might be best defined as an ongoing interaction between the person and their environment
3. Identify the risk and protective factors that underpin the process of resilience
4. Discover some of the practical applications that draw upon the concept of resilience
5. Understand the organisational and individual factors that can drive preferences for practice, including the likely practical uptake of concepts like 'resilience'
6. Learn how resilience-based practice guidance might help organise the ways in which practitioners and organisations engage with vulnerable children and families.

Introduction

Working with vulnerable children and families is a complex and ongoing process. Since vulnerable families often have multiple and complex needs, practitioners who work with them need to try to address both immediate issues such as physical safety and shelter, alongside longer term needs such as promoting good parenting and enabling individual behaviour change away from problems such as drug and alcohol misuse. As the problems that families and children facing hardship endure are complex and multifaceted, practitioners cannot rely on any one single method or theory in their practice, but instead need to adopt a practice philosophy that is able to consider families' strengths, weaknesses, needs, challenges, and priorities in a holistic and coherent way. In this chapter, we will discuss a particular approach to practice that lends itself well to all the different aspects of families' and children's lives, that of a *resilience-based* approach to practice.

Background

Interest in the idea of 'resilience' first developed in the early 1970s, when researchers wanted to identify which traits or contexts might protect 'at risk' young people from developing serious problems such as drug abuse, delinquency or mental illness in later life. The notion of 'risk' in this context relates to settings such as poverty, low education, unemployment, homelessness, parental psychopathology or substance misuse, in children's lives; and is based on an understanding that having just one risk factor is unlikely – risk is cumulative (Newman, 2002). Researchers such as Norman Garmezy (1974), E. James Anthony (1974) and Michael Rutter (1979) saw that some children seemed 'immune' to these problems and risks in their lives, and this led to the notion of 'resiliency' as a particular attribute of children. It should be noted however that being able to maintain behavioural functioning in situations of extreme adversity is not always emotionally healthy – being able to maintain the appearance of good behavioural functioning whilst experiencing great psychological distress has been termed 'apparent resilience' (Newman, 2002).

What is only now being increasingly understood is that resilience is a nuanced and fluid concept, being more of a process that leads to relatively positive outcomes over time rather than a fixed trait of the individual adult or child. In other words, resilience is seen as a relative process that is qualitatively different for every person and is seen to occur when there is relatively good adaptation or functioning despite past or present adversity or risk (Luthar, 2005). Because resilience is relative, it could mean that someone who has not succumbed to a drug addiction is resilient in some contexts, but also that someone who has earned a PhD or become a prominent politician is resilient in another context. It all depends upon the degree of risk and vulnerability in one's life to begin with. Even very socially disadvantaged people can show resilience if they embrace new challenges in positive ways and *thrive* in life.

As researchers tried to understand what particular factors enabled some at-risk children to grow into healthy and competent adults, a number of *protective* factors were developed to explain how risk factors were counteracted. Just like risk factors, these protective factors may be internal or external. A brief outline of various risk and protective factors for resilience as a function of their internal or external status is presented below in Table 3.1 (e.g., see Benard, 2004; Rutter, 2000; Werner, 2000).

As will be seen later in this chapter, contemporary resilience-based practice tends to gear outcomes around positive indicators or the attainment of positive goals, rather than simply the reduction of risk. This differs from more traditional approaches, with the emphasis set upon protective factors

Table 3.1: Internal and external risk and protective factors for resilience

	Risk		**Protective**
Internal	Poor attachment	**Internal**	Security of attachment
	Low self-esteem or self-efficacy		Good self-esteem or self-efficacy
	Male gender		Female gender
	Poor emotional regulation		Intelligence
	External locus of control		Internal locus of control
	Lack of autonomy or purpose		Empathy
	Poor problem-solving		Sense of purpose in life
External	Poverty	**External**	Positive school environment
	Unemployment		Good community connections
	(Parental) drug or alcohol misuse		Social support from friends
	(Parental) mental illness		Educational opportunities
	Sole parenting		Financial stability
	Geographic and/or social isolation		Participatory extended family

such as those listed above. These protective factors for resilience essentially exist across three categories: psychological or dispositional attributes; family support and cohesion; and external support systems (Friborg et al., 2003). The idea is that in casework with vulnerable children and families, workers should attempt to flesh out both the risk and protective factors faced by a family or by individuals within that family. Therefore, resilience-based practice is all about understanding both risks and strengths or resources in people's lives, and then working to minimise risks and increase resources to effect good change or maintain stability for families.

Reflective questions

Have you already heard of the concept of resilience? If yes, in what context? How would you define resilience? How would you assess resilience in a child?

Theories of resilience: strengths, attachment and the ecological perspective

Resilience-based practice aligns very closely with strengths-based and attachment-oriented approaches (as described in the previous two chapters). In Chapter 6, a sustained nurse home-visiting program is described, which draws heavily upon attachment theory and the importance of developing sound and nurturing bonds between mother and child. In this way, the program is promoting a secure base, emotional regulation, physical health and parental self-efficacy, all of which are also protective factors associated with resilience. Early childhood education and care centres, as will be outlined in Chapter 5, are fundamentally based upon child development theory and fostering the developmental gains and strengths of the child. Again, this means that important aspects of resilience, such as good peer relations, emotional regulation, self-esteem, educational opportunities and positive school experiences are also supported. Strengths-based practice that aims to promote and optimise the client's skills, resources and community connections also overlaps with the resilience factors described above.

Resilience research has increasingly adopted an ecological perspective (such as that of Urie Bronfenbrenner, described in Chapter 1), for one cannot minimise the risks facing individuals or promote their resources unless their situation and the *sources* of those risks and resources are also addressed. Thus, to work effectively with vulnerable children and families in a resilience-based way means that practitioners need to focus on the individual, the group (which includes the family and also schools) and their wider community and society at all times. Resilience-based practice also focuses on

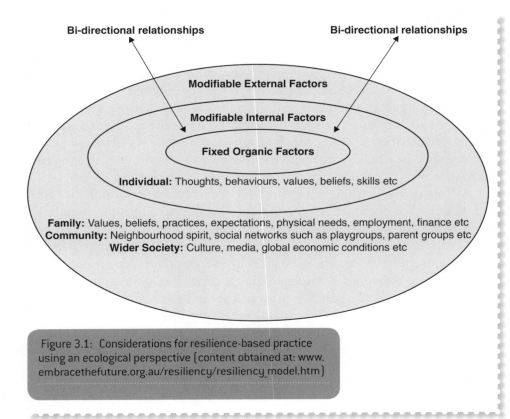

Figure 3.1: Considerations for resilience-based practice using an ecological perspective (content obtained at: www.embracethefuture.org.au/resiliency/resiliency_model.htm)

key transition points in children's lives (e.g., starting primary school, starting high school, parental separation) as these times of children's lives can present both threats and opportunities to develop coping skills and promote resilience (Newman, 2002). Resilience-based work can appear quite circular (e.g., when an outcome in one context such as enhanced self-esteem is also a protective factor for another outcome such as positive peer relationships in a later context) and this needs to be catered for and the wider world considered even when working at the individual level. Some of the ways this work plays out is set out above in Figure 3.1, which shows the resilience-based risk and protective factors that can exist at every level of the ecological model.

This illustration clearly demonstrates the many ways in which the factors at play in the lives of vulnerable children and families might influence one another. These influences need to be harnessed to build a network of support for at-risk children and families, drawing upon the resources of peers, schools, neighbourhoods and the wider community. While non-changeable and internal factors, such as genetic predispositions to illness or addiction, may still play a role in resiliency, ultimately the nature and extent of interpersonal supportive networks is much more important. It should be noted that there are some promising programs that focus on the cognitive underpinnings of resilience, including optimism, problem-solving and autonomy, such as the prominent Penn Resiliency Program in the US (Jaycox et al., 1994). The ecological perspective, however, would say that there are many influences on children's development (not just their own ways of thinking and behaving). And so the ecological perspective to resilience-based practice considers everything from the media and the political agenda, through to school policies and community programs, down to an individual's interests and skills and attributes. Moreover, at all times, the resilience-oriented practitioner must be considering both the strengths and weaknesses in any given situation.

At this point, you might be thinking that 'resilience' sounds like a bit of a catch-all term, meant to encompass all things to all people at all levels of society. Well, it must be said that 'resilience' has been criticised precisely because it cannot be easily defined or broken down into attainable steps for practice. In the past, traditional deficit approaches to practice simply relied on obtaining a 'diagnosis', implementing a 'treatment' or 'intervention' and looking at the overall result. When we talk about deficit approaches, we refer to the traditional approaches of medicine, psychology, social work, nursing and a number of other professions, where practitioners have been almost exclusively focused on what was 'wrong' with the client or patient, such as disease, disorder or delinquency.

The resilience approach, which is typically understood as focusing on individuals' and families' strengths and resources, is often contrasted with the deficit-based approaches from which it originally sprang (Garmezy, 1991). What the most recent resiliency theorists and proponents stress, however, is that a 'best' approach to resilience-based practice needs to incorporate both approaches – to consider risk *and* strength. In order to do this appropriately and thoroughly, and to mitigate some of the ambiguity surrounding the notion of resilience, a number of practitioners and researchers have developed detailed and organised theories and models to guide resilience-based practice. In the next section, we will discuss the main theoretical perspectives surrounding the construct of resilience and then put forward two prominent practice models that are being applied in promising and innovative ways around the Western world.

Activity

Try to identify someone you know whom you would consider to be 'at risk' or vulnerable in some way. Draw two columns labelled 'risks' and 'strengths/resources', and based on what you know about the person, write down every risk and protective factor you can see at play in their life.

Make sure you consider every ecological level and both internal and external factors. Examine whether there are more risks than resources, or vice versa.

Check if you can see how certain strengths might be used to counteract the influence of risks.

Harnessing 'resilience' in practice with vulnerable children and families: imperatives and guidelines

Models of resilience-based practice that have been put forward to date converge around a number of central ideas or principles, and some key imperatives regarding their development and implementation have also been put forward. In terms of program roll-out, the website of the organisation 'Embrace the Future' (www.embracethefuture.org.au), which is a project of the Mental Health Foundation of Australia (www.mhfa.org.au), states 'best practice' resiliency programs are defined as those which:

- Focus on identifying and developing protective factors in the context of past or current adversity
- Target at-risk children, who are most likely to benefit from resiliency programs because they are experiencing significant adversity
- Target their intervention towards times of transition and stress, such as school or puberty transitions, so lessons from resilience programs can be used to assist coping when coping with challenging circumstances
- Have a strong research or evidence base, so that practices are well-founded, reliable and replicable
- Hold a preference for systemic interventions, meaning the entire ecological context should be considered when designing activities or interventions and
- Have evaluation built into the program, so that the efficacy of the program can be documented, funding secured and best practice appropriately disseminated and replicated.

When one takes a closer look at these key features, a number of implications and questions emerge. Specifically, how does one design the actual interventions to take place? How does one appropriately identify and document all the relevant risk and protective factors? How can one ensure that the entire ecological context is addressed? The key challenge here essentially relates to organising the domains of intervention into a coherent framework that lends itself to evaluation and replication. This is critical, as there is not yet a comprehensive evidence base around the concept of resilience-based practice. It is a relatively new and complex area, so any practice and research in the area needs to be carefully developed and organised to ensure that lessons learned may be incorporated into the burgeoning knowledge base. See Tony Newman's (2002) review of effective strategies for promoting resilience in child welfare services for information about specific strategies that aim to decrease risk and enhance protection at the level of the child, family and community.

A small number of researchers have recognised the need to put forward coherent and systematised models for resilience-based practice. Ann Masten and Jennifer Powell (2003) have been instrumental in developing a framework for resilience programs that emphasises strengths over risks (without discarding risk altogether), and focuses on the positive resources, health, and competence of children and young people. Their framework also suggests that programs' goals, models, measures and methods should all reflect a focus on positive adaptation and the natural human capacity for healthy adaptation. Masten and Powell's (2003) specific recommendations are presented in Box 3.1 below.

Box 3.1: Resilience program frameworks (Masten & Powell, 2003)

Mission: Frame goals in positive terms

Rather than focusing on reducing problems or risks, programs should aim to promote competence and shift development toward more positive trajectories.

Models: Include positive predictors and outcomes in models of change

The models used to develop programs should include aspects of health and competence, as well as disorder and dysfunction. There is also a need to focus on normal developmental milestones and recognise protective factors as well as risk factors.

Measures: Assess the positive and the negative

Just as outcomes and predictors should encompass both strengths and competencies and risks and disorders, so too must the measures used to assess the program tap both sides of resilience. Success of a program, however, should be set out in terms of positive outcomes rather than just the absence of problems.

Methods: Develop and implement multiple strategies to address multiple resilience needs

Resilience programs can adopt any one or all of three key strategies: a) *risk-based* approaches, which aim to reduce adversity; b) *asset-based* strategies, which attempt to promote or increase the assets or resources in children's lives; or c) *process-oriented* approaches, which aim to mobilise children's protective resources and thereby improve adaptation and functioning. This last set of strategies could, for example, include improving attachment relationships between children and parents, or increasing parenting capacity through community classes, or by providing extra educational support to children with special needs.

Activity

Try to think of a few ways you would promote resilience for each 'type' of practice approach put forward in the 'Methods' section of Box 3.1: Risk based, asset based and process oriented. If helpful, frame your interventions in reference to someone you know or work with.

Using 'resilience' when working with children and families: snapshots of practice

This summary of resilience program guidelines provided by Masten and Powell (2003) provides a useful theoretical platform from which to explore actual real world approaches to resilience-based practice and the conceptual models that underpin them. In terms of the recommendations set out in Box 3.1, where most contemporary models for resilience-based practice vary is in terms of their methods, or how they develop or organise multiple strategies to address resilience needs. As stated above, Masten and Powell (2003) conceptualised varying methods as being either risk based, or asset based, or process oriented. As will be seen, the following two frameworks developed for resilience-based practice in fact address all three strategic directions in their philosophy, and are arguably two of the most prominent models in the field. The two models (one from the US and one from the UK) will be discussed in this section, including an appraisal of their apparent utility and uptake to date. Finally, an exploration of the UK model in an Australian family and child service will be explained, with results of this research used to provide some insight into the views of practitioners and clients who participated in this resilience-based work.

Henderson's Resiliency Wheel

The approach to working in resilience-based ways developed by Nan Henderson (2008) and colleagues in the US is primarily a conceptual foundation to underpin daily activities across a variety of contexts, including education, social work, aged care and coaching or mentoring. In this sense, this approach is not so much a new theory or model so much as a graphical representation of what is being increasingly understood through research. Specifically, Henderson (2008) draws upon research to put forward a model that is replicable and meaningful across the various contexts mentioned above. Henderson (2008) defines resilience in a way that accords with the general consensus in the literature, as is evidenced by comparing her definition with that distilled by Luthar (2005) from over five decades of resilience research: 'Resiliency can be defined as the capacity to spring back, rebound, successfully adapt in the face of adversity, and develop social and academic competence despite exposure to severe stress... or simply the stress of today's world' (Henderson, 2008, p. 3) and 'Resilience is a phenomenon or process reflecting relatively positive adaptation despite experiences of significant adversity or trauma' (Luthar, 2005, p. 742).

Henderson recognises that resilience is both about identifying and addressing key risk and protective factors, but takes it to a new level by organising those practice imperatives into a useful diagram known as the 'Resiliency Wheel', which is depicted in Figure 3.2 below:

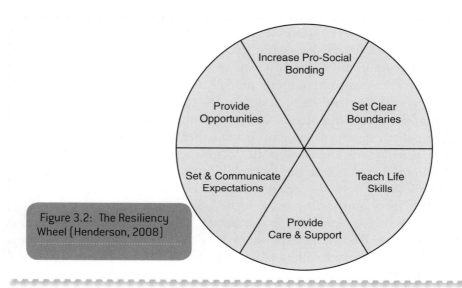

Figure 3.2: The Resiliency Wheel (Henderson, 2008)

To explain this figure further:

- The **provision of care and support** relates to the central importance of caring relations to promote resiliency. This applies to parent–child attachment, as well as the broader supportive environments that are essential for learning and growth.
- **Setting and communicating expectations** relates to developing and upholding expectations of oneself or one's child that are high yet realistic. Such expectations are excellent motivators and can facilitate learning and effective problem-solving.
- **Providing opportunities** refers to giving people, including children and young people, channels for active and meaningful participation. This promotes resilience in a number of ways (e.g., through raising self-esteem and self-efficacy, promoting autonomy and good problem-solving) as individuals take on appropriate responsibility as they identify, plan, evaluate and implement activities.

- Strengthening interpersonal connections through encouraging **pro-social bonding** is an important component of resilience building, as good social support networks are critical for good functioning for young and old.
- It is also important to **set clear boundaries** that are consistent and fair for children and young people, or with whomever one is working. This allows for continuity and some degree of predictability in people's lives, which is important for building stability and trust.
- Finally, people of all ages will encounter and have to navigate certain challenges in their lives, including difficult times of transition (e.g., to school, to a new job, to an aged care facility), so it is essential to **teach life skills** that allow them to approach a situation with good perspective and sound problem-solving. The capacity to address and resolve one's own problems and challenges is central to fostering autonomy and maintaining resiliency.

What is innovative about this approach is that it represents a consistent resilience framework that is promoted as being applicable across multiple settings. Henderson and colleagues have used this model not just as a guideline for therapeutic intervention (Henderson, Sharp-Light & Benard, 2000a), but also as a more generalist platform for resilience building in schools (Henderson & Milstein, 1996; Henderson, Sharp-Light & Benard, 2000b), workplaces (Henderson, 2008), communities (Henderson, Sharp-Light & Benard, 2000a) and even aged care facilities (Henderson, 2008). In this approach, the provision of care and support is seen as fundamental, comprising the resiliency domain that underpins all other segments in the wheel depicted above. This aligns closely with work that emphasises the central importance of secure attachment in resilience paradigms (Cooper et al., 2005; Luthar & Zelazo, 2003), and, as will be seen below, Daniel and Wassell's resilience framework also pays careful attention to secure attachment.

Henderson's (2008) approach to resilience is accessible and popular, and she has authored several books and attended conferences and conventions to disseminate this work. Perhaps its weakness, however, lies in the fact that it is not easily evaluated or investigated, instead forming more a philosophical base from which professionals should operate, rather than a recipe for intervention. Hence, it is more the result of research than the means of furthering research.

In contrast, the resilience model set out below was developed in rigorous and systematic ways, and has been the subject of preliminary investigations and empirical enquiry. This model, originating from the UK, will be discussed in detail, to be followed by an appraisal of recent attempts to embed this approach into a new setting. Ultimately, promising resilience programs need to be rolled out on larger and geographically broader scales, so a sound consideration of adaptability and utility across different contexts and user groups is important – a theme which is explored in Chapter 13 on the diffusion of innovations.

Reflective questions

Does any one of the six areas of the Resiliency Wheel stand out to you as particularly important for fostering resilience? Why or why not? Are there specific areas not present in the wheel that you think should be included? How is culture or could culture be incorporated in this model?

Daniel and Wassell's Six Resilience Domains

Recent work in the UK around the concept of resilience has centred on its practical utility for child protection interventions. Brigid Daniel has been the driving force behind this research, and she and her colleague Sally Wassell have developed a coherent and systematic set of resilience domains that may be seen to underpin child protection case work in theoretically and ecologically valid ways. Daniel and Wassell (Daniel & Wassell, 2002a, 2002b, 2002c) developed their model upon extensive reviews of the literature and studies of best practice, putting forward a set of six domains that are of fundamental relevance to the resiliency of a child.

These six domains are:
- Secure Base
- Friendships
- Talents and interests
- Education
- Positive values and
- Social competencies.

In their model, Daniel and Wassell (Daniel & Wassell, 2002a; 2002b; 2002c) emphasise the commonality of these domains for all children, regardless of their situation in life or the degree of adversity or harm they face. All children require a satisfactory quota of each of these domains in their life, and these domains can also serve protective functions when circumstances become more difficult or inherently harmful, as in the context of child maltreatment. What is meant about their 'protective' value is that if a child has been the subject of abuse or neglect, a practitioner can, after the immediate source of harm has been removed, focus on these domains to help rebuild the child's resilience.

More often than not, one domain or a set of domains is particularly relevant, for example a child may have been kept home to care for a mentally ill or substance abusing parent, perhaps resulting in emotional abuse and a variety of forms of neglect. As the child has not been able to attend school, their domains of friendships, education and perhaps social competencies have been left undeveloped. The practitioner could choose to focus their work on improving the situation in these domains.

In another situation, a young, single and socially isolated mother might be having trouble bonding with her infant. A practitioner from an early intervention service would clearly work to improve maternal attachment, which addresses the *secure base* for the child. In other words, the domains can be used to organise and systematise, rather than prescribe, case work clarifying and articulating the nature of interventions that might usually be left to practitioner experience or intuition or organisational procedures.

As with the previous model, the domain of secure base is set out as having pre-eminent importance amongst the set of six domains (Daniel & Wassell, 2002a; 2002b; 2002c). This is based upon extensive research (e.g., Bowlby, 1988; Cooper et al., 2005; Luthar & Zelazo, 2003), which points to the fundamental importance of a secure attachment relationship in a child's life (as outlined in Chapter 1). The attachment relationship appears to drive later emotional regulation and behaviour throughout the lifespan, which means that any early deficit in this secure base could have far reaching consequences.

In order to gauge the perceived usefulness and uptake of the model in real world casework, Daniel carried out a small pilot study in Scotland that drew upon a set of eight case studies to explore the extent to which the concept of resilience can be operationalised for use with neglected children in the context of statutory child protection work (Daniel, 2006). The study involved caseworkers working with neglected children, and the workers received six days of dedicated training on the resilience framework and its usage. The qualitative data obtained indicated that practitioners were already familiar with the concept of resilience, used the resilience domain model to a greater or lesser extent, and found it helpful (Daniel, 2006). The case studies around the eight neglected children recruited for the study also supported the notion of the central importance of the secure base domain. The comments the practitioners made not only suggested that the secure base might underpin all other domains, but also raised the possibility that careful assessment of the other five domains would help to highlight difficulties with the secure base. In this way, secure base was seen as both a cause and consequence of other realms of children's functioning. Whether other domains in children's lives can be truly and sustainably improved in the absence of a good secure base or attachment relationship is an important future direction for resilience research. These findings contrast with work examining the adoption and application of resilience-based practice by child protection social workers in the UK (McMurray et al., 2008). In that study the workers had not been trained in a specific resilience-based approach and this was reflected in their difficulty in conceptualising resilience and their reliance on a deficit-based approach. These different results highlight the importance of professional education in resilience-based approaches to strengthen understanding and the perceived usefulness of the approach.

Activity

Examine the six domains put forward by Daniel and Wassell, and try to match or align them with corresponding domains in Henderson's model. Do you get a perfect fit?

Consider what is the same/different about these two models for resilience-based practice. Again, think about the relevance of culture to the attachment domains put forward in both models, and think of how it might be incorporated in resilience-based practice to improve outcomes for children.

What does resilience-based practice actually look like?

A number of prominent researchers in the field of resilience have developed explicit principles for resilience-based practice guidance. Rutter (1987), for example, suggested that such practice frameworks should:

- Alter or reduce a child's exposure to risk
- Reduce the negative chain reaction of exposure
- Establish and maintain self-esteem and self-efficacy
- Create opportunities.

Masten (1994) similarly recommended that resilience-based practice should comprise:

- An aim to reduce vulnerability and risk
- Reduce the number of stressors and pile-up
- Increase the available resources
- Foster resilience strings or pathways, and, like Rutter (1987)
- Alter or reduce a child's exposure to risk.

Finally, Benard (2004) has also suggested the need for children to experience as part of their participation in resilience-based practice:

- Caring relationships
- High expectations
- Opportunities to participate and contribute.

Looking at these recommendations, it's possible to see the research under-pinnings of both Henderson's (2008) and Daniel and Wassell's (Daniel & Wassell, 2002a; 2002b; 2002c) models. Both models broadly aim to reduce vulnerabilities and risks while increasing available resources, and the more concrete recommendations provided by Benard (2004) and to a lesser extent Rutter (1987) are clearly reflected in the six domains or foci of each mode.

Below, in Table 3.2, are a number of strategies and interventions that have been identified by UK and Australian practitioners as being examples of resilience-based practice (Daniel et al., 2009). Some were put forward in direct relation to Daniel and Wassell's (Daniel & Wassell, 2002a; 2002b; 2002c) model, and others were described as being part of a diverse, creative and flexible approach to practice.

Activity

Consider which of these strategies seem to align with the two resilience models, and see how well those strategies match the key areas in each model.

Table 3.2: **Examples of resilience-based practice strategies**

Content of strategies	Methods	Intended outcomes
Goal setting	Counselling	Better concentration
Problem-solving skills	Referral to other services and improved interagency responses	Assertiveness
Positive behaviours	Role plays and coaching	Coping skills (e.g., coping with losing games)
Social skills	Play and outdoor activities (including play therapy)	Acceptance of disappointment
Coping strategies	Life story work and journaling	Emotional regulation
Communication skills	Peer support groups	Parent–child bonding
Help-seeking behaviour	Supported play groups	Being able to deal with surprises
'Stranger danger'	Parenting classes to improve attachment relationships	Cool-down techniques and anger management
Parental knowledge about attachment and child development	Quality child care	Problem-solving Friendships
Parenting skills	Providing positive feedback	Community connectedness

(Cont.)

Table 3.2: (*Cont.*)

Content of strategies	Methods	Intended outcomes
Parent–child attachment programs like Marte Meo	Sharing, listening and trust building	Social supports
Understanding the child's history, allowing time for reflection and exploration	Tutoring	
Housing, legal, employment and financial assistance	Advocacy with schools	
Building community connections	Access to medical care	
	Advocacy for parents' educational/training opportunities	
	Mentoring and peer support	
	Reflective techniques and therapeutic writing	

Examining the use of resilience-based approaches in Australia

As was stated above, Masten and Powell (2003) emphasised the essential importance of resilience interventions having some evaluation built into the program, so that utility and feasibility could be documented, further funding secured, and the program rolled out to new settings. The pilot study undertaken by Daniel (2006) served as a rudimentary evaluation of acceptability of the model, at least insofar as being able to determine that practitioners tended to find the six domain approach to resilience assessment and intervention quite helpful. Together with colleagues in the UK, the Australian Centre for Child Protection undertook a research investigation into how well the practice guidance had been transplanted into Australian- and UK-based organisations (Daniel et al., 2009). This took place several months after Daniel visited the sites and delivered three days of training with child protection and early intervention workers, leaving practice manuals and instructive materials with the workers. The shift to a more resilience-based approach to practice was fully endorsed and enabled by the organisation itself at a management level.

Voices of practitioners: the utility of the concept of resilience for practice

The centre's research within the Australian organisation asked participating practitioners how they perceived the application of the concept of resilience within practice. Some interesting implications for how resilience can be used in child and family services were seen. Firstly, in line with Daniel's (2006) earlier study, the practitioners generally had a good understanding of the concept of resilience, saw it as relevant to their work, and thought it was easily applied in practice. The majority of caseworkers understood that resilience was a process, but tended not to discuss the internal and external factors that might serve as risk or protective influences. As with Daniel's (2006) research and our work in Australia (Daniel et al., 2009) practitioners saw a resilience-led approach as a very useful and valid approach to practice. Resilience-based work was described as promoting trust, rapport, and cooperation between client and caseworker. It was also seen as holding unique value for practitioners, helping them to keep focused on gains and goals in the context of considerably challenging and confronting child protection casework.

The only limitations highlighted around the concept of resilience related to it depending on client readiness and cooperation, in the sense that clients needed to be prepared to make positive changes in their lives, and also that it might somehow mask the risks of a situation, if too much focus was given to resilience and positive adaptation. One practitioner noted 'Families need to want to have us on board. They have to be prepared to acknowledge challenges and... to be willing to make some changes. Motivation is a very big thing!' and a second said 'I'm not convinced that resilience is the best framework to apply. It can be a mask on occasions for more maladaptive functioning.'

While practitioners in the main saw resilience as a useful concept, surprisingly the interview data indicated that workers tended *not* to use the formal framework in their actual practice, preferring instead to adopt what was described as a more holistic and eclectic approach that better accorded with their notions of the complex field of child and family welfare. Diverse approaches to practice emerged, including relying on a 'strengths-based' approach, where strengths and resources are emphasised (Saleeby, 2002), using observations and discussions as central therapeutic tools, and striving to connect clients in with social support or community networks as integral to the mitigation of harm (Daniel et al., 2009). Chapter 7 describes the use of strengths-based approaches as a tool for working with fathers.

When asked what sorts of theories or models, including resilience, might direct or influence their casework, both the Australian sample and a comparison UK sample of caseworkers, indicated that attachment theory (Bowlby, 1988) and the Circle of Security Model (Cooper et al., 2005) were the most influential, followed by an adoption of a strengths-based approach (Saleeby, 2002). Attachment theory was generally understood as relating mostly to children having a sense of security and predictability in their life. This was understood as promoting overall resilience. When respondents were asked to give more detail about the strengths-based approach, however, the theoretical differentiations they were making became a lot less clear. Specifically, it varied considerably as to whether practitioners saw strengths-based work as separate from, or complementary with, resilience-based work. This was true for both the Australian and UK samples, and highlighted the degree of variability amongst caseworkers in how they viewed the different models. Here are some examples of participating caseworkers' comments on this: 'We use a strengths-based model... because it gives families total ownership of their problems...'; 'To me, resilience sits side by side with strengths-based work...'; 'The key to resilience or strengths-based work is the relationships you begin with...'

One might ask whether it *matters* that practitioners hold different names for, or perspectives toward, the same type of work. The issue arises, however, when practitioners believe they are undertaking resilience-based work, when in fact they are aligning their work to an interpretation of a strengths-based approach in which only the strengths and resources in a person or situation are highlighted. Hence, there is potential to 'miss half the picture' when practice guidance is misunderstood or erroneously applied. This is not to say, however, that strengths-based work per se is an inferior approach. By no means; rather, it is essential that a practice approach is chosen on the basis of a solid rationale for the work at hand, and all parties then work toward that common goal. Groups of practitioners need to share a common understanding of their program logic and theoretical orientations to avoid confusion, increase transparency and accountability, and bolster the chances of effective dissemination of new approaches.

In part, the diversity of practice approaches seen reflects the complex work carried out in child protection and early intervention work. Practitioners are required to think flexibly, creatively and sensitively to tailor their intervention to the particular set of circumstances facing their client(s). This may lead them to focus on more practical or tangible issues such as legal support, adequate housing, medical care, or employment, as was indeed the case with the practitioners in the Australian research sample. Other mainstays of practice, however, such as focusing on emotions and health, promoting parenting skills and confidence, and reducing social isolation – also very prominent interventions in the research sample – *do* align clearly with resilience program frameworks such as Daniel and Wassell's six domains of resilience-based practice. In this sense, resilience models or frameworks could be used to *organise* one's practice, to create theoretical meaning that might be juxtaposed against practical considerations, and to promote transparency of approach and thus replicability.

Reflective questions

Do you think it is useful to refer to a particular theory when developing and undertaking casework strategies with vulnerable children and families? What are the merits and dangers of aligning our practice to certain methods or models?

Conclusion

This chapter has presented an overview of resilience theory and its applications, shed light on a select number of practice models that have operationalised resilience as integral to strong child and family practice, and described practitioners' perspectives of resilience-based practice. Central to these discussions is the overriding imperative for researchers and practitioners alike to consider both strengths *and* weaknesses in any situation or context, be it casework, model development, or practice framework utility. This onus holds the potential to transform contemporary child and family services as we know them, enabling practitioners and organisations to embrace a degree of holism that is still theoretically powerful and relevant, with the end result of a more balanced and transparent experience for their clients. As society continues to strive to better the lives of its most vulnerable citizens, a wider transformation is also possible, in that as we attempt to bolster resilience for others, so are we also likely to foster our own strengths and resilience. Resilience is an inherently fluid and dynamic process of change and interaction, bouncing off our own experiences and those of people around us. As such, resilience-based practice holds great potential to enable sustainable shifts in the ecological integrity and welfare of individuals, families, groups, organisations and societies of any time or place.

Useful websites

Early Childhood Australia for general information, especially for parents of younger children and infants: www.earlychildhoodaustralia.org.au/ emotional_foundations_for_learning/resilience/about_resilience.html
Embrace the Future: www.embracethefuture.org.au/resiliency
The Mental Health Foundation of Australia: www.mhfa.org.au
Resiliency in Action: www.resiliency.com

References

Anthony, E. J. (1974). The syndrome of the psychologically invulnerable child. In E. J. Anthony & C. Koupernik (eds), *The Child in His Family: Children at Psychiatric Risk*, Volume 3, 3–10. Wiley, New York.

Benard, B. (2004). *Resiliency: What Have We Learned?* WestEd, San Francisco.

Bowlby, J. (1988). *A Secure Base: Parent–Child Attachment and Healthy Human Development*. Basic Books, New York.

Cooper, G., Hoffman, K., Berlin, L. J., Zaiv, Y., Amaya-Jackson, L. & Greenberg, M. T. (2005). *The Circle of Security Intervention: Differential Diagnosis and Differential Treatment. Enhancing Early Attachments*. Guilford, New York.

Daniel, B. (2006). Operationalizing the concept of resilience in child neglect: Case study research. *Child Care, Health & Development*, 32 (3), 303–9.

Daniel, B., Vincent, S., Farrall, E. & Arney, F. (2009). How is the concept of resilience operationalised in practice with vulnerable children? *International Journal of Child and Family Welfare*. Accepted for publication.

Daniel, B. & Wassell, S. (2002a). *Adolescence: Assessing and Promoting Resilience in Vulnerable Children III*. Jessica Kingsley, London.

Daniel, B. & Wassell, S. (2002b). *The Early Years: Assessing and Promoting Resilience in Vulnerable Children I*. Jessica Kingsley, London.

Daniel, B. & Wassell, S. (2002c). *The School Years: Assessing and Promoting Resilience in Vulnerable Children II*. Jessica Kingsley, London.

Friborg, O., Hjemdal, O., Rosenvinge, J. H. & Martinussen, M. (2003). A new rating scale for adult resilience: What are the central protective resources behind healthy adjustment? *International Journal of Methods in Psychiatric Research*, 12 (2), 65–76.

Garmezy, N. (1974). The study of competence in children at risk for severe psycho-pathology. In E. J. Anthony & C. Koupernik (eds), *The Child in His Family: Children at Psychiatric Risk*, Volume 3, 547. Wiley, New York.

Garmezy, N. (1991). Resiliency and vulnerability to adverse developmental outcomes associated with poverty. *American Behavioral Scientist*, 34 (4), 416–30.

Henderson, N. (2008). 'Unlocking the power of resiliency', Resiliency in Action Training and Publications, Resiliency in Action, Inc., Ojai, CA. Available online at: www.center-school.org/Student_Success/documents/Resiliencyhandoutsbestset.pdf

Henderson, N. & Milstein, M. (1996). *Resiliency in Schools: Making it Happen for Students and Educators*. Corwin Press, Thousand Oaks, CA.

Henderson, N., Sharp-Light, N. & Benard, B. (eds) (2000a). *Mentoring For Resilience: Setting Up Programs To Move Youth From 'Stressed To Success'*. Resiliency in Action, Inc., Ojai, CA.

Henderson, N., Sharp-Light, N. & Benard, B. (eds) (2000b). *Schoolwide Approaches for Fostering Resiliency*. Resiliency in Action, Inc., Ojai, CA.

Jaycox, L. H., Reivich, K. J., Gillham, J. & Seligman, M. (1994). Prevention of depressive symptoms in school children. *Behavior Research & Therapy*, 32 (8), 801–16.

Luthar, S. (2005). Resilience in development: A synthesis of research across five decades. In D. Cicchetti & D. J. Cohen (eds), *Developmental Psychopathology: Risk, Disorder and Adaptation* (2nd edn), Volume 3, 739–5. Wiley, New York.

Luthar, S. & Zelazo, L. B. (2003). Research on resilience: An integrative review. In S. Luthar (ed.), *Resilience and Vulnerability: Adaptation in the Context of Childhood Adversities*, 510–50. Cambridge University Press, New York

Masten, A. (1994). Resilience in individual development: Successful adaptation despite risk and adversity. In M. C. Wang & E. W. Gordon (eds), *Educational Resilience in Inner-city America*, 3–25. Lawrence Erlbaum Associates, Hillsdale, NJ.

Masten, A. & Powell, J. (2003). A resiliency framework for research, policy and practice. In S. Luthar (ed.), *Resilience and Vulnerability*, 1–29. Cambridge University Press, New York.

McMurray, I., Connolly, H., Preston-Shoot, M. & Wigley, V. (2008). Constructing resilience: Social workers' understandings and practice. *Health and Social Care in the Community*, 16 (3), 299–309.

Newman, T. (2002). *Promoting Resilience: A Review of Effective Strategies for Child Care Servi ces*. Centre for Evidence Based Social Sciences, University of Exeter, Exeter, UK.

Rutter, M. (1979). Protective factors in children's responses to stress and disadvantage. In M. W. Kent & J. E. Rolf (eds), *Primary Prevention in Psychopathology: Social Competence in Children*, 8, 49–74. University Press of New England, Hanover, NH.

Rutter, M. (1987). Psychosocial resilience and protective mechanisms. *American Journal of Orthopsychiatry*, 57, 316–31.

Rutter, M. (2000). Resilience reconsidered: Conceptual considerations. In J. Shonkoff & S. Meisels (eds), *Handbook of Early Childhood Intervention* (2nd edn), 651–82. Cambridge University Press, New York.

Saleeby, D. (2002). *The Strengths Perspective in Social Work Practice* (3rd edn). Allyn & Bacon, New York.

Werner, E. (2000). Protective factors and individual resilience. In J. Shonkoff & S. Meisels (eds), *Handbook of Early Childhood Intervention* (2nd edn), 115–34. Cambridge University Press, New York.

Working within and between organisations

Dorothy Scott

Learning goals

This chapter will enable you to:

1. Understand current policy directions that are supporting more holistic approaches to working with vulnerable families who have multiple and complex needs
2. Identify the practitioner, organisational and policy related factors which shape practitioner roles
3. Consider the potential for broadening practitioner roles so that they are more holistic and family centred
4. Understand the importance of working across professional and organisational boundaries and the factors that influence this
5. Be able to accept and effectively manage the conflict that can occur in working across professional and organisational boundaries.

Introduction

With the growing realisation that many varied and complex problems, from global warming to crime, infectious diseases and child abuse and neglect, cannot be solved by one service sector or 'silo', there is increasing momentum for 'joined up' approaches to tackle such issues. In relation to socially marginalised people, overarching 'social inclusion' policy frameworks in some countries are focusing attention on how sectors such as health, education, housing, employment and social services can work together more effectively.

This has two main implications for practitioners working with families with multiple and complex needs. One, greater emphasis is being placed on redefining practitioner roles and models of practice so they are more comprehensive. The first part of this chapter therefore explores how practitioner and organisational roles might evolve to respond more holistically to families with multiple and complex needs.

Two, greater emphasis is now being placed on how service providers across different organisations, professions and service sectors work in partnership so that more integrated and 'joined up' services are delivered. The second part of this chapter explores how practitioners need to understand and manage the potential for conflict when working across such boundaries if this goal is to be achieved.

Contemporary policy context

As the close relationship between problems such as poverty, mental illness, homelessness, substance misuse, unemployment, crime, antisocial behaviour, poor health, low literacy and child abuse and neglect is increasingly understood, new ways of thinking and responding to this challenge are emerging. How to develop systems and funding models that get beyond the fragmentation and duplication created by 'single input services based on categorical funding', when trying to serve individuals and families with multiple and complex needs, is a major challenge. At the service delivery level a related challenge is how to tailor services to meet the individual needs of specific families and give the consumers of services greater involvement in decisions in how services are delivered – that is, how do we keep the family, and not the service, at the centre of what we do?

In countries such as the UK, and more recently Australia, 'social inclusion' policies have provided an overarching framework for understanding and responding to 'socially marginalised' individuals, families and communities. Hayes, Gray & Edwards (2008) describe the three commonly accepted forms of social exclusion as:

- *Wide exclusion*, referring to the number of people excluded on a single or small number of indicators (e.g., unemployment)
- *Deep exclusion*, referring to multiple forms of entrenched and deep seated exclusion (e.g., a combination of unemployment, lack of accommodation and social isolation in addition to individual problems such as disability or chronic illness)
- *Concentrated exclusion*, referring to a geographical concentration of social problems (e.g., in urban areas in which the manufacturing industry has

declined, there may be a concentration of unemployment, poor housing, crime and child neglect).

Recent policy trends in the UK are encouraging services across different fields and sectors to 'think family' (see also Chapter 1). Stimulated in part by a crime prevention agenda, a new emphasis is being placed on building the capacity of all services to reduce the negative impact on children of parental substance misuse, crime, mental health problems and unemployment. The Social Exclusion Taskforce in the Cabinet Office led a cross-Whitehall review on families at risk in 2007 and early 2008, which culminated in an initiative called 'Think Family'. Through the 'Family Pathfinder Programme' launched in May 2008, 15 local government areas are testing innovative ways of supporting vulnerable families (Social Exclusion Taskforce, 2008).

The 'Think Family' initiative builds on the foundations of other major policy initiatives such as 'Sure Start' and 'Every Child Matters'. 'Every Child Matters' is the UK Government's response to the inquiry by Lord Laming into the child abuse death of Victoria Climbie, and has a number of elements: a legal requirement on agencies to work together; a common assessment framework; shared performance indicators across portfolios; pooling of budgets through Children's Trusts in local government areas; and an inspectorate model of accountability. Building on these and driven by a number of concerns, most notably crime prevention, the 'Think Family' initiative has a number of core elements.

- *No 'wrong door'* (contact with any service offers an open door to joined up support)
- *Look at the whole family* (services take into account family circumstances and adult services consider clients as parents)
- *Build on family strengths* (relationship- and strength-based engagement)
- *Provide support tailored to need* (no one size fits all).

In relation to socially disadvantaged families with young children, there has been a great deal of interest in tapping the potential of locally accessible universal children's services to be unstigmatised 'platforms' from which early intervention and individually tailored intensive assistance can be offered. This has led to a greater emphasis on working with parents for those employed in traditionally child-focused services such as maternal and child health, and early childhood education and care. This is explored in some of the chapters which follow. It has also led to a greater emphasis on such services working in close collaboration with one another, and on the co-location and integration of early childhood services as well as a range of family support and specialist early intervention services.

Far less attention has been given to how traditionally adult-focused services, in fields such as mental health, drug and alcohol treatment, corrections, domestic violence and homelessness, might become more responsive to the vulnerable children of their adult clients. However, there are some promising approaches in some of these fields, such as enhancing the capacity of adult mental health services to be more responsive to the needs of the children of parents with a mental illness (Cowling, 2004). This has resulted in the development of an Australian Government funded initiative called Children of Parents with a Mental Illness (COPMI), aimed at strengthening the capacity of adult mental health services to address the parental roles of their adult clients and to respond to the needs of their children (www. copmi.net.au). There have also been promising attempts to build better bridges between adult mental health and children's services. For example, Chapter 9 describes an innovative program in which a mental health liaison nurse located in a statutory child protection service works to provide a more informed and coordinated response to families by both child protection and adult mental health services.

Similarly, in the field of drug and alcohol treatment services, there are several encouraging initiatives, including the 'Parents Under Pressure Program' in Queensland (Dawe & Harnett, 2007) and the 'Nobody's Clients' and 'Counting the Kids' projects in Victoria (Odyssey Institute of Studies, 2004). In the words of a practitioner in a child welfare agency who helped establish a therapeutic playgroup in a drug treatment agency, 'Whenever the parents' interests and needs are regarded as antithetical to those of their children and relegated to second place, their incentive to cooperate with services in the care of their children is diminished' (Mohammed, 2003, p. 68).

In fields such as homelessness, there is increasing interest in how best to respond to the needs of children accompanying their parents in emergency housing services. In the field of domestic violence there has also been increasing focus on the needs of children and the impact of domestic violence on the mother–child relationship (Humphreys, 2006). In the corrections field, the Victorian Association for the Care and Resettlement of Offenders (VACRO) has recently published a report that examines the unmet needs of children across the criminal justice system (Hannon, 2007). While these are all promising initiatives, they are relatively isolated examples in their fields. To achieve system-wide reform requires not only the right policies and funding models, but a workforce that is willing to make major changes in the way it works with families with multiple and complex needs.

In relation to working with vulnerable families, most practitioners will be in a setting or have come from a profession that traditionally focuses on the adult or the child. For traditionally adult-focused professions and services, such as mental health or drug treatment services, recognising the needs of children requires major changes. Similarly, for traditionally child-focused professions and services, such as child health nurses and early childhood education and care workers, recognising and responding to the needs of parents requires major changes.

Activities

Consider the policy changes now occurring in a field with which you are familiar. Are there any shifts toward more integrated and holistic approaches in the delivery of services? If so, what prompted this? Do you know how such changes are seen 'on the ground' by practitioners? What might such changes mean for service providers and for vulnerable children and their families?

Choose a traditionally 'child' or 'adult' focused field mentioned above with which you are not familiar. Using the internet, see if you can identify any recent policy directions in that field which may support an approach that is more 'child and family sensitive'. Did you come across any terms and concepts that were new to you? How might you find out what these mean?

Map the traditionally child-focused and adult-focused services in a geographical area you know. Which ones might be serving the same families?

How we play our roles

Practitioner roles need to change in the light of new knowledge and emerging needs but change is not easy. Most of us feel anxious when asked to perform a new role, especially one for which we may not be adequately trained or supported. When there is already a heavy demand on our time, it is even more difficult to embrace such change. On the other hand, extending our knowledge and skills can be stimulating and lead to greater job satisfaction, especially if we can see that it is of benefit to children and families.

Many factors influence practitioner roles: the history of our professions and services; organisational mandates, resources and procedures; professional

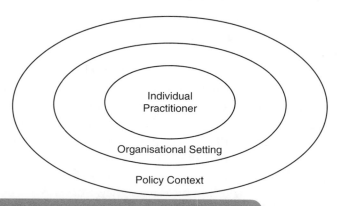

Figure 4.1: Level of analysis for breadth of service provider role performance (based on Scott, 2009)

registration and regulatory processes; industrial issues and occupational vested interests; legislation; the power of other professional groups; government policies and social attitudes. In relation to the latter, what clients using services on a voluntary basis are prepared to accept is a major consideration. These factors are categorised in Figure 4.1 above as relating to the individual practitioner, the organisation or the policy context. In reality of course, the boundaries between domains are blurred.

What at one point in time may be seen as a marginal role for a profession can become a core role, and what may once have been a 'core role' can become marginal or even disappear over time. For example, the recognition of 'new' social problems such as child abuse in the 1960s, the changing roles of women in the 1970s, advances in information and communications technology in the 1990s, the consumer rights movement in mental health, and the increased prevalence of depression and alcohol abuse in the past decade, are just a few factors that have led, and are leading to, significant changes in the roles of many professions and services.

It is possible to analyse service provider roles in terms of their 'core' and 'marginal' functions.

> ... core responsibilities are defined by society's central institutions, and these institutions possess powerful sanctions to ensure that they are fulfilled ... beyond the core are marginal areas in which much more variation is possible. The occupant of the role may ... limit his work to his core responsibilities or extend his involvement with clients to include other aspects of their situation.
>
> (McCaughey, Shaver & Ferber, 1977, p. 166)

Factors relating to the individual service provider that may predispose them to perform 'marginal' role functions related to client well-being include their personality and their beliefs regarding the ideal of service (McCaughey, Shaver & Ferber, 1977). Individual practitioners differ in the degree to which they embrace tasks that transcend the 'bottom line' of their traditional professional role. For example, one child and family health nurse may prefer to stick to the traditional 'paediatric surveillance' role of weighing and measuring infants and checking for developmental disorders, while another may use these important tasks as a means to other ends – to develop a trusting relationship with parents and be responsive to psychosocial problems such as post-natal depression, domestic violence and social isolation (Scott, 1992).

Service providers within a particular occupational group or a service sector can probably be placed along a spectrum of role performance from narrow to broad similar to that suggested by McCaughey, Shaver & Ferber (1977):

- Narrow – core role only ('it's not my concern')
- Somewhat narrow – core role and assessment of 'other needs', leading to referral for the latter ('it's a concern but someone else's job – refer on')

- Somewhat broad – clients' 'other needs' are incidental but unavoidable ('not my core role but I need to do it if I am going to do my core role')
- Broad – 'other needs' are an intrinsic part of core role ('it's all part and parcel of my job').

The breadth with which a practitioner plays his or her role is not just an individual matter but is shaped collectively by the profession or occupation. Role definition is at the centre of occupational identity: 'As an occupational group seeks to establish itself as a profession, it focuses its role around the specialised areas for which its members have training and expertise; in the process marginal tasks are excluded as inappropriate' (McCaughey, Shaver & Ferber, 1977, p. 166).

In response to scientific and technological advances and emerging community needs, professional roles need to evolve and it can be hypothesised that tasks perceived as 'higher status' marginal roles will be more likely to be adopted than tasks perceived as 'lower status' marginal roles.

The way practitioners work is not just a reflection of their individual and professional predisposition. Practice occurs within an organisational setting, a service system context and a particular social policy environment (Figure 4.1). Organisations often compete with one another for scarce resources, and they typically belong to sectors such as 'health', 'education' or 'social services', each with their separate funding sources and policy priorities. This can lead to narrow and rigid silos and 'single input services based on categorical funding'. The emergence of new 'whole of government' approaches to policy and service delivery that attempt to transcend sectoral silos is a source of hope.

Professional boundaries can thus reflect and reinforce sectoral boundaries. The fields of health, education and social services can differ in their values, knowledge and skills, as well as in legal obligations, mandate and status. Such differences may be a great strength in terms of the depth of expertise they bring, but can also be a great weakness in terms of competition and a narrowing of roles and responsibilities. The emergence of an overarching bio-psychosocial perspective across professions working with children and families is another source of hope in addressing these challenges (see Chapter 1).

Other contextual factors that may influence an organisation's capacity to provide a more family-centred service for vulnerable families include:

- Legal requirements, such as mandatory reporting of suspected child maltreatment that may inhibit a service provider from getting 'too involved' in children's needs for fear of endangering a fragile therapeutic relationship with the parent
- Privacy constraints on information sharing between organisations may inhibit a comprehensive understanding of family needs

- 'Single input services' based on categorical funding models will limit the capacity to provide comprehensive responses to families with multiple and complex needs
- Resource scarcity may lead to increased 'gatekeeping' in relation to resource-intensive cases where there are multiple and complex needs
- Strong centralised reform drivers in government and budget pooling across sectors and portfolios may support broader, family-centred service delivery
- Good cost-effectiveness data that demonstrates the value of providing a broader service can provide evidence to support such initiatives.

(Scott, 2009).

Reflective questions

What are the key historical events that have shaped occupational roles in your field?

What are the main influences currently determining what are 'core' and 'marginal' roles in your field? Where would you put yourself on the narrow to broad spectrum in relation to how you 'play your role'? Has this changed? What factors determine whether you are able to perform a broader role?

Working together

Organisations work together in many ways, ranging from the informal to the more formal, and this spectrum has been described as cooperation, coordination, collaboration and integration (Konrad, 1996).

- *Cooperation* is where practitioners in different organisations may informally exchange information about their expertise and services to assist one another to meet the needs of their clients. Being located on the same site can increase the opportunity for people from different services to know one another and cooperate in such informal ways. For example, a pre-school teacher may contact someone at a migrant resource centre to get information that may assist a non-English speaking refugee family, who has just moved into the area, to access the services they may require.
- *Coordination* is when interactions between organisations are governed by formal organisational protocols, such as those relating to the release of information or the making of a referral. For example, in accord with an inter-agency agreement, a child and family health nurse may accompany a parent to a family support service and participate in the intake interview, so that both services and the parent are in clear agreement on the case plan and how information will be exchanged.

- *Collaboration* is sometimes used as a general term for working together, but is also used in a more specific way to describe how services work side by side in an initiative auspiced by both agencies. An example of inter-sectoral collaboration between a child welfare and drug treatment service was the establishment of an innovative therapeutic playgroup for parents and their young children within a Sydney methadone clinic (Mohammed, 2003).
- *Integration* is when a new organisational form is created, sometimes merging what were previously separate services or where a new structure is created. For example, in order to reduce duplication of intake services and to ensure that families are referred to the most appropriate service, a single entry point into all the non-government family services funded by the government in a geographical area was developed (Leung, 2003).

Working across organisational boundaries in a family-centred way can be very challenging as organisations may have different members of their family as the primary client and there may not even be a consensus on the need to communicate or work together. For example, collaboration between a drug and alcohol treatment service and a statutory child protection service raises complex ethical and professional dilemmas (Scott & Campbell, 1994). For the drug and alcohol treatment agency, the parent is the primary client and there may be a realistic apprehension that sharing information with a child welfare service could frighten parents and lead to them withdrawing from a voluntary treatment service. At the same time, professionals have a 'duty of care' to others, such as children, who may be harmed by their client. The priority of the child welfare service, on the other hand, is to assess if it is safe for a child to remain in the home, or whether restoring a child in care to their family is a viable goal. At the same time they need the parent to remain effectively engaged with a treatment agency in order to maximise the child's safety. While there is a growing body of research on inter-agency collaboration between these two fields (e.g., Smith & Mogro-Wilson, 2008), there are no simple solutions. Protocols may help govern the interaction but on their own cannot guarantee the skilled professional discernment and mutual respect that such complex and sensitive situations require.

While it is generally assumed that working together is a good thing, some researchers in this field have argued that:

> *From an agency's viewpoint, collaborative activity raises two main difficulties. First, it loses some of its freedom to act independently, when it would prefer to maintain control over its domain and affairs. Secondly, it must invest scarce resources and energy in developing and maintaining relationships with other organisations, when the potential returns on this investment are often unclear or intangible.*

> *(Hudson, 1987, p. 175)*

That is, to meet their survival needs, organisations have to maximise autonomy and conserve resources. A certain level of conflict between organisations is therefore to be expected and this needs to be accepted rather than avoided.

Having a way of understanding such tensions can help depersonalise the situation, and identify possible solutions. Scott (2005) undertook a qualitative study of inter-agency interaction in child protection cases, and identified five levels of analysis: inter-organisational; intra-organisational; inter-professional; interpersonal; and intra-personal. These levels of analysis are not mutually exclusive, as there are often tensions at multiple levels.

Inter-organisational level

Organisations have a history of past interactions with one another. If the legacy is a positive one, there may be a good store of trust and reciprocity for service providers to draw upon. If the legacy is negative and laden with past conflicts, one organisation may be held responsible by another for the perceived acts of their predecessors. If this is the case, then it may be important to acknowledge the legacy and try to reduce the risk of the past contaminating current attempts to work together.

Understanding the primary source(s) of inter-agency tensions is vital. If the source of the tension is primarily inter-organisational or structural, then this will require a different strategy than when the problem is primarily interpersonal. Undergoing the process of such analysis in itself may facilitate a shift in the perception of the problem and help defuse conflict. For example, what was originally seen as an interpersonal difficulty may come to be understood as predominantly structural in its origin. This is not to say that interpersonal conflicts do not play a significant part in inter-organisational tensions. There is the potential for such conflict in all human encounters. However, what is often experienced as an interpersonal conflict may have strong structural components. The test of this for practitioners is to ask themselves, 'If I changed jobs with the person in the organisation with which I am now in conflict, would we swap sides on this issue?' If the answer is 'yes', then the tension is likely to be structural, not interpersonal.

Policy and funding arrangements are obviously central to tensions arising between organisations. For example, in a service system in which there are many non-government organisations vying for limited government funding on the basis of competitive tendering, it is going to be harder for such organisations to work together in the interests of families.

We see strategies to conserve scarce organisational resources in 'gatekeeping', or attempts to resist referrals from other organisations, particularly if they are likely to be 'resource hungry' and place pressure on staff. For example, organisations may require prospective clients to ring and make their own appointments. This may be justified in terms of principles such as 'client self-determination' and the need to ensure that clients are voluntary and motivated, but if we require this of highly stressed families with multiple and complex needs, they are unlikely to receive a service. The intended or unintended consequence of such criteria is often to exclude the most disadvantaged clients.

Some organisations have greater capacity to 'gatekeep' and to be more selective about the referrals they accept than others. Those with less capacity must nevertheless develop mechanisms to prevent being overwhelmed or they will collapse. For example, statutory child protection services may 'triage' referrals or raise the threshold of eligibility by accepting only those cases that are deemed to require legal intervention. When organisations making the referrals operate on a lower threshold of risk, as occurs when reporting all cases of suspected child abuse is mandatory, the large gap between the threshold for making a referral and acting on a referral can lead to enormous strain between organisations. This is one of the major sources of conflict in the child protection field.

Entrenched gatekeeping problems require policy and service system reform. In Victoria, for example, the *Children, Youth and Families Act 2005*, gives service providers concerned about a child the choice to refer the family to a regional non-government service for assessment or to make a notification to a statutory child protection service. In South Australia, for example, the problem of children in state care having poor access to other government services they needed, such as child and adolescent mental health services or dental services, was addressed by a 'whole of government' policy called 'Rapid Response', giving this group of children priority access to all government services.

While policy and systems reform is necessary, it is difficult to achieve, and practitioners need to continue operating in imperfect systems. Campbell (1999) has proposed some valuable principles and practical processes for building a more collaborative service network under such conditions. Daniel (2004) has also recently proposed a model for a 'protective network' in the field of child welfare in which help for a child can be accessed via any entry point in the network of organisations having routine contact with the child.

Activities

Draw a diagram of a service network, depicting each of those organisations that have an overlapping client population as a separate circle. Insert lines connecting those organisations that you know have direct contact with one another. Why might some organisations that share an overlapping client population not have contact with one another? Answer the following questions for each organisation in the diagram and consider whether the answers help to explain the potential for inter-organisational conflict. Who does each organisation tend to define as the primary client? How does each organisation tend to define its 'core role'? Which organisations are more dependent on other organisations in the network (e.g., for funding, information or referrals)? Which organisations have the most power and influence? Which organisations are competitors (e.g., for funding or clients)? Which organisations have overlapping or blurred mandates or roles?

Consult any documents you can access (e.g., from organisational websites) that establish protocols for how organisations need to relate to one another when they have shared clients. What do you see as the strengths and weaknesses of such protocols?

Intra-organisational level of analysis

Sometimes the source of inter-agency tensions is related to dysfunctional dynamics within an organisation. For example, some teams and organisations generate internal cohesion by making another organisation into 'the common enemy'. This is perpetuated through telling 'atrocity stories' where the narrative is always the same – the failure and incompetence of the other organisation. Such dynamics can also operate between different sections or programs within an organisation.

We have probably all been guilty of telling 'atrocity stories' about another service at some stage. This may seem innocent enough and allow us to vent frustration but it can contaminate the attitudes of new staff before they have even encountered anyone from the other service. A high level of scapegoating of another organisation reflects poorly on the leadership of the organisation doing the scapegoating. Often the leadership skills to address internal tensions or generate cohesion by other means are sorely lacking.

There is usually resistance to looking closely at the factors within a team or organisation that contribute to inter-agency tensions. A change of leadership may sometimes be necessary to bring about a new climate for collaboration. While most management and organisational consultants do not usually operate across organisational boundaries, Roberts (1994) has described the value of consultation in dealing with inter-group rivalry and conflict between health and social services in the UK. Mediation and conciliation processes may also be helpful to address recurrent conflicts.

Reflective questions

Can you recall telling or hearing an 'atrocity story' about an organisation? What function did this serve for those telling the story? What might be the long-term effects of such narratives on service providers and on families?

Inter-professional level of analysis

Sometimes we work across professional boundaries and organisational boundaries at the same time. Tensions similar to those that can occur in a multidisciplinary team within an organisation (e.g., 'demarcation disputes', power struggles and different values), can also occur when professional and organisational boundaries are crossed at the same time. The difference is that when inter-professional tensions occur within an organisation, there is a leadership structure that can potentially address the problem, but this is typically lacking between organisations.

Status hierarchies often get in the way of professions working together. For example, higher status may be accorded to those whose roles are defined as 'therapy', than to those who provide concrete or material services for families, or to those who provide direct care for a child. Those closest to children and families in their day-to-day lives are usually those who know them best yet paradoxically they are usually those least heard in case conferences and least influential in decision making.

There may be differences between professions in their styles of communication and decision making, about which the participants are largely unaware. For example, in a study on child protection case conferences, it was observed that health professionals were cautious about interpretation and speculation, and that police found the discursive consensus-seeking culture of welfare services frustrating (Scott, Lindsay & Jackson, 1995). In such circumstances, just recognising and openly acknowledging such differences may help to defuse the problem.

Reflective questions

Professions and occupational groups sometimes resemble 'tribes', providing their members with a sense of personal identity and belonging. Do you belong to such a tribe? Whose interests are served by in-group and out-group boundaries? What impact may professional tribalism have on our capacity to work together in the interests of children and their families?

Interpersonal level of analysis

Interpersonal factors can help or hinder working across organisational boundaries. This is true everywhere but is particularly obvious in regional and rural settings where personal social networks overlap with professional and organisational networks to a marked degree. This can be a great asset, with positive pre-existing relationships and goodwill facilitating cooperation. When pre-existing relationships are strained, however, inter-agency collaboration may be much more difficult than if people did not know one another. The fear of conflict erupting and rippling through dense social networks may act as a useful curb on conflict but if it just leads to conflict avoidance, it may make it more difficult to address the underlying problem.

Families can also fuel interpersonal conflict between services. For example, a school or a child welfare agency can become the common enemy against which a usually fragmented family may unite. When a practitioner in another organisation joins forces with the family against the service that is the 'common enemy', inter-agency relationships are further weakened. This is not to say that services do not sometimes behave in ways that warrant another agency acting as an advocate for the family, but the risk of families 'splitting' agencies needs to be considered. Sometimes it is tempting to engage a family by siding with them against another organisation but the gains are likely to be short term and to reduce the social capital that is essential to inter-agency collaboration in other cases.

We need to use a high level of interpersonal skills when working across organisational boundaries. The capacity to communicate clearly, to show respect and to build trust are as vital in establishing good working relationships with other organisations as they are with families. Supervisors and team leaders have a key role to play in supporting staff to develop and sustain positive working relationships with other organisations.

Reflective questions

Can you think of an example of inter-organisational conflict? To what degree did interpersonal factors exacerbate or reduce the level of conflict? How might it be possible to reduce the risk of such conflict?

Intra-personal level of analysis

Working with vulnerable children and families can be very distressing and evoke painful feelings for service providers. In the face of strong emotions it is common for defence mechanisms, such as projection and displacement, to come into play. This can intensify inter-agency and inter-professional tensions, and lead to destructive levels of conflict. In a study of inter-agency conflict in a child protection context, it was most intense in those cases in which practitioners felt impotent to protect a vulnerable child (Scott, 1997).

For example, when child neglect was a long-standing problem in the family, or when there were suspicions but little evidence that a child had been sexually abused, deep emotions were aroused in all of the practitioners involved. Each sincerely believed that it was beyond their organisation's ability to protect the child, but some strongly believed that another service had the power to do so, even when there was little rational basis for this view. While this might relate to a lack of understanding of the role and constraints of other organisations, another explanation is that we sometimes cope with strong feelings such as anger and guilt by projecting responsibility or displacing hostility on to others.

In another study that explored the attitudes of different professions to child sexual abuse vignettes, responses were contrary to that expected by professional stereotypes, leading the researchers to comment that:

> *It may be that for the child welfare workers vis-à-vis the court, just as for mental health workers vis-à-vis therapy, repeated exposure to demanding, less-than-successful procedures breeds doubt, and procedures on the other side of the professional fence look brighter.*
>
> *(Wilk & McCarthy, 1986, p. 25)*

Others have tried to explain why it can be so difficult to 'take the position of the other' when strong anxiety is aroused in interaction between organisations.

> *The potential for dissonance and conflict increases the more splitting and denial (i.e., mental partition) is the dominant defence employed by shared clients or patients, and the more their problems occasion high levels of realistic anxiety, stimulating powerful unconscious phantasies in practitioners and their managers. The more threatening the anxiety, the greater and more rigid the practitioners' reliance on socially structured institutional defences and the more fraught it becomes to enter imaginatively into each other's working world for fear of losing hold of their own. Practitioners may then fall back on the 'bedrock' of a narrowly defined primary task.*
>
> *(Woodhouse & Pengelly, 1991, pp. 229–30)*

High quality clinical supervision is vital to deal with such charged situations. We sometimes bring our own issues to these conflicts. For example, there may be personal reasons why we are drawn to identify very strongly with one family member and to work in a particular service, and this can lead to a greater intensity of conflict with organisations that are advocates for another family member. Of course, sometimes it is necessary to be an advocate for a vulnerable member of a family, such as in cases of family violence or child maltreatment, and in those instances a certain level of conflict between the organisations representing the interests of different family members is probably unavoidable. The task then, is to manage the conflict in ways that are least destructive.

While it is important to acknowledge and address conflict in inter-organisational relationships, it is also important not to overstate it. A major UK survey of different professions involved in child protection found that, contrary to the picture portrayed in official inquiries into child abuse controversies, most professionals reported that local inter-professional networks functioned reasonably well (Hallet & Birchall, 1992). Australian research by Darlington, Feeney and Rixon (2004), which explored the interface of child protection and adult mental health services, also found that in at least half the cases shared by both services, collaboration worked well. If we knew more about the conditions under which organisations work together effectively we would be better able to recreate these conditions in other settings.

Reflective questions

Think about high-risk situations that might arise in relation to mental health, domestic violence or child protection issues. What might help practitioners deal with the anxiety such situations arouse so that inter-agency relationships are not weakened? Can you think of a situation where, despite considerable obstacles, people in different organisations managed to work together more effectively than one might have thought possible? What may have made this possible? Are there any lessons that can be learned from this example?

Activity

Adam is two years old and has a history of 'faltering growth' ('failure to thrive'). The identity of his father is unknown. Adam's mother, Alice, is 23 and is six months pregnant. She spent most of her childhood in state care and experienced multiple foster placements. Alice lives with her boyfriend Robert, who is the father of the baby she is expecting. Robert is unemployed and is on probation for drug-related offences. Alice appears depressed and anxious, and seems very emotionally dependent on Robert. They live in private rental accommodation in a large rural town and have no extended family support. A range of services is involved with the family (child and family health nurse, child care centre, non-government family support service, general practitioner, drug and alcohol treatment service, correctional services and statutory child protection services).

In a small group, explore the current and future needs of this family and consider the part each of the services involved might play by having the various services involved represented by different individuals or subgroups in the group. How might the services work together to assist this family? What might be the personal, professional and organisational challenges you could face in working together with this family? What might each practitioner need to fulfil his or her role to the best of his or her ability?

Conclusion

The current policy environment offers some exciting opportunities to redevelop professional roles and services so that they are more holistic and individually tailored to families' needs. There are some inspiring examples of practitioners who have pioneered innovative ways of working with families (see Chapter 9). How these innovations might be transplanted to other settings is a question we explore in Chapter 13. There is increasing recognition that organisations need to work together, especially for families with multiple and complex needs. This is not just a matter of exhorting people to do so – that is much the same as saying to a troubled family 'why don't you smile and try being nice to one another?'! To improve how we work across organisations and sectors, we need to understand the obstacles, identify the opportunities and cultivate within ourselves and our own organisations the values, knowledge and skills to support working together. Given that our work with vulnerable families is so mediated through organisations, there is no alternative. Considering all of the obstacles, especially those at a structural level, it is to the credit of practitioners and a reflection of their commitment to the families they serve that they work with one another as well as they do.

Useful websites

Australian Centre for Child Protection: www.unisa.edu.au/childprotection
Australian Government – Social Inclusion: www.socialinclusion.gov.au
Australian Institute of Family Studies: www.aifs.gov.au
Children of Parents with a Mental Illness: www.copmi.net.au
Social Care Institute for Excellence (SCIE) resources for inter-professional and inter-agency collaboration: www.scie.org.uk/publications/elearning/ipiac/index.asp?dm_i=4O5,1K57,UVZJD,4RQ6,1
UK Cabinet Office Social Exclusion Task Force: www.cabinetoffice.gov.uk/social_exclusion_task_force.aspx

References

Campbell, L. (1999). Collaboration: Building inter-agency networks for practice partnerships. In V. Cowling (ed.), *Children of Parents with Mental Illness*, 203–16. Australian Council of Education Research, Melbourne.

Cowling, V. (2004). *Children of Parents with a Mental Illness: 2. Personal and Clinical Perspectives*. Australian Council of Educational Research, Melbourne.

Daniel, B. (2004). An overview of the Scottish Multidisciplinary Child Protection Review. *Child and Family Social Work*, 9 (3), 247–57.

Darlington, Y., Feeney, J. & Rixon, K. (2004). Complexity, conflict and uncertainty: Issues in collaboration between child protection and mental health services. *Children and Youth Review*, 26, 1175–92.

Dawe, S. & Harnett, P. (2007). Improving family functioning in methadone maintained families: Results from a randomised control trial. *Journal of Substance Abuse Treatment*, 32, 381–90.

Hallet, C. & Birchall, E. (1992). *Working Together in Child Protection: Report of Phase Two, a Survey of the Experience and Perceptions of Six Key Professions*. Department of Applied Social Science, University of Stirling, Stirling, UK.

Hannon, T. (2007). *Children: Unintended Victims of Legal Process: Action Paper*. Victorian Association for the Care and Resettlement of Offenders, Melbourne.

Hayes, A., Gray, M. & Edwards, B. (2008). *Social Inclusion: Origin, Concepts and Key Themes*. Department of Prime Minister and Cabinet, Social Inclusion Unit, Canberra.

Hudson, B. (1987). Collaboration in social welfare: A framework for analysis. *Policy and Politics*, 15, 175–83.

Humphreys, C. (2006). *Domestic Violence and Child Protection: Directions in Child Protection*. Jessica Kingsley, London.

Konrad, E. (1996). A multidimensional framework for conceptualising human services integration. *New Directions for Evaluations*, 69, 5–19.

Leung, J. (2003). Strengthening families: The restructuring of family services in Hong Kong. *Journal of Societal and Social Policy*, 2, 51–68.

McCaughey, J., Shaver, S. & Ferber, H. (1977). *Who Cares? Family Problems, Community Links and Helping Services*. Sun Books, Melbourne.

Mohammed, M. (2003). Woraninta Playgroup. *Developing Practice*, 5, 61–8.

Odyssey Institute of Studies (2004). *The Nobody's Clients Project. Identifying and Addressing the Needs of Children with Substance Dependent Parents*. Odyssey House, Melbourne.

Roberts, V. (1994). Conflict and collaboration, managing intergroup relations. In A. Obholzer & V. Roberts (eds), *The Unconscious at Work: Individual and Organisational Stress in the Human Services*, 187–96. Routledge, London.

Scott, D. (1992). Reaching vulnerable populations: A framework for primary service provider role expansion. *American Journal of Orthopsychiatry*, 62 (3), 332–41.

Scott, D. (1997). Inter-agency conflict: An ethnographic study. *Child and Family Social Work*, 22, 4–5.

Scott, D. (2005). Inter-organisational collaboration: A framework for analysis and action. *Australian Social Work*, 2, 132–41.

Scott, D. (2009). 'Think Child, Think Family': How adult specialist services can support children at risk of abuse and neglect. *Family Matters*, 81, 37–42.

Scott, D. & Campbell, L. (1994). Family-centred practice at the interface between the alcohol and drug field and child welfare. *Drug and Alcohol Review*, 13 (4), 447–54.

Scott, D., Lindsay, J. & Jackson, A. (1995). The child protection case conference: Juggling rights, risks and responsibilities. *Children Australia*, 20, 4–12.

Smith, B. & Mogro-Wilson, C. (2008). Inter-agency collaboration: Policy and practice in child welfare and substance abuse treatment. *Administration in Social Work*, 32 (2), 5–24.

Social Exclusion Taskforce (2008). 'Families at Risk Review'. Available online at: www.cabinetoffice.gov.uk/social_exclusion_task_force/families_at_risk.aspx

Wilk, R. & McCarthy, C. (1986). Intervention in child sexual abuse: A survey of attitudes. *Social Casework*, 67, 20–6.

Woodhouse, D. & Pengelly, P. (1991). *Anxiety and the Dynamics of Collaboration*. Aberdeen University Press, Aberdeen.

Family-centred practice in early childhood settings

Dorothy Scott

Learning goals

This chapter will enable you to:

1. Recognise the potential of early childhood practitioners in health and education settings to engage parents of vulnerable children in ways that will enhance their ability to nurture and protect their children
2. Understand contemporary developments in policy and practice in relation to family-centred early childhood services
3. Learn about some innovative exemplars of Australian family-centred initiatives in early childhood settings and consider what might be applicable to other settings
4. Be sensitive to the needs of children and parents from culturally diverse backgrounds
5. Think about how different professions and services can work together for *and* with vulnerable families and their children
6. Reflect on the professional and personal challenges that may be faced when responding to the needs of vulnerable children and their families.

Introduction

We are in an exciting era of innovation in early childhood services. With the (re)discovery of the importance of the 'early years', new ideas about how early childhood services can be delivered, regardless of whether they are traditionally seen as 'health', 'education' or 'social welfare' services, are blossoming. Strengths-based ways of working with families are influencing how practitioners are reaching out to parents and enhancing their ability to nurture and protect their children (see Chapter 2 for more on family strengths approaches). Policies, programs and face-to-face practice are all in the process of transformation. This chapter provides a background to and overview of some of these developments, describes innovative Australian exemplars of family-centred approaches and their common principles, and identifies some of the challenges involved in working in such ways.

Looking back to see ahead

The early 20th century witnessed major advances in 'child welfare', a term that was then used in a similar way to the term 'child well-being' today, and which crossed the sectors of education, health and social services. The pioneers of the key professions involved were sometimes more family and community centred than those who followed, with the cumulative influences of professionalisation, credentialism and specialisation sometimes combining to narrow the roles of services and practitioners. However, there have always been some individual practitioners in early childhood services who have been passionate about working with families and communities and who have seen this as central to their work with children. In this chapter we shall hear a few of their voices as well as those of parents participating in such services.

In the field of early childhood education, the ideas of Froebel, the father of the kindergarten movement, spread across the world in the late 19th and early 20th centuries (Rogers, 2003). Froebel tended to see the kindergarten as a haven in which children might be freed from parental control, whereas Lillian de Lissa, a pioneer of the kindergarten movement in Australia who went on to become an international figure in the field, embraced parents as partners. Historian Helen Jones has brought to light how Lillian de Lissa helped mothers to become ambassadors of progressive ideas and practices about health and education in their local Adelaide communities.

> *Through mothers' clubs, the first begun in Franklin Street in 1906, these women co-operated in ancillary tasks for the free kindergartens and also gained useful knowledge of child rearing and health. Most lived in very poor circumstances; their experience was widened through contact with the kindergartens and in seeing the improvement in their own children's physical development and general abilities. Out of the Franklin Street Free Kindergarten mothers' club came not only personal advantages for members, but their own acts of altruism which extended the benefits of kindergartens to others.*

> *(Jones, 1986, p. 173)*

In the field of infant health, there is evidence of similarly progressive thinking by the founding mothers. During the economic depression of the late 1920s and early 1930s in Victoria, Dr Vera Scantlebury Brown and Sister Muriel Peck established the statewide system of infant welfare centres (later called maternal and child health centres). Dr Scantlebury Brown was also responsible for Victorian pre-schools. In her 1940–41 *Director of Infant Welfare Report*, Dr Scantlebury Brown noted that parent clubs, mothers' clubs, get-together clubs and infant welfare leagues were flourishing in some infant welfare centres and that there were large numbers of volunteer helpers (Victorian Commission of Public Health, 1940–41). She also noted the close collaboration between infant welfare centres, the Lady Gowrie Pre-School Child Centre and other early childhood services. Family- and community-centred practice in maternal and child health nursing, now often seen as a very recent development, had strong roots in its origins. Interestingly, it was often the same women who campaigned for, and established, both infant health and kindergarten services.

In the field of social services, much of the innovation in the early 20th century was the result of philanthropic initiatives rather than government. In the economic depression of the 1890s, the plight of unmarried mothers and their infants was dire (Swain, 1995), with no government benefits to protect them from destitution. Extreme poverty, lack of contraception and the intense social stigma surrounding illegitimacy resulted in the abandonment of many newborn babies in lanes and along riverbanks of our cities, and led to the practice of 'baby farming'– the placement of several infants in private homes in impoverished neighbourhoods where babies frequently died as a result of malnourishment and neglect (Swain, 1995).

In response to deep social concern about 'baby farming' and the plight of these children and their mothers, women of private means in places such as Sydney and Melbourne established charitable 'day nurseries' where infants and children under school age could be cared for while their unmarried mothers went out to work. These day nurseries were the earliest forms of organised child care in Australia. One of these, the Sydney Day Nurseries Association (now known as SDN Children's Services), will be highlighted later in this chapter in relation to its current innovative work with very vulnerable families with infants and pre-school children.

Throughout the history of early childhood health, education and social services, there have been many changes, some resulting from advances in technology and knowledge. For example, by the 1920s the development of 'babies' homes' became possible because of infant formula. In some places, church organisations established homes to 'rescue' infants from the 'social evils' of the slums. Paradoxically, later developments in knowledge were an important factor in helping to close such institutions. For example, by the 1970s research by Bowlby and others on the effects of institutional care on infants was influential in bringing about the closure of babies' homes, as well as liberalising the very rigid parental visiting policies and practices in children's hospitals.

The 1970s was an era of exciting changes in social policy and human services in Australia. When I was a social work student at the Methodist Babies Home in Melbourne in the early 1970s I had the privilege of designing a new initiative for the Uniting Church to replace the old babies' home. Supported by generous funding from the Whitlam Labor Government, Copelen Street Family Centre provided very high quality early childhood education and care for infants and pre-schoolers, and parenting education and support for their families, mostly living in the inner urban public housing estates of Richmond and Prahran. A multidisciplinary team of trained mother-craft nurses (nowadays described as qualified child care workers), pre-school teachers, social workers and child health nurses was developed. Staff reached out to vulnerable families, often collecting children from their homes, which provided informal opportunities to build rapport with parents.

Many of the parents, mostly single mothers, were struggling to nurture their children under difficult circumstances such as their own childhood of deprivation and neglect, financial stress, substandard housing, and poor physical and mental health. The parents were strongly encouraged to come to the centre, which had a special room for parents, and to participate in its activities. Children were not segregated by age, but belonged to home groups of five children, with two caregivers to each group who were warm and consistent figures in the parents' lives as well as their children's lives. Many 'teachable moments' occurred every day that provided opportunities for enhancing responsive and sensitive parenting. Unfortunately this service, similar in nature to the famous Perry Pre-School in the US, came to an end in the 1980s due to a loss in government funding. Twenty years later, this type of family-centred early childhood service is the model that is being rediscovered, hopefully in a policy climate that will prove more conducive to its sustainability.

The 1970s also saw the emergence of the playgroup movement that aims to provide enriched opportunities for parents and young children to interact with one another in a local setting. While most playgroups are self-governing, in 'supported playgroups' a paid facilitator is involved until the group is well enough established to become self-sustaining. Supported playgroups usually meet on a weekly basis and are aimed at reaching families with additional needs, including those from culturally and linguistically diverse backgrounds, Indigenous families, families where a parent or a child has a mental illness or a disability, teenage parents and families who are socially isolated and disadvantaged. Supported playgroup coordinators also provide parenting information and help to link parents to other services they may need. Playgroups are especially valuable in providing a non-stigmatised and accessible service for families with very young children who are in the age group which falls between the predominantly infant-focused child and family health services and pre-school or kindergarten services.

Contemporary policy context

Political support and a strong policy framework are thus vital if family-centred early childhood services are to be sustained and 'scaled up' to reach all vulnerable children and their families. The UK Government's initiative, Sure Start, which was developed in 1999, is an example of a policy framework that seeks to bring together early childhood education and care, health and family support, with a focus on outreach and community development. It is focused on families with children under four years of age living in areas of social disadvantage. There is great diversity in Sure Start Local Programmes but the following principles are seen as important for all:

- Involving parents as well as children
- Non-stigmatising
- Multifaceted, transcending 'education', 'health' or 'parenting' interventions
- Locally driven, and based on consultation with parents and communities
- Culturally appropriate and sensitive to the needs of children and parents.

Initial evaluations of Sure Start have raised concerns that the most disadvantaged families are not accessing the services. A variation between the outcomes for different services was also found and the possible reasons for this explored (www.ness.bbk.ac.uk/impact/documents/1183.pdf).

New Zealand has also shown leadership in developing strong early childhood services with higher standards than Australia in relation to staff–child ratios. Most Australian states and territories now have 'early years' policies, and some, such as South Australia, have pioneered the development of 'integrated' children's centres in primary schools in low income areas that bring together a range of programs and organisations, with a community development focus as well as direct service delivery.

In 2008 the Rudd Labor Government made a commitment to developing and funding child and parent centres on a large scale, and to improving standards of care. Historical divisions between the early childhood education and child care sectors, and between federal and state responsibilities, have been major obstacles to integrated early childhood policies and services in Australia.

In relation to child and family health services, which are a state and territory responsibility, there is enormous variation in the degree to which there are universal services that reach families with infants. There is also significant variation in the degree to which they are narrowly focused on paediatric surveillance (monitoring infant and child growth and development) as well as how the social and emotional well-being of families and communities are addressed. There is also variation in the degree to which such universal services have been developed to act as non-stigmatised platforms through which vulnerable families with complex additional needs can receive a more intensive and individually tailored service.

In some states and territories, targeted child and family health nursing services have been developed and are offered to families with complex needs. Some of these are based on the Nurse–Family Partnership Model (Olds et al., 1997). One of these, the South Australian Family Home Visiting Program, is described in the next chapter. The Australian Government, through the Office of Aboriginal and Torres Strait Islander Health, has also recently funded Aboriginal health services across Australia to deliver the Australian Nurse–Family Partnership Program in Aboriginal communities.

Some non-government organisations have also pioneered the use of universal early childhood education and care services as 'platforms' from which more specialist services can be offered to families with more complex needs. Through the Australian Government's 'Invest to Grow' initiative, Lady Gowrie Centres have pioneered the 'Through the Looking Glass Project', an early intervention strategy in five child care settings across Australia for families where there is an impaired parent–child attachment relationship. The 18 week program provides intensive support, therapeutic intervention and high quality child care for families where there are multiple risk factors including anxiety, depression, social isolation and early trauma in the parent's own life. A therapist and child care worker collaborate closely with each other and the family. The program also helps to build social bonds between families. The results of an interim evaluation are encouraging (www.throughthelookingglass.org.au).

Families from culturally and linguistically diverse backgrounds may not be familiar with Western models of early childhood services and it is sometimes challenging for early childhood services to become welcoming and 'culturally safe' places for such families. One innovative initiative, the Refugee Family Resource Program of the Victorian Cooperative on Children's Services for Ethnic Groups (VICSEG), pioneered the placement of bicultural and bilingual staff for a day or so a week in early childhood services in local communities. These workers engaged refugee and recent immigrant families in the service system, and helped to enhance the cultural sensitivity and competence of mainstream early childhood health and education practitioners by working alongside them (Chapters 6 and 8 also describe the need for such culturally competent practice).

Activities

Think about your own pre-school years and then talk to other people about what it was like for them. If you went to an early childhood service, explore the similarities and difference of your experiences and memories. What strikes you about the service now compared with your child's eye view of this small social world back then?

Talk to people who work in the early childhood field and ask them how they see their role in relation to working with parents and communities.

Innovative exemplars

There are many innovative and inspiring exemplars of early childhood health and education services being developed by committed and skilful practitioners. While some of these have been subject to substantial evaluation, others are yet to be fully evaluated so our understanding of whether they are effective, and if so, why they may be effective, is undeveloped at this stage.

Whilst most program evaluations focus on the nature of the program's interventions, there is increasing awareness that it is the people behind a program, and the processes of working together in ways that enhance high morale and hope, that may be as critical, if not more critical, ingredients of success.

The following four exemplars have been subject to varying degrees of evaluation, and have been selected for their geographical and disciplinary diversity. As you read them, however, see if you can identify what they may have in common in relation to their underlying values and principles.

Townsville Aboriginal and Islander Health Service 'Mums and Babies Program'

Several different organisations delivering antenatal care for Indigenous women formed a 'Mums and Babies Program' at the Townsville Aboriginal and Islander Health Service. The goal was to address the low level of use of child and family health services by Aboriginal and Torres Strait Islander families as a means to reduce very poor perinatal outcomes such as premature birth and low birthweight. A multidisciplinary and cross-cultural team of doctors, nurses and Aboriginal health workers was developed, with the latter playing a crucial role in encouraging pregnant women of Aboriginal and Torres Strait Islander backgrounds to use the service.

Transport was provided and access was on a walk-in rather than an appointment basis. A culturally sensitive and family-centred ethos was nurtured and efforts were made to make the centre an attractive and enjoyable place for mothers and children. Photographs of new babies were put on display to celebrate their arrival into the community and educational toys and a weekly playgroup were provided for children.

The program is based on common sense, continuity of care, cultural currency and a family-friendly environment, and also capitalises on the cultural safety aspects of an Aboriginal Medical Service and the co-location of mental health, dental, and social support services.

(Panaretto et al., 2005, p. 515)

Indigenous women employed as health workers collaborated closely with non-Indigenous female doctors and nurses to create a clinic with a more informal and home like atmosphere. The Indigenous workers used what one might call 'opportunistic engagement' strategies – for example, if they saw an Indigenous woman who was pregnant in the supermarket they would go up to her, introduce themselves if they didn't already know the woman, and encourage her to make use of the centre. It wasn't long before the numbers increased and by word of mouth they kept on increasing, such that a new building had to be found!

Following the introduction of the program there was a marked increase in the use of antenatal services by Aboriginal women, rising from 23.8% of eligible women in 2000 to 61.2% in 2003. The number of antenatal care visits per pregnancy increased from three to seven and there was a significant reduction in preterm births compared with contemporary controls (Panaretto et al., 2005). Those evaluating the program conclude:

This study shows that integrated services delivered in a 'safe' environment increase access to antenatal care in the Indigenous community. Increased access to antenatal care should afford the opportunity to establish programs that minimize risks such as tobacco and alcohol use, possibly leading to reductions in the prevalence of low birthweight and perinatal mortality in future, particularly if the reduction in preterm births can be sustained. This model may be adaptable to other urban centres with significant Indigenous populations.

(Panaretto et al., 2005 p. 518)

First-time parent groups, Victorian Maternal and Child Health Service

Maternal and child health services in Victoria are delivered by local government and largely funded by the state government. It is a very well respected universal service with approximately 98% of all families with an infant using the service in the first year. In the past few decades the service has evolved from one that was almost exclusively focused on infant health and development to one that is also focused on family emotional and social well-being and strengthening social support.

The capacity of maternal and child health services to strengthen social networks at the neighbourhood level is now recognised and all first-time parents in the state are offered the opportunity to join a series of approximately eight group sessions facilitated by their nurse at their local maternal and child health centre. Group sessions cover a broad and flexible range of topics such as: adjustment to first time parenthood, women's health post birth, child safety in the home, infant 'settling' techniques, baby massage and nutrition. Two thirds of first-time mothers join such groups (Scott, Brady & Glynn, 2001).

Victorian maternal and child health nurses have been trained to facilitate groups in non-didactic ways to maximise group interaction and cohesion so that they are likely to continue of their own accord (Edgecomb et al., 2001). A follow-up study in two outer urban local government areas of Melbourne found that over three quarters of the groups were still regularly meeting on their own, mostly in group members' homes, 18 months to two years after the nurse-facilitated groups had ended. Where groups ended due to women returning to paid employment, significant one-to-one friendships continued in most cases (Scott, Brady & Glynn, 2001).

In-depth interviews with the maternal and child health nurses in two outer suburban government areas identified how nurses actively encouraged mothers to participate in the groups through the one-to-one relationship they had established with them in routine visits.

> *The reasons nurses gave mothers for attending the group ranged from being child-focused (for example, the benefits to the baby of information on feeding or CPR) to mother-focused (for example, social contact), and nurses varied the reasons according to what they thought would appeal to the women. For example, one described how she emphasised the practical aspects of the content of the sessions saying that 'some of them don't want the gossip thing'. Another conveyed the idea of group participation as a normative expectation but did so in a subtle and unpressured manner. 'You promote it as something for all new parents and give some information and then gradually turn it around to meeting others and transition to parenthood issues. I think it would put them off if I wasn't low key.'*

> *(Scott, Brady & Glynn, 2001, p. 24)*

Some nurses saw the purpose of the group as being primarily community building, with social contact and peer support being more important than information provision. This was how some mothers saw it as well. The nurses therefore facilitated the group in informal and unstructured ways to help the group 'gel'.

> *'My overall aim is to get them connected with one another … I don't give information directly, I draw out their experiences' said one nurse. This was echoed by another who commented that 'Sometimes they don't want information and I have to balance that – they want the social experience'…*
> *Nurses facilitated participation in the group in a number of ways. Some introduced themselves as mothers, thus minimising the social distance between them and the other women, and modelling limited and appropriate self-disclosure ('I give a little anecdote and if people don't talk I'll tell them mine and draw them in'). Many nurses emphasised the importance of doing*

the introductions well and ensuring that the members actually got to learn one another's names … Some nurses deliberately underscored what the mothers had in common in order to strengthen the cohesion of the group, and avoided drawing attention to differences.

(Scott, Brady & Glynn, 2001, p. 26)

Some maternal and child health nurses in this study were highly successful in engaging harder to reach groups such as fathers, young mothers and immigrant families. For example, one nurse in a low income urban–rural fringe community wrote to all the fathers of new babies and invited them, along with their partners and babies, to come to an evening session on 'how to save your baby's life'. Offering practical skills in infant resuscitation was what got the men through the door but once there, the nurse used her warmth, humour and down-to-earth manner to engage them in more sensitive issues such as the impact of a new baby on couple relationships, and the serious risks associated with shaking babies. For many of the families such evenings nurtured new friendships and so strengthened neighbourhood social support.

In relation to young mothers one nurse confessed 'With the real teenage mum I haven't had much success – the one looking for Mum thinks I am wonderful but the one rebelling against Mum thinks I am terrible' (Scott, Brady & Glynn, 2001, p. 27). In contrast, another nurse had been able to engage young mothers in a group by not trying to mix them in with other women but offering a group especially oriented to their needs.

These groups were described as being very different from other groups ('I serve coke instead of tea!') and less reflective and more action oriented ('we just sat on the floor and made toys and they loved it'). One nurse said she avoided using videos (DVDs) as the adolescent mothers just 'switched off as if they were back in the classroom'.

(Scott, Brady & Glynn, 2001, p. 27)

A DVD documentary produced by the Rural Health Foundation in 2008 captures how a maternal and child health nurse and a youth worker in Mildura, in rural Victoria, have worked together to set up and facilitate an on-going group for young mothers. These young women often struggle to nurture their babies in a context of low income, relationship breakdown, poor transport, housing difficulties and social isolation. The two practitioners take it in turns to facilitate alternate weeks of the group, with the youth worker dealing with issues such as sexuality and substance misuse, and the nurse doing the more child-focused sessions (www.rhef.com.au/programs/program-1/?program_id=31). In the documentary both practitioners talk about how they respond to crises in the young women's lives and through the trusting and non-judgemental relationships they have established with them; how they can help reduce the situational stressors in the lives of these young women which, if unaddressed, could impair the way they care for their babies.

Some nurses described working effectively with immigrant mothers, either linking them into ethnic specific women's groups, which were mostly conducted in their own language, or having English speaking groups for women from a range of different countries.

> *One nurse was excited about one of her groups in which ethnic diversity was actually what gave the group its cohesion. 'There are virtually no Anglo-Australians and it's a real multicultural group and they're mixing really well together' she said, adding that the husbands had also joined in regular social occasions which the group had organised. Another nurse described how 'in one group there was only one 'Anglo" and they were a very diverse group'… the most popular session she had run for that group was on the theme of 'parenting in a new land' in which the members had shared similar experiences.*

> *(Scott, Brady & Glynn, 2001, p. 27)*

SDN Children's Services Parent Resource Program

SDN Children's Services, which originated as one of the subsidised day nursery associations a century ago, has created a family support program within a mainstream early childhood service (Udy, 2005). It provides good nutrition and a high quality early childhood program for very vulnerable children who do not usually use any form of child care, and reaches out to parents struggling with problems such as poverty, social isolation, drug and alcohol abuse, mental health problems and domestic violence. The program has four key elements (Udy, 2005):

- Scholarships that enable children to attend up to three days a week at a mainstream early childhood education and care centre
- Additional on the job training, coaching and professional supervision for early childhood education and care staff in how to work with 'hard to engage' parents who often present as 'demanding' and 'difficult'
- A warm and welcoming climate to encourage these parents to participate in information sessions where there are opportunities to make friends with other parents
- Inter-agency networking and referrals to link families with the range of services they need, and help to coordinate an integrated response to the family's needs.

A range of positive outcomes for the children, families, staff and the community have been identified in an evaluation of the program that has captured rich qualitative data on the perceptions of different stakeholders (Goodfellow et al., 2004).

Some of the quotes from parents include the following:

They seem to let you into their lives – the personal things. I think that it's really nice that they're open with parents. I like it. I think this is important because we're prepared to do it ourselves so it's nice to get it in return. I think that it's important that they can be honest.

The staff tend to be interested in talking to you not only about the child but even in you personally. Sometimes they ask 'How are you going?' and say 'This was a wonderful thing that happened today.' I notice that they take enough interest to remember things. And that's quite important. People sometimes treat things as a job and have their cut-off points whereas I don't find that here … I like the stability of the staff as well.

The staff always tell me things and that makes me comfortable. They always tell me what Alan has done in the day and they get his book out and show me the photos of what he has been doing. And his teacher will say 'he has done this today'.

Udy (2005) argues that for such a program to become successfully integrated in mainstream early childhood services the following elements are necessary:

- Consistent, committed staff
- Support and mentoring for staff
- A mix of professional disciplines
- Inter-agency engagement and involvement
- Time to release staff to attend meetings, receive training, reflect on their practice and spend time with families
- Management expertise as performance expectations are raised.

'Pal' – Napranum, Far North Queensland

Between 2000 and 2002 in Napranum, near Weipa on the Gulf of Carpentaria in Queensland, a home-based outreach program called 'Pal' was developed by staff in the pre-school centre in close partnership with local Indigenous women. Napranum is a very deprived Indigenous community and parents had asked for help to prepare children better for starting school. Pal stands for 'Parents and Learning', and local women with pre-school aged children are trained and employed as tutors to deliver kits to participating families over a two year period. The focus of the program is on coaching parents to do enjoyable exercises based on carefully chosen books and materials each week, in order to build their confidence in themselves as their children's first educator. The program is an 'indigenised' adaptation of the original Israeli HIPPY Program.

The Pal Program has two levels – pre-school and the first year of primary school. There are 60 weekly Pal kits, each one developed in close consultation with community members and comprising a high quality story book, related educational activity and a simple to understand instruction card.

The parent works with the child each week during the school term, reading the book and working through the activities. The Pal tutors deliver and pick up the kits each week and show parents how to use the materials, based on the training and support they themselves have been given.

While ostensibly an early literacy program, Pal is also aimed at strengthening parent–child relationships by creating opportunities for enjoyable interaction. A process analysis of the program found that the program operates in ways that build on the knowledge and skills within the community (Hanrahan, 2004). Pal has also provided opportunities for some of the women in the community to engage in paid employment and occupy respected roles, thus strengthening their ability as community leaders. The Pal Program has been adopted in a number of Aboriginal communities across several Australian states in the past few years.

Common principles

While the practices highlighted in these exemplars may not be possible to implement holistically in all early childhood services, the underlying principles that they have in common are applicable to all early childhood settings and are explored throughout this book.

They include:

- Positive partnerships between service providers and families
- Building on families' strengths and aspirations
- Responding holistically to the needs of children and families
- Strengthening links between families to create social support
- Collaborating across professions and services to provide comprehensive responses
- Embodying and expressing an ethos of hope and optimism.

Reflective questions

If you were a parent, what elements in the physical environment and the emotional climate of an early childhood service would make you feel comfortable or uncomfortable? How might the barriers to parents feeling comfortable be overcome?

Read the notes below of a conversation with a group of maternal and child health nurses working in a 'standard' community service for all families rather than a special program for vulnerable families. Can you identify any of the common principles listed above in their approach to their work?

Over lunch a group of maternal and child health nurses (Patricia Glynn, Fiona Hunter, Vivienne Thomas, Carol McIntyre and Nicole Carver), who work in the outer western suburbs of Melbourne, talked about several issues relating to how their roles had changed in response to new demands, and how they grappled with the complexities and challenges of their work. I started by asking them about the cultural diversity of the communities they served. One nurse spoke about a Karen refugee family from Burma, who had been featured in a recent television program. It had shown the mother and her six children in an overcrowded refugee camp in Thailand, living in a tiny space and washing from a bucket surrounded by a sea of other families. Then the program showed the family arriving at Melbourne airport and going straight to a four bedroom house in a new outer suburb. Her nurse remarked 'It was going from poverty and community to affluence and isolation.'

Another maternal and child health nurse spoke, with warmth and great admiration, about the massive adaptation that was required of such families. 'These are earth mothers. They are brilliant – wonderful, natural responsiveness to their children. 'What can I teach them about parenting?' I said to the NGO worker running a group for Karen families who asked me to come and speak with them! But there were challenges for them – like not letting a four year old take care of a two year old, and the importance of road safety, and eight year old children not going out walking on their own as they would have in a village when collecting wood. This is a different context and creates challenges for traditional childrearing which works in a setting where neighbours would all care for the children of the community.'

We discussed the enormous isolation such families face, especially in new suburbs, where there was no contact with neighbours. 'It's about adjusting our expectations and our views as well – we're learning as much from them… we have to be careful not to be paternalistic', said one maternal and child health nurse. 'They are so grateful – one of our Karen mothers named her child peaceful country in her language' said her nurse, who obviously derived a great deal of satisfaction from working with families from culturally diverse backgrounds.

The maternal and child health nurses were sensitive to how bewildering our services might seem – 'to have a health system that looks after you when you are not even sick!' There was an interesting discussion about how the families saw the nurses. 'Sometimes it is hard initially as the parents may be suspicious, feeling that they are under surveillance as some are so scared… and making the transition from being visited at home to coming to see us in the centre … sometimes it is a challenge to find their way by public transport – it can seem very daunting.'

I asked them how they engaged immigrant mothers in the First Time Parent Groups that they offered. One nurse spoke about a group she facilitated which had mothers from China, Sri Lanka, India, Iran and local Australian mothers, including young mothers, in which they all got along well. Another spoke about the importance of encouraging immigrant women to join the groups but that if this was not appropriate, for example, because of language difficulties, how they might still be able to connect them with another family from a similar background. 'Some mothers are not confident enough in their English to join new mother groups but we have been able, with their permission, to link them with other families from the same background on a family to family basis and that can work very well.'

Another challenging aspect of the work for the maternal and child health nurses in the communities in which they worked related to problems such as domestic violence, mental health, drug and alcohol abuse and child protection. 'We need more one-to-one time with some families. Sometimes referring them to the enhanced maternal and child health service (a more intensive outreach service) is not desirable or possible as they have the relationship with us, but it can still be good to consult with the enhanced maternal and child health service about the situation.' Another nurse commented that 'maternal and child health nurses now get clinical supervision in a group on a regular basis and that is very helpful.'

Another said that she needed to know more about what other services did. 'I don't know enough about what other people do – what child protection workers actually do for instance.' They contrasted this with how they had come to know about practitioners in some of the new co-located service centres. 'In the new co-located centres, it is much easier to make referrals – you just walk across the corridor and introduce the parent. The other worker is a real person, not just a name and a telephone number – to you and to the parents.' Another nurse said 'co-location means that others on the site can give you support. For example, the kindergarten teacher and I will go for a walk together at lunch time and we can talk about our families.'

Conclusion

Early childhood services have enormous potential to enhance the well-being of vulnerable children and their families. To fulfil this potential, skilful engagement of parents by practitioners, an organisational ethos of developing partnerships with other service providers, and a supportive policy framework and funding arrangements are required. There are many promising family-centred approaches in early childhood services currently being developed in Australia but they need to be rigorously evaluated for their effectiveness and for their transferability to other contexts. Working with vulnerable families can be professionally and personally challenging but also immensely fulfilling.

Useful websites

Australian Research Alliance for Children and Youth: www.aracy.org.au
Bernard van Leer Foundation: www.bernardvanleer.org
Centre for Community Child Health, Royal Children's Hospital Melbourne:
  www.rch.org.au/ccch

The Family Action Centre: www.newcastle.edu.au/research-centre/fac
Playgroups Australia: www.playgroupaustralia.com.au
Rural Health Education Foundation: www.rhef.com.au
St Luke's: www.stlukes.org.au; www.innovativeresources.com.au
Through the Looking Glass, Lady Gowrie Centre: www.throughthelookingglass.org.au
What Works for Children?: www.whatworksforchildren.org.uk
Wilfrid Laurier University: www.wlu.ca/index.php

References

Edgecomb, G., White, S., Marsh, G., Jackson, C., Hanna, B., Newman, S. et al. (2001). *First Time Parent Group Resource and Facilitation Guide for Maternal and Child Health Nurses.* Victorian Department of Human Services, Melbourne.

Goodfellow, J., Camus, S., Gyorog, D., Watt, M. & Druce, J. (2004). *'It's a Lot Different Now': A Description and Evaluation of an Innovative Family Support Program within Mainstream Early Childhood Services.* SDN Children's Services, Redfern, NSW.

Hanrahan, C. (2004). *Rethinking Parent Participation: A Process Evaluation of the Parents and Learning Program in Napranum.* James Cook University, Townsville, Queensland.

Jones, H. (1986). *In Her Own Name: Women in South Australian History.* Wakefield Press, Adelaide.

Olds, D. L., Kitzman, H., Cole, R. & Robinson, J. (1997). Theoretical foundations of a program of home visitation for pregnant women and parents of young children. *Journal of Community Psychology*, 25 (5), 10.

Panaretto, K. S., Lee, H. M., Mitchell, M. R., Larkins, S. L., Manessis, V., Buettner, P. G. et al. (2005). Impact of a collaborative shared antenatal care program for urban Indigenous women: A prospective cohort study. *Medical Journal of Australia*, 182 (10), 514–19.

Rogers, E. (2003). *Diffusion of Innovations* (5th edn). Free Press, New York.

Scott, D., Brady, S. & Glynn, P. (2001). New mother groups as a social network intervention: consumer and maternal and child health nurse perspectives. *Australian Journal of Advanced Nursing*, 18 (4), 23–9.

Swain, S. (1995). *Single Mothers and their Children: Disposal, Punishment and Survival in Australia.* Cambridge University Press, Melbourne.

Udy, G. (2005). SDN's Parent Resource Program: Reflecting our heritage, responding to present needs, reinventing the future for and with struggling families. *Developing Practice*, 12, 22–30.

Victorian Commission of Public Health (1940–41). 'Report of the Director of Infant Welfare'. Unpublished.

Sustained nurse home visiting with families of Aboriginal children

Fiona Arney, Kerrie Bowering, Alwin Chong, Virginia Healy and Bob Volkmer

Learning goals

This chapter will enable you to:
1. Develop an understanding of strengths-based approaches to working with Aboriginal and Torres Strait Islander families
2. Understand the importance of cross-cultural partnerships when working with Aboriginal and Torres Strait Islander families
3. Consider the cultural, social and emotional needs of Aboriginal and Torres Strait Islander clients when delivering services
4. Understand the need to take a 'whole of family' approach to improve outcomes for Aboriginal and Torres Strait Islander children
5. Recognise the characteristics of practitioners that are key to developing positive relationships with families.

Introduction

Australian Aboriginal and Torres Strait Islander families show remarkable strength and resilience. Australian Aboriginal culture is the world's oldest living culture, with knowledge systems evolving over many thousands of years and in adaptation to the changing Australian environment (Gostin & Chong, 1998). Knowledge about cultural practices (including childrearing), spirituality, relationships to land and nature, kinship networks, laws, lores, and rites, have been passed down within and between different cultural groups through ceremony, story, art, dance and song (and today through literature and electronic media) for millennia.

Today, Aboriginal and Torres Strait Islander people are estimated to make up 2.5% of the Australian population, with approximately half (53%) of the Indigenous population living in cities or inner regional areas (Australian Bureau of Statistics, 2008a). Children and young people make up a greater proportion of the Aboriginal population than of the non-Aboriginal population, with approximately half of the Aboriginal and Torres Strait Islander population aged 21 or under, compared to half of non-Aboriginal people being aged 37 or under) (Australian Bureau of Statistics, 2008a). Aboriginal people are more likely to live in a family household than are non-Aboriginal people (81% compared with 68%); with the households more likely to have multiple families living in them (5% of Aboriginal households compared with 1% of non-Aboriginal households) and to be headed by a sole parent (30% compared with 10% of non-Aboriginal households) (Australian Bureau of Statistics, 2008b).

Features that have been identified as common childrearing principles across a range of Aboriginal and Torres Strait Islander communities include the importance of: relationships, connections, balance, harmony, caring, sharing and respect (Department of Family and Community Services, 2005). 'Growing children up strong' includes the behaviours and actions that promote, enable and sustain positive growth and development of Aboriginal and Torres Strait Islander children, and includes a holistic approach to children's physical, emotional, spiritual and cultural well-being as well as promoting and sustaining children's safety (Borg & Paul, 2004; Warrki Jarrinjaku ACRS Project Team, 2002). The recognised diversity between (and within) communities and cultural groups highlights the needs for diverse approaches to reach these common goals.

Activity

Find out some more details about traditional and contemporary Aboriginal and Torres Strait Islander childrearing practices using the resources listed at the end of this chapter and other sources. How do these practices promote children's physical, emotional, spiritual and cultural well-being and their safety?

Challenges to childrearing

Childrearing that promotes optimal outcomes for Aboriginal children can be compromised by a wide range of factors. Professor Judy Atkinson calls for an 'educaring' approach to address the multiple and complex needs of Aboriginal and Torres Strait Islander people (e.g., drug and alcohol misuse, mental health problems and suicide, physical health problems and shorter life expectancy, financial concerns, unemployment, social isolation, and community and family violence) (Dawe, Harnett & Frye, 2008). Such an approach requires an understanding that these inter-generational problems are a legacy of the impact of socio-political factors such as colonisation, assimilationist policies that included the forced removal of Aboriginal children from their families, racism and discrimination, and the exclusion of Aboriginal and Torres Strait Islander people from paid employment (Human Rights and Equal Opportunity Commission, 1997). Recognising how these factors impact upon the health and well-being of Aboriginal and Torres Strait Islander people and using this knowledge to create approaches to address the grief, loss, trauma and dehumanisation resulting from these experiences, is of the utmost importance.

The impacts of socio-political factors on childrearing in Aboriginal and Torres Strait Islander families have led to:

- Changes in cultural norms and traditional parenting styles
- The inability for traditional childrearing practices to be passed down or practised from one generation to the next (because family members were forcibly separated)
- If traditional practices were able to be passed down, such practices not being understood or endorsed by the dominant culture in Australian society (e.g., a lack of understanding about the role of extended family and kinship networks in raising children may lead to biological parents being seen as neglectful in their parenting roles by non-Aboriginal Australians)
- Family contexts (as described above) that are not ideal for child development and well-being.

(Borg & Paul, 2004)

This has led to situations where Aboriginal and Torres Strait Islander children are far over-represented in the child protection system. Australia-wide, Aboriginal and Torres Strait Islander children are more likely than non-Aboriginal children to be the subject of a substantiated notification (at six times the rate of non-Aboriginal children) and almost nine times as likely to be placed in care (Australian Institute of Health and Welfare, 2009). A South Australian study has identified that by the time they were 15 to 16 years old in 2007, 57–76% of Aboriginal children born in 1991 had been the subject of a notification (based on the estimates of the proportion of Aboriginal children born in South Australia in 1991 as between 3–4%) compared with 22.5% of all children born in that year (Hirte, Rogers & Wilson, 2008). Even more alarming was that the rate of such notifications was increasing, with 56% of Aboriginal children born in 2002 already having been notified by the time they were four years old (compared to 11% of non-Aboriginal children). Aboriginal children were also more likely to: be the subject of more serious notifications of abuse; be notified for emotional abuse and neglect; have a first notification at a younger age; and be notified on multiple occasions (Hirte, Rogers & Wilson, 2008).

Aboriginal children, when compared with their non-Aboriginal peers, have also been shown to be more likely to have poor health outcomes and health concerns such as preterm birth, low birthweight, hospitalisations, higher mortality rates, more recurring infections, chronic ear infections and poor nutrition (Australian Bureau of Statistics, 2008c).

These poor outcomes for children speak to the need for public health and population approaches to promote Aboriginal child health, safety and well-being (O'Donnell, Scott & Stanley, 2008). Such an approach requires the ability to engage with and provide services to Aboriginal and Torres Strait Islander families that are respectful of culture, are based on evidence of what has worked in the past, and which have a sound theoretical basis for what might work in the future.

A number of characteristics of successful approaches to working with Aboriginal and Torres Strait Islander families have been identified – from the literature, from service providers, and most importantly, from the families themselves (Borg & Paul, 2004; Warrki Jarrinjaku ACRS Project Team, 2002). In terms of supporting the health and development of Aboriginal and Torres Strait Islander children, services and resources are needed that enhance and support the strengths of parents and families to care, support, provide for, teach and protect their children. The characteristics of the most useful approaches to supporting Aboriginal and Torres Strait Islander families have been identified as:

- Informal service delivery – services encourage informal talk and activities such as preparing a meal, sharing a coffee or cup of tea. They may also deliver programs in a secondary manner, such as supported playgroups delivered during health service visits, rather than providing the program as a separate activity.
- Community based – services respectfully identify and value the positive role of community including, parents, grandparents, cousins, uncles, aunties, Elders. Services work *for* communities as well as *with* them, and services are based on the strengths and the needs of communities.
- Culturally respectful, relevant, supportive, competent and safe for clients and staff – a culturally safe service is one that is also identified as being welcoming to Aboriginal and Torres Strait Islander clients – for example, it may have posters written in the Aboriginal language/s of the client group and provides translation services, it has 'friendly Aboriginal faces' and provides a culturally comfortable environment with Aboriginal employees in visible roles. The service works to build relationships of trust with individuals, families and communities. Support is provided for Aboriginal staff working in mainstream agencies.

- Supportive of families – services embrace the context(s) of Aboriginal families (e.g., recognising that raising a child in an Aboriginal family is a shared responsibility). Priorities are determined by families' circumstances and social and familial obligations, and services build on the knowledge and skills of parents and families and build their capacity to acquire new skills. Support and advice is provided not 'training' on how to parent.
- Inclusive of Elders – services recognise Elders' respected status in the community and value the shared knowledge they hold.
- Partnerships – services work in partnership with families, with their extended families, with their communities and with other agencies. Services are coordinated, and are complementary rather than competitive.
- Community controlled – services have elements of community control. This acknowledges the importance of community and contributes towards the goal of self-determination, empowering community members as decision makers and valuing their decisions.
- Learning organisations – services promote good practice examples and explore (to understand) why some services/delivery methods do or don't work. Services evolve to address multiple disadvantage and changing needs.
- Holistic – approaches integrate rather than separate the spiritual, emotional, physical and cultural aspects of life.

Reflective questions

Thinking of a public health approach that includes primary prevention (services that are available to everyone and aim to prevent a problem from occurring), secondary prevention (services that are aimed at a specific target group who may be more likely to develop a problem) and tertiary prevention (services to help respond when the problem has occurred and to prevent it recurring), what might a public health approach to improving the health and well-being of Aboriginal and Torres Strait Islander children look like?

Think of a service that you know that works with Aboriginal and Torres Strait Islander clients. What features does it have of those listed above? How might it be adapted to have more of these features?

Promising approaches to working with Aboriginal families

There are a growing number of promising programs and practice forming the evidence base and supply of resources regarding Aboriginal childrearing and ways to support families and communities in culturally competent ways (Child and Youth Health, 2004; Victorian Aboriginal Child Care Agency,

2006). However, it seems that when agencies implement new or existing supports and services with Aboriginal families and communities they have little access to the evidence base and little access to each other to share learning and resources. This is consistent with the research utilisation literature that suggests that it is often difficult to translate research into practice, particularly in reactive service systems such as child and family welfare, where the evidence is sometimes unclear or requires complicated solutions (Lewig, Arney & Scott, 2006) (see Chapter 12). Projects to promote the sharing of learning from a range of initiatives for Aboriginal and Torres Strait Islander children and their families include:

- The Secretariat for National Aboriginal and Islander Child Care (SNAICC) Report on the Indigenous Parenting Project (Borg & Paul, 2004) and the SNAICC Resource Service: srs.snaicc.asn.au
- 'Success Stories in Indigenous Health', Australians for Native Title and Reconciliation (ANTAR): www.antar.org.au
- 'The Rio Tinto Child Health Partnership: Delivering Improvements in Aboriginal and Torres Strait Islander Child and Maternal Health': www.ichr.uwa.edu.au/files/user6/RTCHP_Final_Report_Web.pdf
- 'Promising Practices in Out-of-home Care for Aboriginal and Torres Strait Islander Carers, Children and Young People: Profiling Promising Programs': www.aifs.gov.au/nch/pubs/reports/promisingpractices booklets/menu.html

Where no evidence exists, we must build the capacity of sites of practice to share promising practices, create and share new knowledge, and build the evidence base (Foster et al., 2006). Given the tremendous disadvantage that Indigenous children face, the dissemination of evidence-based approaches to family support work is less likely to do further harm and has the potential to make a substantial impact on the health and well-being of Indigenous families and communities. The following section describes a preliminary investigation into an initiative for improving the health, well-being and development of Aboriginal children in South Australia. It is only one example of such initiatives. Exciting work is being done in a range of other regions and services across Australia. Other promising programs aimed at promoting a healthy start to life for Aboriginal and Torres Strait Islander children and their families include the 'Anangu Bibi Program' in South Australia (Stamp et al., 2008), the 'Strong Women, Strong Babies and Strong Culture Program' in Western Australia (Smith et al., 2000), the Nganampa Health Council's 'Antenatal Care Project' in the Anangu Pitjantjatjara Yankunytjatjara Lands in Central Australia (Department of Health and Ageing, 2001), the 'Southern Aboriginal Maternity Care Project' in South Australia (Power, Nixon & O'Donnell, 2008) and the Townsville Aboriginal and Islander Health Services 'Mums and Babies Program' in Queensland (Panaretto et al., 2005) which was described in Chapter 5.

Activity

Find out about one of the programs named above and identify the elements of the program/service that relate to the features of best practice programs for Aboriginal and Torres Strait Islander families. Are there any other features that you might add to the list? Has the program/service been evaluated? What outcomes were obtained?

The Family Home Visiting Program in South Australia

In 2006, the Family Home Visiting Aboriginal Research Partnership was formed in order to examine a potentially promising approach to delivering child health services to Aboriginal families from a mainstream service (Sivak, Arney & Lewig, 2008). The partnership included formal agreements between the Aboriginal Health Council of South Australia, the Australian Centre for Child Protection at the University of South Australia, the Children, Youth and Women's Health Service (South Australia), and the Department of Families, Housing, Community Services, and Indigenous Affairs (Research & Analysis Branch); it also included representation from Nunkuwarrin Yunti of South Australia Inc., the Aboriginal community controlled health service in metropolitan Adelaide.

At the time, a greater proportion of Aboriginal families were engaging with the Family Home Visiting Program than were non-Aboriginal families, and the partnership was interested to examine why this was so. What did families perceive as the purpose and benefits of the program? What were some of the characteristics of the program and program staff that made it attractive to Aboriginal families (if this was indeed the case)? Were there things that families thought could be improved with the service? This section describes what the Family Home Visiting Program involved at the time and what the findings were from the research examining the program from the perspective of the families of Aboriginal children and is based on information from the full report of the pilot exploration of the program (Sivak, Arney & Lewig, 2008). It should be noted that this research was conducted three years ago and the Family Home Visiting Program model has since evolved (more details about this appear later in the chapter). The Children, Youth and Women's Health Service in Adelaide can be contacted for more information on the current model for the program.

Home visiting

'Home visiting' is a catch-all term describing programs delivered to families in their homes and can include a range of different services. Because home visiting programs can be very different, researchers have tried to examine the features of successful home visiting programs that enable them to improve outcomes for child health and development, parenting practices and the prevention of child abuse and neglect (Bennett et al., 2007; Caldera et al., 2007; Gomby, 2007; Holzer et al., 2006; Sweet & Appelbaum, 2004).

More effective and acceptable programs are those which: are more intensive; are of longer duration; contain content that is targeted at specific outcomes (e.g., content regarding child development, parent–infant attachment, strategies to improve child safety and to decrease the use of physical punishment); use trained professionals (or a combination of trained professionals, such as nurses, partnered with community health workers); use partnership approaches to work in client needs-driven ways; use staff from the same cultural backgrounds as the client group (e.g., the use of Indigenous paraprofessionals in the Apache and Navajo communities in the US); and are targeted for specific service users (Barlow et al., 2006; Barnes-Boyd, Norr & Nacion, 2001; Bennett et al., 2007; Caldera et al., 2007; Duggan et al., 2007; Gomby, 2007; Harvey-Berino & Rourke, 2003; Olds et al., 1999; Olds et al., 1998; Roman et al., 2007). Chapter 13 specifically examines the spread of home visiting models in a range of Australian contexts.

One particular program, the Nurse–Family Partnership, has been implemented since the 1970s and has demonstrated, through a series of randomised controlled trials in the US, that prenatal and early childhood home visitation by nurses can significantly decrease children's antisocial behaviour later in life when they have focused on assisting disadvantaged, first-time mothers to access antenatal care, promote their child's health and development, and develop economic self-sufficiency (Olds et al., 1999; Olds et al., 1998). When there is no or little domestic violence in a family, the program has also been reported to lead to reduced rates of child abuse and neglect (Eckenrode et al., 2000).

Building upon previous home visiting programs for Aboriginal families in metropolitan Adelaide (the Aboriginal Education Foundation, an Aboriginal-run, community-based agency, delivered in-home support for mothers and families from 1972 until early in the 1990s; Brice et al., 1992) and upon learning from Olds' Model of Home Visiting, the South Australian Children, Youth and Women's Health Service adopted and adapted a model of family home visiting. Since 2004, the family of every newborn baby in South Australia has been offered at least one visit by a qualified community child and family health nurse in the first few weeks of the child's life. During the visit, parents (usually mothers) are invited to complete a 'Pathways to Parenting Questionnaire' with the visiting nurse, which asks a range of questions about the mother, the baby and the rest of the family. From this information and from other details obtained prior to and during the visit a decision is made about whether to offer the family the more sustained Family Home Visiting Program. This decision will be made if it is thought that Family Home Visiting, a nurse-led preventive two year parenting program, will benefit the family above and beyond what normal service delivery would be likely to achieve (e.g., attending a local child and family health clinic). There are some characteristics in the South Australian program that mean the family will be offered Family Home Visiting, including the mother being less than 20 years old; the infant being of Aboriginal descent; the mother having poor attribution toward the infant; and/or the mother being socially isolated. The program is not designed for families who are in very chaotic situations, because parents are unlikely to be able to pick up the key principles of the program if they have many problems at the point of crisis. Other forms of support are needed for these families. Data from 2006 show that approximately 12% of families were offered Family Home Visiting and of these there was a take up rate of 77.9% among non-Aboriginal mothers and 83.6% for mothers of Aboriginal babies (Scott, 2006). Retention rates 12 months into the program were 79.3% and 85.5% for non-Aboriginal and Aboriginal families, respectively.[1]

Family Home Visiting aims to build attachment between infants and primary caregivers in a non-judgemental manner and in a non-threatening environment to meet the needs of parents and children in a way that both predicts and responds to family needs. Family Home Visiting has six modules: Building Relationships; Your Social Baby; Becoming a Separate Being; Getting Mobile; The Who Am I Phase; and Toddling On (Children, Youth and Women's Health Service, 2005). In all, a family may have up to 34 visits that are scheduled to start off weekly in the first six weeks, fortnightly for the next six months and monthly visits after that. Family Home Visiting focuses on child health and development and parent–child attachment and is scheduled to continue from the first visit to the family up to the child's second birthday. In order to provide a more inclusive service, Aboriginal and African families are offered the services of cultural consultants who work alongside the child and family health nurses who deliver the program. The home visiting professionals are also supported by a multidisciplinary team of psychologists, social workers, family support coordinators, and through referral to other health professionals and community services.

The visits are usually provided in the family's home, but can happen wherever the family feels most comfortable (e.g., another family member's home or the local child and family health clinic). The program also aims to link families to other programs and services in their local community so that families are supported by and connected to others during and after the Family Home Visiting Program. While Family Home Visiting is based on the learning from Olds' model of home visiting, important differences exist. For

---

1 Please note, in this chapter we have often used the term 'Aboriginal' to refer to people of Aboriginal and Torres Strait Islander descent to reflect the predominant cultural background of the Indigenous people of South Australia.

example, Family Home Visiting does not start during pregnancy, but builds upon the services provided by a midwife. Commencing in the first few weeks after the child is born; Family Home Visitors include cultural consultants as well as child and family health nurses; and whereas the US model exclusively targets first-time mothers, only the majority of Family Home Visiting clients are first-time parents.

A key component of Family Home Visiting is the training staff receive in using a strengths-based approach, which is based on Hilton Davis' 'Working in Partnership with Parents Model' (Davis, Day & Bidmead, 2002) to work with families towards the goals that the family set around their child's health and development. Staff also receive extensive training in attachment, child development and socio-emotional issues facing families.

What do families think of the Family Home Visiting Program?

The pilot research exploring Aboriginal families' perceptions of Family Home Visiting involved 60 participants living in the northern and southern regions of the Adelaide metropolitan area. The 60 participants represented a convenience sample of 52 families (14%) out of the approximately 380 Aboriginal families who had enrolled in the program since its commencement in 2004.[2] Forty-seven of the participants took part in focus groups and 25 did one on one interviews (12 took part in both a focus group and an interview). Focus groups took place in community settings and the one on one interviews took place where the participants felt most comfortable (e.g., at home, the child health clinic, or another family member's house). The participants included mothers and fathers of an Aboriginal infant who had been or were still involved with the Family Home Visiting Program, and extended family members such as grandmothers, aunties and uncles who had supported family members in the program. Half of the parents who took part in the study were receiving Family Home Visiting for their first child. Participants were recruited by Family Home Visiting child and family health nurses and Aboriginal cultural consultants who had met frequently with the research staff.

The service

The Family Home Visiting Program flows on from the first visit (universal contact visit) that all families are offered by a community child and family health nurse. Some families find out about the program while pregnant or because of previous experiences with nurse home visiting teams.

---

2 The collective term 'family' is used at times in this chapter to refer to the mothers, fathers and extended family members who took part in focus groups and interviews representing the views of those receiving Family Home Visiting and/or supporting recipients of the service.

Well [the child and family health nurse] has been close to the family for about…'cause of my little brother who's five now, so I knew her beforehand, but straightaway when [my daughter] was born [the child and family health nurse] phoned the hospital after I'd had her and then she just turned up on my doorstep when [my daughter] was 2 days old. Yeah, she followed up on what I was doing… – Mother

For some families, the process of being offered the program was a bit confusing at first, and it was important for Family Home Visiting child and family health nurses to reassure families that they were not associated with child protection services – a key point for families who had had previous experience with child protection. For families who took up the program despite any initial fears, they felt well rewarded.

It [Family Home Visiting] needs to be more easily approached. Because all of my other girlfriends relate it with their child get[ting] taken from them. So they're like, 'We don't want them coming around our house.' So that's what happens. So you need to get that wiped off. Somehow. Because I only get a positive experience, that's what I get out of it. And I tell everyone, 'No, they're so good. You can open up. You can tell them anything, and they're there for you. They're going to help you. And don't get scared' and all that. – Mother

The engagement process was enhanced by the qualities of the child and family health nurses and the Aboriginal cultural consultants. At times, the consultants were able to help bring the families and non-Aboriginal staff together, which otherwise might not have happened. Giving families the choice about whether to take part in Family Home Visiting or not was also seen as crucial to successful engagement with the program.

I reckon [Family Home Visiting staff] have to…love what they do and they would have to love being involved with the families…and to put up with how some families are…because they can't be too judgmental. All families are probably a bit rude to start off with because they don't know who you are, how you are, what's going on in your head…and you are going to be with their child…so…like all of them are going to love the program…they love the program now and they love the people who work for them. It's about respect and earning that respect to start off with. – Mother

I might not necessarily get on well with that particular person [Aboriginal cultural consultant], but they're a lot more likely to get in my home [than a non-Aboriginal nurse on her/his own], you know what I mean, because we're on the same level. We're on the same level in the ways we think, and how we do things. They know what lines to draw and we know what lines to draw, so it's very much needed that you have an Aboriginal worker with anyone that come to do that [in your home]. – Extended Family Member

I wasn't too sure what it was about. [But the Aboriginal cultural consultant] explained everything to me like, 'Oh no, it's not that. You've got a choice to be in the program or not', and that made me feel good. And she came out and that was really good. – Mother

The families involved in the research spoke very positively about the program, speaking of it as a highly valuable service that was able to promote positive child development and parent–infant attachment in a responsive, convenient and flexible way. The convenience of being visited in the home was seen as especially important for the families involved, particularly given the other commitments that families may have had and the difficulties of having visits in clinic settings.

> *Yeah, it [Family Home Visiting] was definitely my saviour, and even my partner said, if he could be here, he'd even comment on how much we sort of got out of it. – Mother*

> *And so I found that joining the program meant that I didn't have to change the other children's routine. I felt like I could – you could feed the baby, and give him a feed, and do all of that, and you didn't have to get the nappy bag ready, get the baby ready, get yourself ready, work out how you're going to get to, say, Child and Youth Health. And you didn't have any of those problems. You stayed in your own routine. And that's like the immunisation, and weighing and everything. – Mother*

> *Yeah. Having the other two children – they're 11 and 13 – I had to take them to visit the [maternal and child health] nurse, and I had to – well, at the time we only had one car, which my husband-at-time drove to work. So I had to walk to visit the lady. And yeah. The first one was a prem baby, and so she was absolutely tiny when she came home. And juggling a little baby, and all the health and stuff that goes with that, was hard. But then when the second one came along, there was a toddler and a baby, so juggling that, and trying to get to the nurse… And it's easier in your own home, because the baby can continue to play, and do what it does. And you can freely talk. Whereas, if you go into someone else's environment, they [children] want to touch everything, and inevitably touch everything they're not allowed to. And you try and occupy them. And it makes you rush through the visit – and they're [health staff] probably on a restricted time frame, whereas with the visiting nurse, she stays for a long time. So you can talk about lots of issues that you wouldn't normally talk about. So that's really good, I think. – Mother*

The flexibility of the program was also greatly appreciated by families and seen as very respectful of the families' situations. This included the scheduling and location of appointments to suit family needs and routines, the length of the home visit, and the child and family health nurses' flexibility and responsiveness around the needs of the family for information and referrals.

> *And she rings you first and organises a time that suits you. So not just, 'Oh, yeah, I can only come at this time.' She contacts me and lets me know what time, so it suits me. Or if I want to see her again that week or whether I just leave it to the Tuesday when I see her. – Mother*

> *When they [Aboriginal cultural consultant and child and family health nurse] come here, like over the last fortnight I was a bit tired. Yeah. Because I didn't have much sleep the night before, and when I was feeding I just dozed off.*

And they didn't stay very long because they knew I was tired. So they go, 'Well, since you're tired, we'll just do a little bit and then we'll leave.' So they know when… So, if I'm not feeling too good when they come, because they – what time – they come about 9:30, and they don't leave until like 11. So they're here for awhile with you. But if I'm tired or something, I'll just say, 'Yeah, I think we should just catch up another time.' Yeah, so it's good like that. So I just stop at any time. – Mother

She sort of does what we want to do. So if we have something we need to talk about, or if we want the baby to be weighed or something, then she's happy to do that, or whatever we want. So she sort of takes the lead from us, and what our needs are. – Father

In addition to health and developmental checks for the child, Family Home Visiting provides families with information about child development, parent–child attachment, nutrition, community links, and referral to other services (including health information for mothers and other members of the family). Such referrals may include services such as physical and mental health care, housing, child protection, higher education and children's playgroups. Families who feel comfortable being videotaped will also have recordings made of their interactions with their infants and sometimes the whole family gets involved. All of these activities were highly valued by parents – both first-time parents and those who have older children.

The developmental stuff. They're always up to what they should be, and how they're interacting, and what you can be doing to stimulate them, and what they're seeing – you know, like when they can only see 30cm in front, and then they can see further – so what you can be doing, and what activities. And they did like a video, they did a little video, and they give you the DVD, with a little picture of [our son] on the cover. And then they make you a little folder, and you've got all your information that you need. And it's good. – Father

And Nungas [Aboriginal people] have a lot of kids but we don't always get taught [about 'development']. Like one of the exercises for my son is throwing a ball from one hand to the other, and the reason why they're doing that is that it kind of links up both sides of the brain – and I never knew anything like that until now. Because I hadn't done anything like that, you know what I mean. – Mother

Yeah other agencies. And that's what I'd like you to hear. They've plugged us into sports, kindies, health, […] hospitals, specialists…wherever the women in the program are, and I've met most of the women in the program, whenever they hear of a good idea, doesn't matter where or what it is, they [the child and family health nurse and Aboriginal cultural consultant] will pass that information onto you because they care about you and your child. – Mother

They do DVDs with the families, and they do a lot of stuff showing how you're interacting with your baby, and things. Like you can learn from what the baby's doing, and see things that, when you're doing it, you don't notice. That probably is one of the really good things. – Mother

> *Oh, knowing that I've got support, and if I needed any questions for my baby, I'm doing it alright. [It's doing it] all over again, because it's been four years since I had one! (laughing) – Mother*

The content of the service (e.g., the information which was given and the service referrals) was important, but the way in which this content was delivered to families was just as important. Using the strengths-based partnership approach, families were encouraged to identify the information they would like to have and the home visiting team would provide this. The knowledge that families already had was also highly respected by the child and family health nurses, and families were supported in their decisions through the full provision of information about an issue, with the child and family health nurses providing a range of alternatives.

> *And yeah, but she doesn't say well, 'You should never smack your child! And if I ever see you, I'll report you to the Child Services!' Something like that. It's more like, 'This is one of the things that happens with smacking children, and this is another way of approaching it, if you don't want to do it that way.' – Mother*

The cross-cultural partnership between the child and family health nurses and cultural consultants provides cultural connections and cultural information for families whilst helping families access a mainstream service (Chapter 2 explains more about the importance of maintaining cultural strengths for families). This was especially important for families who may have had limited connections to the Aboriginal communities of Adelaide. The cultural safety provided by having Aboriginal staff involved in service delivery meant that families felt comfortable with the service and were able to more fully understand the information they were given.

> *I'm Aboriginal [but not from Adelaide], and I don't know much about the Aboriginal people here. So, if they're going to give us an Aboriginal worker, it's good for her to come. Because I don't know much about what I can do here. I mean, she told me about the dads' group, but that's about all. But other things, like the things that are going to happen around here, like important things, meetings or get togethers with other families and that. – Father*

> *You know, I hardly ever actually get an Aboriginal worker coming to my home. [...] No, I want [the Aboriginal staff] to come, because the only Aboriginal people my child gets to see is from the Early Learning Program. That's a playgroup, where they come out and play with him once a fortnight. But that's it. I think [the Aboriginal cultural consultant] has come out, I think two or three times maybe? But that's about it. So my baby sees no black fellas at all. It sucks. (laughing) – Mother*

> *Well with the Aboriginal workers, I like how you can talk about your culture more with the Aboriginal workers around, and how you feel – like, with the non-Aboriginals you can, but with the Aboriginal ones, how you're feeling. – Mother*

Auntie [Aboriginal cultural consultant] will put it in the terms I understand. But yeah. [...] Because sometimes if [the child and family health nurse] doesn't understand what I'm saying, Auntie [Aboriginal cultural consultant] will put it into the perspective so [the child and family health nurse] knows, so yeah. [...] Oh, I just look at [the Aboriginal cultural consultant], she just... I'm not sure how she does it, but yeah. – Mother

Home visiting staff would also accompany parents and children to appointments, which was beyond families' expectations. So too was the support that staff provided in transporting families and at times making appointments with other services for family members. While this was highly valued by the families who received this extra service, it was beyond the scope of the service model and raised implications for the ability of the service to sustain such levels of support and the expectations and dependency it might raise on the part of clients.

Maybe I would've got back on my feet and back out in the world, maybe later on – I don't know. It probably would've taken me a bit longer, if it wasn't for [the child and family health nurse] to sort of like, you know. And because – I think it helped me get there quicker, because [she] said, 'I'll go there with you. Come on, you know, I'll be there, so...' So that helped that initial ice-breaker – Mother

I didn't expect they'd be so nice! (laughing) And I didn't expect her to drive me to my playgroups and everything, and help me out that way. And like, answer my phone call at 7:30 at night or something. – Mother

Yeah, [my baby] still has to go to hospital now [...] have appointments at 9.00am. Sometimes we don't get home 'til 4.30pm and they [Family Home Visiting staff] pick me up at 8.30am and we get to the hospital and they are with me all day [...] They're [Family Home Visiting staff] good, excellent. – Mother

Parents also appreciated that the frequency of visits became less just as parents were feeling that they needed the support less often from the service.

I think they have a little plan where it's once a week for some weeks, and then they go fortnightly for a while, and then it's... And I found that when they went fortnightly I was just ready for fortnightly visits. It was just good timing. – Mother

Participants also spoke of the way that the program and the child and family health nurses were able to respond to their family situations (including positive and negative circumstances, and the larger family size in some households) in ways that were both respectful and empowering, and took a whole family approach. This included providing parenting information for grandmothers who were also involved in raising their grandchildren and who didn't have such information available when they became parents. Staff also spoke of the importance of a whole family approach when working with families in the Family Home Visiting Program, and the need for this to happen more.

> *Yeah, it's not just children, youth and women – there's men involved. You can't just have children without men! (laughing) …It's families! And dads should be encouraged to participate with their children. – Mother*

> *And just another thing, before they [Family Home Visiting staff] came, I felt like there was just no room for baby. Like families really seemed to be worrying about themselves, and so having the workers coming to the home, they gave the message that new baby was a very important part of the family as well. That's a big thing for me, because they [people in the household] didn't really care about babies' routines. I mean people would just rock up when they want, and especially after the money and that, baby bonus, you know. Everybody would come around, 'humbugging' [annoying us] … It's good having them [Aboriginal Family Home Visiting staff] there, because your neighbours don't…and the community, you've got that backup, 'Yeah babies are really important'. – Mother*

> *We have four generations here, and that's got to be very rare in Aboriginal communities. So he [baby] is just spoiled rotten, but he's a really good child. And I think, being an older mother, and I'm sure the other grandmothers agree, that you can be a better mum with your grandchildren than you were with your children. […] So, it's about you [grandmother] too, learning to be a good parent. I've not always been a good parent. – Extended family member*

> *Well for the first year of my daughter's life, I lived with my mum. So my mum was there most of the time for the visits. And what was helpful was my mum hearing this information from [the child and family health nurse], and taking that on board as well. So she had more of an understanding. Because it's been a long time. And I mean, she's got grandkids – but she didn't live with them like she did with my little one. […] Well, I don't know if it [nana's being present at the visits] stopped her [from giving advice]. (laughing) But she had more of an open mind with things, just with how things are done differently than they were 20 or 30 years ago. – Mother*

> *The whole family, the whole family. Because it's ridiculous if you're just over there to do a health check, and the baby is okay and the mother's okay. But she's worried she doesn't have anywhere to live, and she's busted up, and they're starving, and – you know? – Aboriginal cultural consultant*

> *What I was getting at is, we've got an organisation, it's the mother and the child. But we've had a couple of families, like the husband does everything! And it's the mother that bashes the husband. And the husband is saying, 'Um, I'm really the caregiver of the child. And I need help around relationships, you know counselling, for both of us, to make it change.' You know? So it's how you look at the scenario. But sometimes when you listen to nurses and managers, it's all focused on the mother and child, the mother and child. And the father is sort of like pushed right back? And you've got fathers out there that are screaming out for help. – Aboriginal cultural consultant*

A number of issues were identified that Family Home Visiting was able to support families to deal with including: problems with housing, a lack of transport options, experiences of having been in state care, social isolation and a lack of connections to the Aboriginal communities in Adelaide, mental health problems and substance misuse, family conflict and domestic violence, a lack of cultural identity for parents and for children, and the inter-generational impacts of child removal, family conflict and grief and loss. The ability of the child and family health nurses to liaise with other agencies around some of the concerns families had (e.g., providing support with housing, mental health and child protection services) provided a holistic approach to working with families around their health and well-being, and enabled parents to focus on their roles in their children's lives. The community child health nurse has a significant part to play in linking families with other providers to assist their needs being met, jointly working with their family so that they can build up their skills and their trust in other providers. This supports a model of independence.

> *Housing, they done like a support letter for me. Yeah, just to say that I was one of their clients, and that I was on my own and just had a newborn baby. But yeah, that was good like that way, to help me push for housing – Mother*

> *Because, and they've seen my parenting, they [child and family health nurse and Aboriginal cultural consultant] know that if I'm not well and when I'm well. Because I've got depression, if I'm well, I'm going to my appointments, and everything's 'deadly' [great], then all good. But they know too that when I'm sick, that I won't make appointments, I'll cut it, I won't be home. So they'll keep coming back. They won't worry about being disappointed with you, 'She wasn't there.' (laughing) – Mother*

> *Because some girls have nobody. But I'm more isolated than them. I only rely on my foster mum – I don't have aunties, uncles, cousins, so. They did a lot for me, you know. And most of my girlfriends don't even know half the things that are around in the community for them. If it's depression, or if it's malnutrition – all sorts of things. Just lots of information, you don't even have to ask, they'll offer. You know what I mean? If you're shy or you can't, you don't even have to think about asking. They know, they're aware, and they'll offer it. – Mother*

As a result of the program, parents reported an increased sense of confidence in their parenting role (and in themselves generally) as they were treated as the experts about their baby and their family. This was especially true for parents who might not have had other role models or supports to turn to for advice about parenting.

> *I think it just gives you more confidence that you know what you're doing, you can get through the next week. And like, with all [my son's] changes, because he's growing and changing so much! Like, even when you have a hard week, just knowing that that's – you know, you can go back to your information*

chart, and go,' Oh yeah, he's supposed to be a bit unsettled this week.' And you know, it makes you just feel a little bit more in control, I think. – Mother

Thinking…maybe, 'Am I doing the right thing?' and having that reassurance that, 'Yeah, I am a tops mum, and I am doing the right thing.' So, yeah. Having [the child and family health nurse] to say, 'Yeah you are doing the right thing.' It has definitely helped boost my confidence as a parent. – Mother

I reckon it's opened me up to more talking. Because, when I first come to Adelaide I wouldn't go out or talk to hardly no one. And since [the child and family health nurse has] been coming and that, and [the Aboriginal cultural consultants] and that, I've been out in the open, and there are other areas for me to go to and all that. – Mother

Oh yeah, because I didn't really have any idea about what to do with a baby. Like I had my instincts but [the child and family health nurse] has just helped me with stuff like, she says things like, 'That's normal, this is normal', like, 'Don't worry about that'…helping me which is good. It's good to have her just one-on-one because my family aren't around – Mother

Family Home Visiting is designed to work primarily with the mother and child, but families also spoke of the way in-home support was also able to be provided for fathers, other children in the family and extended family members such as grandmothers to support the baby's/child's development. This was a very valuable part of the service delivered to families, although often fathers' schedules and the hours of the programs didn't allow a large amount of involvement in the program. (Chapter 7 describes strategies to engage fathers more in services for children and their families and describes a home visiting program specifically targeted at fathers.)

Yeah, 'cause, a lot of it for him [my partner] was difficult as well. Um, like a lot of the information we got and the questions that we asked [the child and family health nurse] were from him as well. So it was a great help for him and he, like, the amount that [the child and family health nurse] helped us, he's just as thankful as I am. Every time she came around and he was home she'd really encourage him to join in and… […] With all the sleep stuff she's encouraged him to come and help, like, 'This is what you do.' – Mother

And with these workers here, what happened is, they came one day, at one visit, and we were talking, something about my diabetes, and the nurse said she'd bring one of the diabetes health workers down, to have a talk with me when they came on their next visit, you know. Which I just thought was great. Because, they could've said, 'We'll make an appointment for you', and I'd say, 'Yeah, I'll go to it', and I probably wouldn't end up going to it, you know? But they brought the worker to me. You know? – Extended family member

Where possible, the program aims to have the same staff member/s provide all of the visits to a family, unless the family requests a change, the staff member leaves employment or the family move to a different Family Home Visiting region. Families very much appreciated this continuity, which enabled strong bonds to be formed between families and the home visiting staff, and a deeper understanding of the lives of families. Some families who had changes in staff delivering the program commented on the process of changing workers.

> *I think, like, you could have any nurse come and do it, but it's nice to have the same person coming to your house all the time, and they get to know your baby a bit, and know your family, and know your background. Like some families have bigger problems than others, and some have personal issues – and we all have financial issues! (laughing) – Mother*

> *Because [Family Home Visiting] was an ongoing thing, and it was a regular visit, [my daughter] built trust and a relationship [with the child and family health nurse]. And like I said before, [the Family Home Visiting nurse] was like an auntie [...] [My daughter] just loves her. So she has become part of [my daughter's] world. – Mother*

> *No, they're all good. The only thing I didn't like was like you get to know one worker and what they're like and then [...] And she left. [...] She moved somewhere else. [...] I think [the second nurse] felt it too. – Mother*

> *Oh that's right. And that's why you were upset. Because you see, you build that relationship with the person [Family Home Visiting staff member]. You know. [...] That one person. And then, like I said, when they leave, you know, it's like, 'Now I've got to build this all up again.' – Extended family member*

> *Somebody with the same goals, the same principles, the same, you know, on the same wavelength. Because I moved from [a different site of roll-out] where I had [Aboriginal cultural consultant] – as my worker she was "deadly" [...] in her role as the Nunga worker, she was fantastic! And [the child and family health nurse], the non-Aboriginal worker, she was deadly too. And then moving here, it was just a really smooth transition. Like they had rung auntie [Aboriginal cultural consultant] and [the child and family health nurse], and said, 'She's on her way!' (laughing) – Mother*

The end of the program (e.g., when children became two years old) was seen by some families, particularly those with fewer social connections, as a difficult time. This illustrates how highly valued the service, and more particularly, the key role that staff play in the lives of families, but also suggests that managing the transition well and linking families to other services for their families is critical. A success of the program is how well families have been linked into their local community, and how they seek out help if they need it in the future.

> *I won't know what's happening now 'cause nobody will tell me, unless she [Family Home Visiting staff member] tells me. Informing me about it, like, she's always informing me about everything. Maybe I'll have to go out and find out on my own. (laughing) – Mother*

> *Yeah, it was like, 'This is our last visit.' And we got a little certificate for [my daughter]. [...] And I don't know. Some people might handle it better than me.*

I can only speak for myself, but I found it really hard to break free from that. [...] Yeah, so whether or not it was the last meeting, or if it was a whole day spent together doing activities and the video, yeah. I think it still would've been the process of it ending anyway – that grieving process. Mm. – Mother

I know [my daughter] misses [the child and family health nurse]. She still says, 'Are we going to see [nurse's name] today?' Or, 'Is [nurse's name] coming over?' She does. And I know she would have been grieving. She would've gone through a grieving process, and missing her. She had a birthday and, 'Is [nurse's name] coming to my party?' So, she's [nurse] made a huge impact in her life. And mine as well. And she's like an auntie, like my auntie as well. A dear friend that I have a lot of respect for, and really do look up to, and admire. – Mother

The child and family health nurses and the Aboriginal cultural consultants

Families' views about the program could not be separated from their appreciation of the staff – their qualities and abilities as practitioners were seen as the key to engaging families into the program, to effective service delivery and to promoting child health and well-being throughout the program. Families had a real sense of being cared about and valued – as parents and as individuals, and parents felt that the staff loved their children and had a passion for working with children, and with Aboriginal families in particular. Child and family health nurses and Aboriginal cultural consultants were seen as family members and friends of the families with whom they worked, although parents were quite aware of the boundaries of the relationship. These experiences were often contrasted with poor interactions with other services or staff members – often where families felt they had been told what to do by staff, felt talked down to, and felt that they were not valued by the child and family health nurses.

To me they're more like family, interested in you like family. They're not just in a job, but they're interested in your child. And really, really – and I've seen people doing their job, it's their job and they've got to do it, early childcare workers – but these [Family Home Visiting staff] are like genuinely concerned about our children, and they love them like they're their own family. So it's... might be the empathy thing, I don't know. – Mother

I thought [having a baby] was going to be so difficult – like to try to get around on public transport and like, 'What if something happened?' Because I don't want to call [my partner's] mum. Because I'm really independent, and I don't want to have to be relying on someone. But it's good to have someone coming here. But I haven't really become reliant on [the child and family health nurse] – to do everything all the time – but it just makes life a lot easier. Than having to get to the doctor, and get to the doctor's surgery, every fortnight or whatever (laughing) [...] But she does give me other services. And I wouldn't call her like, really late – because she's given me this 24 hour parent line and... – Mother

She's [nurse] really placid. And so she's not really, 'Do this and do that' overbearing. She's just – I suppose she just lets me do the talking! (laughing) And so, whatever I've got, she'll just listen and then start giving information and stuff. And yeah, I think that's what I like about her the most. Because a lot of people just tell you what to do. And they might be right or it might be wrong, but they just don't let you come to that place by yourself. – Mother

The personal and professional qualities of child and family health nurses and Aboriginal cultural consultants that were highly valued included:

- Being non-judgemental
- Showing empathy and relating their own childrearing experiences
- Being respectful and listening to families
- Following through on promised actions
- Demonstrating expertise in child health and development
- Being open and honest, friendly and down-to-earth
- Showing passion for their roles and commitment to their work
- Including the whole family
- Being positive about the family
- Being committed to working with Aboriginal families, and doing so in a way that acknowledges the expertise of families.

These qualities align almost exactly with those included in the Family Home Visiting Service Outline (Children, Youth and Women's Health Service, 2005) and those in international research examining successful partnerships with families (Barlow et al., 2006; Davis, Day & Bidmead, 2002; Kirkpatrick et al., 2007), specifically: having non-judgemental respect for others, an ability to develop health and caring relationships, having warmth and being genuine, being client focused in decision making, effectively assessing families' strengths and needs, and being able to work collaboratively with other colleagues.

No. I've never experienced [the Family Home Visiting staff having 'attitudes']. They've always been really nice, really outgoing. Speaking to you all the time. Yeah, and not when – and if I do something wrong, they're not doubting me about it. They're telling me a right way that I can understand. – Mother

[The child and family health nurse] has an interest in children and she has a passion for what she does. She was just meant to be. How she treats the children her passion shows through. – Mother

But they never say anything negatively. Or anything like that. It's always very, very positive. ... And no one's tried that like that before. – Mother

And the main thing is that she is always positive, finds positives. Especially when things are... You know, young girls are very vulnerable to negativity, hugely vulnerable, and [the child and family health nurse] will just find things all the time with them that are positives. And [the nurse] will just talk to them.

And you see [the young mums] once they have lifted themselves up [the nurse is] like, 'Well maybe you can try this now.' – Extended family member

Well the other one, she – I don't know – sort of had the attitude like she didn't really care about her job; she just wanted to get it over and done with, and she's more in it for the money, I thought. Because she had no heart in it. As opposed to this one now: she thinks the world of her job. She loves it. – Mother

[…] You get somebody who knows what your life is like, and they want to support Nungas. You know what I mean. – Extended family member

Sometimes we get off on a tangent because her children have similar abilities to my older ones…and we've talked to her about that. We were having a good discussion about that […] And how she handles it, because she's got kids that are similar. So, that's quite good. She's not just the nurse, she's a mum. And she has trials and stuff with her own children, like everybody, which is good because sometimes professionals come across as though their children are perfect and she doesn't do that. (laughing) Because no kids are perfect. – Mother

A very important point to remember regarding the involvement of the Aboriginal cultural consultants as part of the home visiting team is the role that the staff have within their own families and communities. There are high levels of accountability to the community about who gets the service and why or why not someone is considered eligible. Because of their roles as health care providers and their relationships with communities, it's very difficult for the Aboriginal staff to refuse the service to Aboriginal families and for some practitioners this has meant they have provided service to families who weren't eligible. The role for Aboriginal staff working in Aboriginal health (and other sectors focused on Aboriginal health, safety and wellbeing) is one that does not get left at the office door at the end of the working day. It is a 24 hour, seven day a week role. This needs to be acknowledged by workplaces and support provided for staff accordingly.

And the other thing too, is you get people coming up to you saying, 'Oh, well, how come my cousie is doing that Family Home Visiting Program, but I've got twice as much kids as her, and I need more and more help, and how come I can't be a part of it?' And then you have to explain. […] Just that 'Due to too many crises that keep occurring, you don't really fit into the Family Home Visiting Program, but what we can do is offer you other supports.' And I always say, 'We're not giving up on you! If you ever need to call me, give me a call.' – Aboriginal cultural consultant

Conclusion

In this chapter we have emphasised the important characteristics of services and programs to support the health and well-being of Aboriginal and Torres Strait Islander children. Family inclusiveness, cultural respectfulness and programs that recognise the strengths and address the needs of families as identified by those families are very important. Also of great salience for the families included in the research examining Family Home Visiting was the need for program convenience (e.g., being delivered in the home), flexibility and Aboriginal staff who were the bridge bringing together Aboriginal clients and a program from a mainstream service. These findings are of great relevance as a number of Australian states and the Australian and New Zealand Governments are currently adopting or developing home visiting approaches (e.g., the Australian Office for Aboriginal and Torres Strait Islander Health's Health at Home Program) to optimise outcomes for Indigenous children and their families. A feature of program success that is consistently emphasised throughout this book, not least in this chapter, is the need for staff who embody the principles of relationship-based practice outlined in Chapter 1 – empathy, respectfulness, genuineness and optimism. Approaches that emphasise the strengths and expertise of Aboriginal families, and work together in partnership with them, are far more likely to successfully engage families and therefore have more chance of optimising the health and well-being of their children. The Family Home Visiting Program in South Australia, used as an example of how to incorporate principles into practice, has been and will continue to evolve since its commencement in 2004. Lessons learnt have been incorporated into training, criteria for entry has been refined, and the focus on the development of partnerships, to promote upskilling and independence for families, and appropriate referral to other providers, has been strengthened. Seeking feedback and working closely with Aboriginal communities is embedded now into the program as it is rolled out into communities in rural and remote South Australia. A prospective study to examine the effectiveness of the Family Home Visiting Program is currently underway, with two groups of families enrolled. The prospective study involves those in the program and a comparison group of families in regions where the program had not yet been rolled out at the time of recruitment. The evaluation aims to establish the effectiveness of the program with regards to child health, development and safety, and maternal health as well as allowing for comparisons within the groups of families.

Useful websites

The Centre for Parent and Child Support: www.cpcs.org.uk
'Footprints in Time – Longitudinal Study of Indigenous Children': www.fahcsia.gov.au/sa/indigenous/progserv/families/lsic/Pages/default.aspx
Nurse–Family Partnership: www.nursefamilypartnership.org
Secretariat for National Aboriginal and Islander Child Care: snaicc.asn.au
Warrki Jarrinjaku Jintangkamanu Purananjaku 'Working together everyone and listening': www.waltja.org.au/default/warrki.html

References

Australian Bureau of Statistics (2008a). 'Population characteristics, Aboriginal and Torres Strait Islander Australians, 2006'. Available online at: www.abs.gov.au/ausstats/abs@.nsf/productsbytitle/2B3D3A062FF56BC1CA256DCE007FBFFA

Australian Bureau of Statistics (2008b). 'Experimental estimates of Aboriginal and Torres Strait Islander Australians, Jun 2006'. Available online at: www.abs.gov.au/AUSSTATS/abs@.nsf/DetailsPage/3238.0.55.001Jun%202006

Australian Bureau of Statistics (2008c). *The Health and Welfare of Australia's Aboriginal and Torres Strait Islander Peoples ABS 4704.0.* Australian Bureau of Statistics, Canberra.

Australian Institute of Health and Welfare (2009). *Child Protection Australia 2007–08.* Australian Institute of Health and Welfare, Canberra.

Barlow, A., Varipatis-Baker, E., Speakman, K., Ginsburg, G., Friberg, I., Goklish, N. et al. (2006). Home-visiting intervention to improve child care among American Indian adolescent mothers. *Archives of Pediatric and Adolescent Medicine*, 160, 1101–7.

Barnes-Boyd, C., Norr, K. & Nacion, K. (2001). Promoting infant health through home visiting by a nurse-managed community worker team. *Public Health Nursing*, 18 (4), 225–35.

Bennett, C., Macdonald, G. M., Dennis, J., Coren, E., Patterson, J., Astin, M. et al. (2007). 'Home-based support for disadvantaged adult mothers (Review)', The Cochrane Collaboration. Available online at: www.cochrane.org

Borg, T. & Paul, A. (2004). *Indigenous Parenting Project.* SNAICC, Melbourne.

Brice, G., Radford, A. J., Harris, R. D., Van Der Byl, M., Neeson, M. & Monten, H. (1992). 'One Community, One Grief: Aspects of Aboriginal destructive and self-destructive behaviours, their 'prevention' and 'causality''. In S. McKillop (ed.), Preventing Youth Suicide: Proceedings of a Conference 24–26 July 1990 (AIC Conference Proceedings; no. 13). Australian Institute of Criminology, Canberra.

Caldera, D., Burrell, L., Rodriguez, K., Shea Crowne, S., Rohde, C. & Duggan, A. (2007). Impact of a statewide home visiting program on parenting and on child health and development. *Child Abuse and Neglect*, 31 (8), 829–52.

Child and Youth Health (2004). *Pathways to Parenting the Indigenous Way.* Government of South Australia, Adelaide.

Children, Youth and Women's Health Service (2005). *Family Home Visiting Service Outline*. Government of South Australia, Adelaide.

Davis, H., Day, C. & Bidmead, C. (2002). *Working in Partnership with Parents: The Parent Adviser Model*. Harcourt Assessment, London.

Dawe, S., Harnett, P. & Frye, S. (2008). Improving outcomes for children living in families with parental substance misuse: What do we know and what should we do? *Child Abuse Prevention Issues*, 29.

Department of Family and Community Services (2005). 'Growing up culture strong: National Indigenous child rearing and good practice in service delivery'. Workshop Proceedings. Department of Family and Community Services, Canberra.

Department of Health and Ageing (2001). *Better Health Care: Studies in the Successful Delivery of Primary Health Care Services for Aboriginal and Torres Strait Islander Australians*. Australian Government, Canberra.

Duggan, A., Caldera, D., Rodriguez, K., Burrell, L., Rohde, C. & Shea Crowne, S. (2007). Impact of a statewide home visiting program to prevent child abuse. *Child Abuse and Neglect*, 31 (8), 801–27.

Eckenrode, J., Ganzel, B., Henderson, C., Smith, E., Olds, D., Powers, J. et al. (2000). Preventing child abuse and neglect with a program of nurse home visitation: The limiting effects of domestic violence. *Journal of the American Medical Association*, 284 (11), 1385–91.

Foster, D., Williams, R., Campbell, D., Davis, V. & Pepperill, L. (2006). 'Researching ourselves back to life': New ways of conducting Aboriginal alcohol research. *Drug and Alcohol Review*, 25 (3), 213–7.

Gomby, D. S. (2007). The promise and limitations of home visiting: Implementing effective programs. *Child Abuse and Neglect*, 31 (8), 793–9.

Gostin, O. & Chong, A. (1998). Living wisdom, Aborigines and the environment. In E. Bourke, C. Bourke & B. Edwards (eds), *Aboriginal Australia: An Introductory Reader in Aboriginal Studies* (2nd edn), 147–67. Queensland University Press, Brisbane.

Harvey-Berino, J. & Rourke, J. (2003). Obesity prevention in preschool Native-American children: A pilot study using home visiting. *Obesity Research*, 11 (5), 606–11.

Hirte, C., Rogers, N. & Wilson, R. (2008). *Research Report – Contact with the South Australian Child Protection System*. Department for Families and Communities, Government of South Australia, Adelaide.

Holzer, P., Higgins, J. R., Bromfield, L. M., Richardson, N. & Higgins, D. J. (2006). *Child Abuse Prevention: What Works? The Effectiveness of Parent Education Programs for Preventing Child Maltreatment*. Australian Institute of Family Studies, National Child Protection Clearinghouse, Melbourne.

Human Rights and Equal Opportunity Commission (1997). *Bringing Them Home: Report of the National Inquiry into the Separation of Aboriginal and Torres Strait Islander Children from Their Families*. Human Rights and Equal Opportunity Commission, Sydney.

Kirkpatrick, S., Barloe, J., Stewart-Brown, S. & Davis, H. (2007). Working in partnership: User perceptions of intensive home visiting. *Child Abuse Review*, 16, 32–46.

Lewig, K., Arney, F. & Scott, D. (2006). Closing the gap: Research utilisation in child and family services. *Family Matters*, 74, 12–19.

O'Donnell, M., Scott, D. A. & Stanley, F. (2008). Child abuse and neglect – Is it time for a public health approach? *Australian and New Zealand Journal of Public Health*, 32 (4), 325–30.

Olds, D., Henderson, C., Kitzman, H., Eckenrode, J., Cole, R. & Tatelbaum, R. (1999). Prenatal and infancy home visitation by nurses: Recent findings. *The Future of Children*, 9 (1), 44–65.

Olds, D., Pettitt, L., Robinson, J., Henderson, C., Eckenrode, J., Kitzman, H. et al. (1998). Reducing risks for antisocial behavior with a program of prenatal and early childhood home visitation. *Journal of Community Psychology*, 26 (1), 65–83.

Panaretto, K., Lee, H., Mitchell, M., Larkins, S., Manessis, V., Buettner, P. et al. (2005). Impact of a collaborative shared antenatal care program for urban Indigenous women: A prospective cohort study. *Medical Journal of Australia*, 182 (10), 514–19.

Power, C., Nixon, A. & O'Donnell, K. (2008). *Evaluation of the Southern Aboriginal Maternity Care Project: 'Ngangkitta Ngartotdli Karpandi' (Supporting Mums and Babies)*. Flinders University, Adelaide.

Roman, L., Lindsay, J., Moore, J., Duthie, P., Peck, C., Barton, L. et al. (2007). Addressing mental health and stress in medicaid-insured pregnant women using a nurse-community health worker home visiting team. *Public Health Nursing*, 24 (3), 239–48.

Scott, D. (2006). 'Family Home Visiting: The way forward'. Presentation at Parenting Imperatives II: The 2nd National Parenting Conference. Adelaide, May 2006.

Sivak, L., Arney, F. & Lewig, K. (2008). *A Pilot Exploration of a Family Home Visiting Program for Families of Aboriginal and Torres Strait Islander Children*. Australian Centre for Child Protection, Adelaide.

Smith, R. M., Smith, P. A., McKinnon, M. & Gracey, M. (2000). Birthweights and growth of infants in five Aboriginal communities. *Australian and New Zealand Journal of Public Health*, 24, 123–35.

Stamp, G., Champion, S., Anderson, G., Warren, B., Stuart-Butler, D., Doolan, J. et al. (2008). 'Aboriginal maternal and infant care workers: partners in caring for Aboriginal mothers and babies', Rural and Remote Health, 8. Available online at: www.rrh.org.au

Sweet, M. & Appelbaum, M. (2004). Is home visiting an effective strategy? A meta-analytic review of home visiting programs for families with young children. *Child Development*, 75 (5), 1435–56.

Victorian Aboriginal Child Care Agency (2006). *Working with Aboriginal Children and Families: A Guide for Child Protection and Child and Family Welfare Workers*. East Brunswick, Victoria.

Warrki Jarrinjaku ACRS Project Team (2002). *Warrki Jarrinjaku Jintangkamanu Purananjaku – Working Together Everyone and Listening: Aboriginal Child Rearing and Associated Literature*. Department of Family and Community Services, Canberra.

Including fathers in work with vulnerable families

Richard Fletcher

Learning goals

This chapter will enable you to:

1. Recognise the potential of child and family practitioners in health and education settings to engage fathers (and father figures) of vulnerable children in ways that will enhance their ability to nurture and protect their children
2. Understand how community and staff perceptions, social policy and institutional practices may act as barriers to fathers' participation in child and family settings
3. Become familiar with recent research evidence pointing to fathers' positive influence on children's well-being and consider the implications of this
4. Recognise the complexity of changing service procedures and practice to include fathers fully in a way that enhances family well-being
5. Reflect on the professional and personal challenges that may be faced when attempting to include fathers in services targeting vulnerable children and their families.

Introduction

Involving fathers in the lives of children is consistent with the goals of nearly all family services. Child and family services routinely declare that they wish to form partnerships with *parents* to ensure the best outcomes for children and most practitioners would consider that having both partners involved in parenting programs is likely to be associated with better outcomes than if services rely on the mother to relay information and ideas to her partner. The reality, however, is that while staff might wish to see fathers involved, when services say *parents* they usually mean *mothers* and when evaluators record *family* involvement in the service it is the mothers' involvement that is assessed. The focus on mothers reflects the history of public support for families with young children through maternity services and mothers' clubs and while the language and naming of services has changed to reflect a broader view of family practice the reality is that participants are overwhelmingly mothers and staff in child and family services are mostly women.

In previous times the focus on mothers might not have presented a problem but community values have shifted to endorse fathers' involvement with young children and the science of infant development has challenged the exclusive focus on mother–infant interaction by demonstrating an independent effect for father–infant and father–child relationships. At the same time, however, increasing awareness of sexual abuse and domestic violence perpetrated by men has added to the complexity of involving fathers in child and family services. In this chapter the context of family service provision to fathers is explored before describing recent research evidence pointing to a new role for fathers in child development. Examples of practice are used to illustrate some of the complexity involved when family-related services begin shifting their practice to include fathers while also remaining committed to mothers' and children's well-being.

Has fathering changed?

It is now common to notice fathers in shopping malls pushing strollers or walking with children in the park and to see advertisements for everything from computers to life insurance now include images of young, well-toned fathers nursing happy infants or holding happy young children. Community surveys regularly report strong endorsement of the value of fathers taking an equal share of the care of children, and governments in many countries advocate for parents to share home duties and work opportunities equally through gender equality quasi-government commissions, boards and the like. We have new services such as antenatal groups for fathers (Chapter 13 describes the spread of one such program in Australia), fathers' parenting classes and fathers' websites and forums that did not exist for earlier generations. Recent changes to family law in Australia have stressed the right of children to an ongoing relationship with both parents in the absence of violence or abuse, and there is debate about the extent of paternity leave that should be offered to new fathers. The enthusiasm of the media for stories featuring fathers means that any changes in fathers' behaviours or new developments in fathers' roles are widely promulgated.

However, while the amount of time that fathers spend with their children seems to be increasing in most Western countries, the role of fathers in all societies remains clearly different from that of mothers. This is particularly the case in the period surrounding childbirth; it is mothers who develop a special relationship with their infant through the pregnancy – a relationship that cannot be duplicated by fathers. Another female domain is breastfeeding, which, whether sustained or not, also clearly defines the mother as nurturer and father as 'support person'. The different roles for male and female parents are reflected in work patterns surrounding the birth. Even in countries that have strenuously promoted gender equity policies and encouraged fathers to take leave from their work to care for their children, the primary role of mothers in infant care remains, in no county do fathers take as much time away from their work and careers to care for children as mothers do.

One way to gain some perspective on the changes in the social definition of fatherhood is to examine the content and interpretation of family law as it applies to fathers and fatherhood. Legislation covering the whole gamut of family relations, from inheritance and probate to incest and child custody incorporates definitions of who is a father and what are his rights and obligations. By defining the 'father' through his roles, rights and responsibilities, the law sets in train a discourse that permeates the fine grain of society; legal debate surrounding fatherhood can provide an indication of changes in our social definitions.

Fatherhood in the law

New legislation has been introduced in many Western industrialised countries that alters the legal basis of paternity and helps to shape fathers' options in rearing their children. Nordic countries have pioneered paid paternity leave for fathers as part of their efforts for more equal gender relations in families (Gíslason, 2007). A second wide-ranging shift has been led by the United Nations in its *Convention on the Rights of the Child* which emphasises, among basic needs for care and protection, children's right to ongoing personal contact with both parents in the event of separation. Countries who are signatories to the convention (140 have signed) have made changes to their laws regarding children including those dealing with separation and divorce. In 2006, Australia passed the *Family Law Amendment (Shared Parental Responsibility) Act 2006* making both parents responsible for decisions about their child through the concept of 'equal shared parental responsibility' (Caruana, 2006, p. 56). A third important change has been the development of artificial conception procedures that have required separating legal fatherhood from biological fatherhood. Legislation in some states of Australia for example expressly deems that a sperm donor should not be considered the father of a child conceived through the use of his sperm (Fletcher & Willoughby, 2002).

However, as historians have noted, new conceptions of social roles that may be incorporated into legislation are not universally adopted; rather than swapping one idea of fatherhood for another, different or even contradictory notions of fathers and fathering may coexist for considerable periods of time.

The task for child and family workers

Those working in child and family services have to navigate between the competing notions of what society, and what individuals, expect of fathers. Clearly some aspects of fathers' roles have changed but many have not. The evidence that most men and women in the community (including most service providers) want fathers to be involved and yet few fathers are engaged with child and family services suggests that involving fathers must be a complex task, one that cannot be accomplished by simply inviting fathers to participate alongside mothers. When staff of an organisation make the decision to include fathers, it is important to appreciate the scope of the task and the considerable changes that may be involved.

Practitioners who have attempted to recruit fathers on the basis that everyone agrees with father involvement and therefore all that is required is an invitation, have often been disappointed in fathers' responses. In many cases these practitioners have put in extra time and effort to hold the event after hours and often to prepare the food, displays and activities. When only a few fathers turn up, the staff are then tempted to conclude that there is no interest from the men and to withdraw from the task of including fathers saying 'Get fathers in? Yes we tried that…it didn't work.' Two important, initial steps to include fathers are a) identify the barriers that currently exist to prevent services addressing the needs of fathers and b) develop an evidence-based rationale for why fathers should be involved in the first place.

The internal, systemic and organisational barriers to including fathers are described in the following sections along with implications for service providers. Recent research on father–infant and father–child relationships is then outlined to provide an evidence base for including fathers.

Barriers for fathers: internal constraints

Qualitative studies using convenience samples in the US and the UK have documented men's feelings of frustration, helplessness, anxiety, discomfort and nervousness in the context of antenatal classes and their resentment at feelings of being ignored at the birth (Chapman, 2000; Henderson & Brouse, 1991; Jordan, 1990; Nichols, 1993; Smith, 1999). Australian research has also shown that new fathers are often unprepared for the relationship changes occasioned by the birth, and that they are unaware of services available after the birth that are able to assist families (Fletcher, Silberberg & Galloway, 2004). Yet, when expectant fathers are surveyed about hospital services they are generally very positive and when a large representative sample (n=1000) of Australian fathers was asked to identify their needs the most common responses were 'don't know' (16%) and 'nothing needed' (14%), with only 3% identifying a need for more assistance from services (Russell et al., 1999).

Rather than conceptualising help seeking as an individual, singular decision, researchers in the mental health area describe 'help-seeking pathways' involving multiple social interactions to identify and assess the psychosocial need and multiple decision points leading to engagement with services and treatment (Aoun, Palmer & Newby, 1998). Services may underestimate the lack of informal knowledge among fathers of how family support services operate. Fathers may not seek help because they (correctly) believe that their infant's crying or their child's unsettled behaviour will probably subside over time. They may also expect that their own distress will be temporary. Fathers' lack of experience in managing family relationships with new children may also make the recognition of child development or relationship problems by fathers less likely. Fathers' perception of the risk of embarrassment might be another factor, deterring them from seeking help from services or preventing the discussion of help for parenting problems within their social networks.

Barriers for fathers: opportunity constraints

In contrast to mothers, who of necessity attend antenatal and post-natal services, fathers' attendance is optional. Fathers do not need to have health professionals assess their weight, blood pressure and so on, and so do not need to attend clinics for procedures or consultations. Work patterns and social values also mean that it will probably be the mother who contacts the health or welfare services for support with any problems to do with the children. As a result, a major obstacle to engagement with fathers is the lack of regular contact with health and welfare services.

Although there are no published statistics of fathers' attendance at perinatal health visits, men are less likely than women to visit general practitioners during the primary parenting years and are less likely to contact telephone parenting services for information and support. In the welfare area the reluctance of practitioners to contact biological or stepfathers in cases where a child is considered 'at risk' is well documented (Scourfield, 2006).

Fathers also face considerable time pressure. Fathers in Russell et al.'s (1999) survey most frequently cited lack of time and the competing demands of work as a barrier to becoming involved with their children. However, the lack of time is, to some extent, a subjective judgement influenced by the father's perception of the importance of the activity concerned. For example, the prediction of a father's involvement with children from the father's workplace demands – such as the number of hours worked – is relatively weak; the amount of involvement is not simply a result of his lack of availability. The experience of father-involvement programs is that once the fathers see the point of the activity then ways to manage work demands are often found (Fletcher, 2004).

Barriers for fathers: service constraints

From the time that a pregnancy is confirmed, the mother becomes the client of the health service and her pregnancy becomes the focus of visits with her general practitioner or to the antenatal clinic. Hospital data collections may not record the father's name, and the materials given to mothers during her hospital stay may not even mention fathers, referring instead to mothers and their 'support person'. Analysis of popular commercial childrearing information in North America found that fathers were rarely mentioned, and when they were their role was depicted as predominantly ancillary to mothers and voluntary (Fleming & Tobin, 2005). A recently completed review of parents' information needs in Australia found that perinatal parenting information is usually directed explicitly to mothers and that there is widespread recognition among service providers that the father's role is considered an 'add on' and insufficiently addressed (Centre for Community Child Health, 2004).

Evidence from a wide range of studies also suggests that the attributes of staff and the design of services may unintentionally inhibit a father's participation. A review of fathers' access to family services identified 13 barriers to fathers' participation (Fletcher, Silberberg & Baxter, 2001). Professionals' attitudes to fathers, their lack of skills to engage with men, and the lack of appropriate models of male service delivery, were identified as hindering fathers' involvement. A paucity of appropriate information and resource materials targeting fathers and service providers' lack of knowledge about men were also noted (Fletcher, Silberberg & Baxter, 2001). The lack of knowledge about men may derive, in part, from the gendered nature of the workforce in health and family services. Although there is no evidence that male clinicians provide better care to males, the need for family services to reflect the diversity of the clients being serviced is gaining recognition. In Western industrialised countries fathers are unlikely to encounter males in any of the front-line areas of midwifery, paediatric nursing, or among nurses making home visits in the weeks after the birth. Social workers, family workers and welfare workers also tend to be female.

Interaction of barriers

The way that these factors might interact to marginalise fathers was recently described as part of an invited contribution to a special issue of *The Medical Journal of Australia*' on men's health:

> When Michelle and Anthony attend Michelle's GP after the positive pregnancy test, Anthony expresses his support but asks few questions. When asked about the couple's intentions for pregnancy care Anthony's quick glance toward Michelle flags his uncertainty. For the next visits Michelle attends the clinic alone. Anthony does participate in the ultrasound consultation and he joins in when asked during the antenatal classes but he accepts that the emphasis throughout is appropriately on the mother and a successful birth. During the birth he wonders if he is in the way and is grateful in the end to have a healthy mother and baby. Post-birth, when the home-visiting nurse arrives, Anthony goes to make coffee and misses most of the discussion. His return to work precludes him attending the check-ups for mother and baby at the doctors.
>
> Anthony's minimal role with health professionals is mirrored at home and in social settings. Michelle reads the books, brochures and magazines and tells Anthony about popular names, baby development, and the dangers of SIDS [Sudden Infant Death Syndrome]. Anthony is affectionately ribbed by workmates about sleep deprivation and nappy changing and although one of his mates has just become a father Anthony has little chance to learn about the business of fathering. Social time with the new baby is dominated by eager mothers or girlfriends and there are few opportunities for Anthony to try out 'holding a new baby' without drawing attention to himself.
>
> (Fletcher, Matthey & Marley, 2006)

Some of the limitations of programs for families of young children in engaging fathers have been discussed in Chapter 6. Developing new father-inclusive models of service will require addressing all of the above barriers: fathers' lack of experience with infants and children's care and poor understanding of services; the lack of contact between family-based services and fathers; and the paucity of father-inclusive models of service delivery.

Implications for services

There is an important lesson here for any family service that is attempting to attract men to activities or programs at a centre – check the walls to see what message they are sending to the families. Health and welfare centres, for example, frequently have posters about domestic violence or sexual assault, important issues that need to be raised. But for many services these are the only messages directly talking to men. Young Indigenous fathers told us, when we interviewed them about their experience of community services surrounding the birth, that all the posters in the waiting rooms were about domestic violence, sexual abuse, stalking women or drug and alcohol abuse. As one father put it 'All they think about when they see a father is the bad things he done' (Hammond et al., 2004).

Changing the messages from the walls is relatively simple. Over recent years a variety of posters promoting involved, positive fatherhood for services have been developed, including posters for specific groups such as Indigenous fathers and many are available at low cost (see the useful websites at the end of this chapter). Of course, posters are not the only channel for the environment to give a message to fathers. Some child and family centres have taken the next step of examining the colour schemes and general décor in the centre for how it might appear to a father. Most centres strive for a soft pastel look that reflects the 'normal' environment for mothers and children; the colours that might make the space more male friendly can be seen in advertising for products that are aimed at male customers – they are often bolder and include greater contrasts.

In other places centres have created a 'dads' corner' where photographs of fathers using the centre and notices directed explicitly to fathers can be displayed. Using photographs of 'real' fathers has the added bonus of underlining the normality of fathers' involvement. Posters or images of sports stars or celebrity fathers have their uses but locally produced images of 'ordinary' fathers can send the important message that 'fathers who are just like you' get involved at this service.

Some services have used notices to make their processes, which mothers already know, clearer to fathers. For example, when a father, who doesn't usually pick up his child, arrives at the early childhood centre he may not know whether he is supposed to take home all the material alongside his daughter's bag or leave it, he may not know where the sign-out book is or that he should fill out the form for photographs or tomorrow's excursion to the park and leave it in the box near the director's office door. Having clearly set out instructions (information that mothers who attend often will already know) can reduce the father's sense that he is out of place.

An extension of this idea is to examine how fathers gain knowledge of a service before they walk in the door or attend an event such as a parenting course or clinical appointment. What pamphlets, advertisements or publicity might they have seen that explains who the service is for? How does the induction or referral process suggest who is expected to attend? What comments might their family or friends have made about the style of the service that will help form their attitude to the service?

An important point to grasp in answering these questions is that although services intend to include everyone when using the words 'parent' or 'family', that is not how these words are understood in the community. It would be usual, for example, for any letter arriving at the home addressed as 'Dear Parent' to be handed to the mother, who is the one most likely to be dealing with family matters. Services wanting to communicate with the fathers in the families have sometimes added 'Dad this means you' after '"Dear Parent' or added a 'Message for Dads' with a separate section highlighting information for fathers.

For many services the first contact with a father might be by phone and the following scenario is one that I have used in many training workshops for early intervention staff wishing to hone their skills to effectively reach fathers:

Scenario

Kerry works at XYZ Early Childhood Service. Jennifer Farmer has been in contact with her seeking a place on Monday, Tuesday and Wednesday for her two year old daughter Jasmine. Kerry is calling to inform the family that these days are now available and to ask if a place is still required. As it happens Mr Farmer answers the phone. The following conversation takes place:

Father: Hello?

Kerry: Hello – is that the Farmer residence? I am calling about a place for Jasmine…

Father: Who is this?

Kerry: Hi. This is Kerry from XYZ Early Childhood Service. I am calling about a place for Jasmine…

Father: Ummm…

Kerry: Mrs Farmer put Jasmine's name down for Monday to Wednesday….

Father: Oh….OK…

Kerry: And we'd like to know if you still want the three days for Jasmine…

Father: OK. Hold on and I'll get Jenny for you…

Many child and family practitioners find this scenario very familiar. It is often mothers who search out which services are available and then negotiate the best arrangements for the family. The telephone contact with the father in this example presents an opportunity to convey to the father that he is also seen as important by the service.

In the father-inclusive practice training workshops the participants role play various ways of engaging the father in this brief window of contact. The task for Kerry in this scenario is to convey that, for this service, the involvement of the father is seen as important. Strategies suggested during the workshops include asking him about the things that Jasmine likes to do, asking if he knows where the XYZ Early Childhood Service is located or discussing who will be dropping Jasmine off or picking her up. In the role plays participants often falter when the role-playing father asks why the service wants to involve him because his partner Jenny has always handled these things in the past. In spite of the enthusiasm for fathers' involvement with children's care few services have developed any detailed rationale for including fathers and staff are frequently at a loss if they are required to articulate the thinking behind efforts to reach them.

Activities

Consider how you would explain the importance of including fathers to colleagues who are concerned about their ability to work with fathers; a manager who requests evidence for allocating resources to work with fathers; a father who is unsure about whether to undertake a 'fathering' activity; and a single mother.

Visit a child and family service. Try to see the physical layout as a new, relatively inexperienced father might. What messages about the service would stand out? What, if anything, would tell the father that the service is actively seeking his involvement?

Evidence of fathers' impact

The task of involving a father in a home visit, a parenting group or even in a conversation about the best course of action for his child may be made difficult because it takes place against a backdrop of previous experiences like those of Michelle and Anthony described above. If things are to change it will require considerable effort and thought by practitioners wishing to refashion services to include fathers alongside mothers in supporting their children.

The question which follows is: 'Why should this service invest precious resources in implementing changes to include fathers?' Developing new procedures has cost implications as including fathers implies taking on additional clients or additional tasks to support families. The evidence of fathers' impact on children's development is crucial therefore in two ways. Firstly if services are to allocate resources to refashioning procedures, skilling staff to engage fathers and reach out to fathers then the evidence that this will improve family well-being is essential.

Equally important will be the practitioners' understanding of the differences between mothers' and fathers' roles. Shifting the basis of the work from 'mother as central and father as helper' to an approach that includes father–infant and father–child relationships will mean grappling with how fathers' interactions influence both the child and the mother–child relationship. The recent developments in our understanding of how fathers' positive interactions can foster children's development will be important knowledge for managers, service planners and practitioners alike.

Studies assessing fathers' impact on development have followed families over several years measuring fathers' interaction at an early age and then children's well-being some years later. In a study by the National Institute of Child Health and Human Development in the US, which examined parental factors that predicted school readiness, children who had fewer behaviour problems and higher social skills came from families where the fathers were sensitive and supportive of autonomy. An emotionally intimate marital relationship also added to the positive effect of these factors (NICHD Early Child Care Research Network, 2004).

A more recent study, also from the US, compared the influence of fathers and mothers from a low income sample on their children's cognitive development. Children with two supportive parents scored highest on measures of maths and language while those whose parents were both unsupportive scored lowest. What was also clear, however, was that the positive effect of having one parent supportive did not depend on whether that parent was a mother or a father. Elevated cognitive abilities were just as likely to be apparent amongst children with a supportive father as those with a supportive mother (Martin, Ryan & Brooks-Gunn, 2007).

Fathers' effects on well-being do not stop at childhood. As part of the US National Longitudinal Study of Adolescent Health a nationally representative sample of adolescents was tested from Grade 7–12 to measure their relationship with their fathers and mothers and their level of depression. Over the five years of the study the quality of the father–adolescent relationship, as judged by the adolescent, was found to be equally predictive of the adolescents' mental health as the mother–adolescent relationship (Videon, 2005).

Studies such as these provide a powerful argument for recognising a role for fathers separate from that of mothers, and for challenging the notion of father as 'helper' to the mother. It has long been assumed, for example, that the mother–infant bond was the template for the father–infant bond, and that while the relationship with the mother was fundamental to children's well-being the relationship with the father was an optional extra. For their part, fathers assumed that they had no role to play with young children until they could be physically active or could 'kick a footy'.

Recent research has challenged the assumptions of practitioners and fathers alike. Infants' secure or insecure attachment, for example, is now thought to be largely independent for mothers and fathers. When the results of several studies assessing the attachment of infants were analysed, it was recognised that while many infants did have a secure attachment to both their mother and their father, they could be securely attached to the mother but insecurely attached to the father or the reverse. Contrary to the 'helper' notion of fathers, an infant may form a secure attachment to the father alongside an insecure attachment to the mother (van Ijzendoorn & De Wolff, 1997). What is more, when a new father is depressed (and therefore less responsive and affectionate) the effect on the well-being of the infant is similar to when the mother is depressed.

Since the early 1980s we have known that depressed mothers' early parenting, specifically their insensitivity to infant cues and inability to provide effective emotional regulation, is associated with the development of insecure or disorganised infant–mother attachment and subsequent reduced social competence and increased behaviour disorders (Ashman & Dawson, 2002). What has recently been established is that fathers' depression is also an important factor in children's development. When over 8000 fathers were tested for depression eight weeks after the birth and their children's behaviour assessed at three and a half years of age, those children whose fathers recorded depressive symptoms in the clinical range two months after the birth were found to have double the risk of behavioural and emotional problems (Ramchandani et al., 2005). The effects of the father's depression was independent of whether the mother was depressed and independent of the father's later mental health suggesting that having a depressed father in the early months of life can have a long-lasting negative effect on children's emotional and social development.

In summary recent research shows that:

- Father involvement can have a significant and important effect on the well-being of children
- Fathers influence their children's development directly rather that solely as a 'helper' to the mother
- Infants respond to fathers as well as mothers and benefit from their relationships with fathers independently of their relationships with their mothers
- Infants/children do best when they have a secure relationship with both mother and father and when the relationship between mother and father is warm and affectionate.

What about 'bad' dads?

The evidence for early intervention with mothers is now strong enough for governments of all persuasions to endorse programs and policies that aim to support vulnerable families with young children. However, although the evidence for fathers' impact on children's development is also now well-founded, and in many areas policies and programs are moving to include a focus on fathers within early interventions for vulnerable families, the provision of support for fathers remains problematic. One reason for the faltering progress of father inclusion is described above – societies and individuals continue to hold contradictory notions of fatherhood and practitioners frequently underestimate the changes required to incorporate fathers fully into mainstream services. As well, the research on a father's role in child development is relatively new, so that training and theoretical support for father inclusion is still emerging.

However there is also the important issue of violence and abuse to incorporate into any changes seeking greater father involvement. Particularly in vulnerable families, practitioners may be well aware that part of the difficulty facing the family is violent behaviour from the father. In this situation it will be important to avoid any simplistic approach that ignores difficult issues of violence or abusive behaviour, thereby ignoring the needs of the mother. Equally futile however, is the approach that ignores the father and his relationship with the children because the father is (or once was or might be) violent. In a recent example from my own work, a parenting skills program refused to provide educational sessions for parents in a housing estate program because there may be men attending the course. 'They'll be wife bashers' was the only explanation offered for the refusal.

As part of the reconceptualising of fathers' roles, researchers have questioned the exclusive emphasis on providing safety and comfort for young children and have turned their attention to how parents can foster children's confidence and exploration. Fathers' 'rough and tumble' play has been identified, not only as common among fathers and children in many cultures, but as beneficial for child development (Paquette, 2004). There has also been the suggestion that fathers' interactions with young infants are typically less modulated than mothers' with more unexpected peaks of excitement, again with positive developmental implications (Feldman, 2003).

However, for those working with vulnerable populations, the notion of encouraging fathers' energetic play with children may seem too risky. Indeed, there is evidence to support practitioners' caution with simply encouraging more involvement (of any type) from fathers. A study of over 1100 fathers and their five year old children found that for children whose fathers had high levels of antisocial behaviour, the more time they lived with their father, the more behaviour problems they exhibited (Jaffee et al., 2003). In this study the problematic fathers were defined as having high levels of antisocial activity warranting a diagnosis of antisocial personality disorder and so would form a rather small group within the population of fathers. A potentially larger group among those coming into contact with child and family services are fathers who might be involved in domestic or family violence. However, practitioners in child and family services may feel ill-equipped to address the complexity of issues in a situation of family violence or even of family anger. As a UK volunteer expressed during a training session for home visitors:

...you go to a house and you could hear dad shouting inside, what would you do? Well I'm sorry but I'm only a volunteer – I keep saying that to myself – I

would get back in the car and I would ring the office. It's not our place to go into somewhere where a) we don't know the situation and b) we could be putting ourselves in danger…

(Evangelou et al., 2008, p. 74)

The risk of confronting antisocial or angry behaviour should be taken seriously when providing family-based services. The possibility of encountering an angry or even violent parent requires care in the overall design of the service, in training and support for staff, and in establishing safety protocols and procedures. However the risk that there may be domestic violence should not preclude the family having contact with services, nor should it prevent the service including strategies for engaging with the father around his role in the family. Addressing violence and conflict as part of a comprehensive response to family difficulty can enhance services' effectiveness with families facing serious disruption and stress. For example, this is how the manager of an all-female early intervention service for families with multiple problems (substance abuse, criminal history, parental history of abuse and neglect) described the effects of adopting a focus on fathers:

There was a lot of domestic violence and the emphasis on fathers actually led to us developing a much better policy around domestic violence … We'd talk to the whole family about it not being safe in the family and that we weren't willing to send a worker into the family until things were safer, but we would still see them in a café or at our rooms. We didn't drop them and we made it clear that we really wanted the man to work on his own stuff …We also asked two male therapists to talk to us about our own issues – about how we (the staff) didn't talk about our own fathers, and how the women staff members felt quite confronted by working with fathers.

(Edwards, 2004, p.9)

Strengths-based practice with fathers

The notion of 'strengths-based practice' has been coined to describe ways of interacting with families that do not ignore any risk of harm to children, or the need at times for outside agency involvement, but which assume that family members have the capacity to develop supportive and healthy relationships that will enable their children to flourish. Applying this approach to fathers in vulnerable families implies a shift in emphasis from seeing the father as simply a problem – the irresponsible or drug abusing father who is a major cause of the child's vulnerability – to picturing a father with his own vulnerabilities and needs as well as someone whose behaviours may be damaging to family well-being.

As described in the section 'Barriers for fathers' above, a number of factors might make it unlikely that fathers would be involved in initial assessments or discussions. However practitioners' training, experience and skills can also influence how inclusive services are of fathers. In the following account an experienced family worker describes how she encourages the father's involvement once it has been established (through telephone contact with the mother) that there is no current violence between the couple.

> When I first visit a family I would see the person who made the referral, generally the woman, we'll call her Betty. The first visit would probably happen within business hours, during the day when the kids were at school and Betty's husband (or partner) was at work. The husband generally knew that I was coming. For example, I generally asked, 'Does your husband know that I am coming today?' If Betty responded 'Yes', I then might have said, 'What does he think about you asking for an agency's support around this?' Betty might have said something like, 'Oh he's okay, he doesn't really like talking about these sorts of things but he doesn't mind if I do.'
>
> From here, I would talk with the woman about how she thought I might be able to support them and generally the woman would have some ideas about that. For example, I might have asked Betty what her husband thought, and for her husband's name. Let's say, for example, Betty's husband is John. What I tended to do then was to include John's name in the conversation a lot. I would say something like, 'If John was here now, what would he be telling me about what's happening between you two?' Betty would then say something like, 'Well, he thinks it's probably my fault because I get depressed and I get down and I get fairly dependent and I can't cope.' And we would continue to talk.
>
> Those first visits were often short because I established that the work went a lot better if the man was present. For example, I would ask the woman when her husband would be willing to participate, and the woman would generally say that she had to ask him. My intention at this point would be to convey to the woman that I was interested in her husband's opinion as well, that I was interested to see both of them together, and, that I wanted both of them to be comfortable with me. I would make a time for the next visit, which may have been after hours.

(Cantwell, 2004, pp. 94–5)

The ongoing work with vulnerable fathers as part of the support for families will, of course, require more than one conversation and may take a variety of forms depending on the service type and target. There is now recognition, for example, that modifying services to include fathers or father figures of families where children have disabilities may enhance the well-being of all family members. Two examples of ongoing work with fathers, one through home visits and one through centre-based group work are described below. In the first, a pilot attachment-based program for fathers, ultilising videotaping of father–infant interaction is described. In the second, a group program for men addressing anger and violence offers insights into how facilitated discussion can shift fathers' ways of handling family tensions and conflicts.

A pilot home visiting service for fathers whose partners have post-natal depression

The service was advertised as 'a free service for new fathers' who may have 'a wife or partner who is not doing so well'. No specific therapy or subsequent action was promised, however, a home visiting model (with a male visitor) was offered at the first interview if appropriate. The practice framework for the intervention, which was developed with mothers, uses videotape to record the parent doing 'whatever they enjoyed' with their infant and then viewing the tape together to discuss questions such as 'What is the baby thinking here?'. Father-specific aspects of the intervention were guided by the emerging research on fathers' roles in infant development: fathers' attachment styles with their infant are likely to develop independently to those of mothers; fathers' use of play interactions will be particularly important; and, negotiating a place in the father–mother–infant triangle is a key task for fathers.

A father contacted the service three months after the birth of his child requesting help to be a 'better father'. Although his partner had suffered severe post-natal depression she was not requesting or receiving any professional support at the commencement of the home visits. During the 10 home visits the father's interactions with his infant were videotaped and reviewed in an attachment-based framework. At the conclusion of the home visits the mother and father were interviewed about their experience of the program. The father concluded:

> being a good parent is something that you can train yourself to do …anybody can change a nappy, anybody can pick him up if he is crying … but what I am looking for out of this is the interaction that you are missing…and that's what I am picking up. Through the DVDs and the video I am picking up those little signals that William wants to interact. Which I think in the long run will bring William and I a lot closer and improve our relationship and that's the whole point of the exercise.

> *(Fletcher, 2009 p. 99)*

In this case, the positive outcome for the father also had a 'knock on' effect for the mother's relationship with their infant. The mother reported:

> I think that you [indicating the father] taught me to be more aware. I think that I spent the first months going 'Oh there is this to do and that to do and everything to do' and because [the male home visitor] would ask you 'What do you think he's doing there?' then you would ask me 'What do you think that he is doing there?' and it actually made me more aware that he is actually thinking about things…not this lump that just … I think that made me love him even more because I stopped thinking about all the things that had to be done…

> *(Fletcher, 2009, p. 100)*

A group program for men to end violent and abusive behaviour

Stuart Anderson coordinates the Men's Resource Centre in Northern New South Wales. Using transcripts from men's groups (recorded and transcribed with their permission) he describes the potential for group processes that engage men on the challenges of parenting. Names have been changed to ensure anonymity.

The course offered for men focuses on ending violent and abusive behaviour. An alternative way to describe this focus is that the course assists men to increase safety, trust, respect, care and love within their family. Parenting issues and skills are addressed in the program not because it has dedicated parenting segments but because the desire to be a better dad comes up in nearly every group session. It's like a steady undercurrent that each man is struggling with in some way. One man telling a story about his children fires up all present to think about the dilemmas and frustrations involved in parenting. Even the men who don't have children are stimulated to participate as they recall traumas in their own childhood. It's very rare to hear any of the men talk about a violence-free childhood.

Here is an example of how the group process can assist fathers to rethink their approach to fathering.

Geoff begins with his concern about his wife yelling at their children:

Geoff: Case in point, two girls in the back of the car coming home the other night, yabba yabba yabba. Told half a dozen times by their mother to keep quiet. They're starting to tick me off. I've been driving for four hours. I just put my foot on the brake two kilometres from home, stopped the car. 'Would you girls like to get out and walk now?' 'What for Dad?' 'Because you just won't shut up.' 'We'll be quiet Dad.' Off we went, peace and quiet. I don't want to yell at the girls, I don't want to have a confrontation. It is a conscious choice, I don't want to do this. I just came around the problem in a different way. Their mother was already tense and tired, she was up the anger scale.

Others in the group acknowledged that Geoff made a significant shift from how he used to yell and berate his kids. That he kept his voice calm was seen as great. The facilitators were keeping an eye on this, would others in the group speak up or would they intervene with some further questions? As it happened this group had several men who had attended for a few months and they found it easy to challenge each other. Gary thought that Geoff could do better.

Gary: Do you think you were threatening your kids?

Geoff agreed there was an element of threat in it, but said his voice was calm and he was not angry at the kids himself. He talked about his fear that his wife would abuse the kids because he could see her rising anger. In the following discussion several ways for Geoff to get the message across to his kids were explored.

Fred who has a back injury and, therefore, is the house husband said that he was in a similar situation the other day. He told the group that at that time he said, 'You are making your mother very angry, is that what you want to do?'

This response was thought by group members to have that same old language that seems to indicate that the kids are responsible for mum's anger. They asked Fred what he would say if he was taking responsibility for his own feelings. Fred struggled with this shift of focus. His habit was to blurt out his ideas on what and who was wrong. It took several attempts before he could name his feelings of anxiety and fear. In that session he only partially succeeded in putting together a sentence that satisfied the other group members. Another man, Nick decided that telling his own story might help Fred.

Nick is a creative steel and metal worker who speaks quietly and firmly. It would be easy to assume that he had never had a problem with anger or abusive behaviour. He related how much of a relief it was not to buy into other people's stress. He used to yell at his wife and daughter to try and stop them arguing.

Nick: It's just easier to stay out of the fights. I'm here if they've finished the fighting and come and talk sense, I'm here for that. I'm not here to get dragged into their fights. My wife said to me, 'It was so great that when we were having that fight you didn't get involved.' It really sunk into her that while she and my daughter were having that fight I was sitting over the other side of the room calmly having a coffee. My quietness allowed her to see what she was doing. She came over and said: 'Thank you. I appreciate that you stayed out of it and looked after yourself, that allowed me to have some insight.'

One person taking care of themselves had an effect on the whole family or household. The discussion continued exploring the benefits of a relaxed, calm, whole-picture view rather than the tunnel vision that develops as anger rises.

Nick: It's funny isn't it? When we start putting pressure on ourselves we start falling apart, then all the rest start falling apart and it multiplies – it makes it worse and worse. What I've found is a calmer approach has made everything else calmer. Even the kids are looking at me different, which is good.

(Anderson, 2004, pp. 54–5)

Activity

Kerry is seven years old, and has been displaying very challenging behaviours such as frequent tantrums, fighting with other children, and stealing and swearing at her teachers. She lives with her mother Julie and half siblings who she is made to care for (four year old twins and a two year old). An unsubstantiated report notes that Kerry was left alone in the house to care for her siblings during the day for some hours in the school holidays.

Julie received several periods of respite care when she was unable to cope with Kerry. With the new baby (three months old) Julie requests respite with the same Department of Community Services carers as before as Kerry liked them. Julie did not want another child but is against abortion. After having the twins, she was diagnosed with post-natal depression, however, no record is available on any treatment or support offered to her or taken up.

Julie's mother lives two hours away and sometimes helps out but finds Kerry's behaviour distressing. She said she won't come to stay as Kerry gets on her nerves.

Eduardo is the father of Kerry but not Julie's other children. He has been away working interstate for the last four years and returned home some months ago. He has taken Kerry out occasionally. Eduardo shares a house with his mate and lives close by but the house is too small to have Kerry over to stay. There is conflict between Julie and Eduardo, however Eduardo pays child support when he can and always remembers Kerry's birthdays and Christmas.

Eduardo emigrated 10 years ago but all his family still live in Ecuador. He works regular day shifts at the local petrol station three days a week and is hoping to get work in the Goodyear franchise next door.

Julie is advised by the duty child protection case worker that there are no respite carers available. After discussions with Julie, the case worker contacts Eduardo and asks if he would be willing to regularly read to Kerry at bedtime to help her settle into a routine. Eduardo agrees and for the first week arrives at the arranged time to read Kerry a bedtime story. After one week he misses a night, then reads again for three nights then misses a night, then reads for two and misses a night, reads for one night and then stops coming. Julie rings the caseworker and explains that 'He is too unreliable.'

What is your first guess at why Eduardo stopped the reading sessions? What factors or experiences might push Eduardo away from staying connected with his child? Who or what might encourage Eduardo to stay connected with Kerry?

Conclusion

While the damaging effects of children experiencing or witnessing abusive behaviour deserve continued recognition, the potential of fathers to promote positive development in children justifies concerted action to expand services' ability to include fathers. Maximising support for vulnerable children will require shifting the policies, procedures and practices in child and family services to be inclusive of fathers.

Useful websites

About the Fathers Program, Family Action Centre, University of Newcastle provides training, resources and research on father-inclusive practice: www.newcastle.edu.au/research-centre/fac/programs/fathers

The Canadian Father Involvement Initiative develops policy and resources for father-inclusive practice: www.cfii.ca/fiion

European Fatherhood presents research and policy on improving gender equality for fathers: www.european-fatherhood.com

Fatherhood Institute (UK) provides policy and practice materials for father-inclusive practice: www.fatherhoodinstitute.org/

Head Start is a national program in the USA that promotes school readiness: www.acf.hhs.gov/programs/ohs/index.html

Institute of Family Practice provides training courses relevant to men and family relationships: www.ifp.nsw.edu.au

Men and Family Relationships Services work alongside men to assist them to manage a range of relationship issues with partners, ex-partners and children: www.fahcsia.gov.au/sa/families/progserv/FRSP/Pages/mfr-men_family_relationships.aspx

Mens Line Australia provides 24 hour family relationships counselling: www.menslineaus.org.au

Sure Start is a UK Government programme aiming to deliver the best start in life for every child: www.dcsf.gov.uk/everychildmatters/earlyyears/surestart/whatsurestartdoes/

References

Anderson, S. (2004). Men's anti-violence programs also improve parenting. In R. Fletcher (ed.), *Bringing Fathers In: How to Engage with Men for the Benefit of Everyone in the Family*. University of Newcastle, Newcastle, NSW.

Aoun, S., Palmer, M. & Newby, R. (1998). Gender issues in psychosocial morbidity in general practice. *Australian Journal of Social Issues*, 33 (4), 335–53.

Ashman, S. & Dawson, G. (2002). *Maternal Depression, Infant Psychobiological Development, and Risk for Depression*. American Psychological Association, Washington, DC.

Centre for Community Child Health (2004). *Parenting Information Project Volume 3*. Australian Government, Canberra.

Cantwell, S. (2004). Involving men in a home visit. In Fletcher R (ed.), *Bringing Fathers In: How to Engage with Men for the Benefit of Everyone in the Family*. University of Newcastle, Newcastle, NSW.

Caruana, C. (2006). Shared parental responsibility and the reshaping of family law. *Family Matters*, 74, 56–9.

Chapman, L. L. (2000). Expectant fathers and labor epidurals. *The American Journal of Maternal Child Nursing*, 25 (3), 133–8.

Edwards, J. (2004). Making the change towards fathers: The example of the Benevolent Society's Early Intervention Program. In R. Fletcher (ed.), *Bringing Fathers In: How to Engage with Men for the Benefit of Everyone in the Family*. University of Newcastle, Newcastle, NSW.

Evangelou, M., Sylva, K., Edwards, A. & Smith, T. (2008). *Supporting Parents in Promoting Early Learning: The Evaluation of the Early Learning Partnership Project*. University of Oxford, Oxford.

Feldman, R. (2003). Infant–mother and infant–father synchrony: The coregulation of positive arousal. *Infant Mental Health Journal*, 24 (1), 1–23.

Fleming, L. & Tobin, D. (2005). Popular child-rearing books: Where is daddy? *Psychology of Men & Masculinity*, 6 (1), 18–24.

Fletcher, R. (2004). Bringing fathers in: How to engage with men for the benefit of everyone in the family. In R. Fletcher (ed.), *Bringing Fathers In: How to Engage with Men for the Benefit of Everyone in the Family*. University of Newcastle, Newcastle, NSW.

Fletcher, R. (2009). Brief report: Promoting infant well being in the context of maternal depression by supporting the father. *Infant Mental Health Journal*, 30 (1), 95–102.

Fletcher, R., Matthey, S. & Marley, C. (2006). Addressing depression and anxiety among new fathers. *Medical Journal of Australia*, 185, 461–3.

Fletcher, R., Silberberg, S. & Baxter, R. (2001). *Fathers' Access to Family-Related Services.* University of Newcastle, Newcastle, NSW.

Fletcher, R., Silberberg, S. & Galloway, D. (2004). New fathers' post-birth views of antenatal classes: Satisfaction, benefits, and knowledge of family services. *The Journal of Peri-natal Education*, 13 (3), 18–26.

Fletcher, R. & Willoughby, P. (2002). *Fatherhood: Legal, Biological and Social Definitions*: Family Action Centre, University of Newcastle, Newcastle, NSW.

Gíslason, I. (2007). *Parental Leave in Iceland. Bringing the Fathers in: Developments in the Wake of New Legislation in 2000.* Ministry of Social Affairs and Centre for Gender Equality, Akureyri, Iceland.

Hammond, C., Lester, J., Fletcher, R. & Pascoe, S. (2004). Young Aboriginal fathers: The findings and impact of a research project undertaken in the Hunter Valley. *Aboriginal Islander and Health Worker Journal*, 28 (5), 5–8.

Henderson, A. & Brouse, A. (1991). The experiences of new fathers in the first 3 weeks of life. *Journal of Advanced Nursing*, 16 (3), 293–8.

Jaffee, S., Moffitt, T., Caspi, A. & Taylor, A. (2003). Life with (or without) father: The benefits of living with the biological parents depend on the father's antisocial behavior. *Child Development*, 74 (1), 109–26.

Jordan, P. L. (1990). Laboring for relevance: Expectant and new fatherhood. *Nursing Research*, 39 (1), 11–16.

Martin, A., Ryan, R. & Brooks-Gunn, J. (2007). The joint influence of mother and father parenting on child cognitive outcomes at age 5. *Early Childhood Research Quarterly*, 22, 423–39.

NICHD Early Child Care Research Network (2004). Fathers' and mothers' parenting behavior and beliefs as predictors of children's social adjustment in the transition to school. *Journal of Family Psychology*, 18 (4), 628–38.

Nichols, M. (1993). Paternal perspectives of the childbirth experience. *Maternal–Child Nursing Journal*, 21 (3), 99–108.

Paquette, D. (2004). Theorizing the father–child relationship: Mechanisms and developmental outcomes. *Human Development*, 47 (4), 193–219.

Ramchandani, P., Stein, A., Evans, J. & O'Connor, T. (2005). Paternal depression in the postnatal period and child development: A prospective population study. *Lancet*, 365, 2201–5.

Russell, G., Barclay, L., Edgecombe, G., Donovan, J., Habib, G., Callaghan, H. et al. (1999). *Fitting Fathers into Families: Men and the Fatherhood Role in Contemporary Australia.* Commonwealth Department of Family and Community Services, Canberra.

Scourfield, J. (2006). The challenge of engaging fathers in the child protection process. *Critical Social Policy*, 26 (2), 440–9.

Smith, N. (1999). Antenatal classes and the transition to fatherhood: A study of some fathers' views (Part 1). *MIDIRS Midwifery Digest*, 9 (3), 327–30.

van Ijzendoorn, M. & De Wolff, M. (1997). In search of the absent father – meta-analysis of infant-father attachment: A rejoinder to our discussants. *Child Development*, 68 (4), 604–9.

Videon, T. (2005). Parent–child relations and children's psychological well-being: Do dads matter? *Journal of Family Issues*, 26, 55–78.

Parenting in a new culture: working with refugee families

Kerry Lewig, Fiona Arney, Mary Salveron and Maria Barredo

Learning goals

This chapter will enable you to:

1. Understand the experiences of refugee and newly arrived migrants
2. Reflect on the personal and professional challenges that may be faced when responding to the needs of refugee and newly arrived migrants
3. Develop an understanding of the cultural and parenting differences that may contribute to parents and families from refugee backgrounds being involved with the child protection system
4. Recognise the potential of practitioners to engage parents from refugee backgrounds in ways that will enhance their ability to parent in Australia
5. Learn about an innovative exemplar of working with refugee families
6. Think about how different professions and services can work together for and with refugee families.

Introduction

The house was full of women and children and since we were one of the last ones in, we had to sleep under the roof. It was very unsafe where we tried to fall asleep. We lay next to an open area, which looked down on to the first floor. Since the house wasn't finished it didn't have a fence on the stairs or that area where we slept. The noise of grenades and guns made it impossible for us to fall asleep because they were basically falling somewhere near us. You could feel them and sometimes it felt that bullets were knocking on the roof, which was right above our heads. I was lying there on the floor covered by my mother's body, praying to God that one of those grenades or bullets wouldn't hit through the roof.

(Zana Mujenovic, aged 17, in Dark Dreams, 2004)

As a result of political upheaval and persecution in their own countries, many people (individuals and families with children) are forced to flee to neighbouring countries for asylum, where they are placed in refugee camps. Many of those recognised by the United Nations Refugee Agency (UNHCR) as refugees eventually go back to their own country and a number will be assisted to resettle in a third country such as Australia, Canada and the US.

As well as contending with previous traumatic experiences such as loss of family members, torture, displacement and starvation, resettled refugee families may also face many complex challenges including parenting in a new culture. For some refugee children and adolescents, parents represent the only consistent feature in their lives. However, parents who are refugees face significant additional challenges to those of mainstream Australian parents. Many of the factors associated with parenting difficulties in mainstream Australian families are also experienced by refugee parents (parental mental health problems, poverty, physical health problems, social isolation, children's behavioural problems) (Centre for Community Child Health, 2004). In addition, refugee parents confront stresses associated with the experience of torture and trauma, separation or death of family members, resettlement, language difficulties and different cultural expectations about behaviour and parenting (Gonsalves, 1992; Lamberg, 1996).

Working with families from culturally and linguistically diverse (CALD) backgrounds can pose a number of challenges and opportunities. When families have had to flee their countries of origin because of persecution, war or natural disaster, this can add to the level of complexity. The unique circumstances of refugee families pose a special challenge to practitioners working in child and family services. Drawing on the published literature and interviews with child protection practitioners and members of refugee communities this chapter provides a background and overview of the refugee experience and presents practitioner and refugee community perspectives about working with refugee families.

Who are refugees?

The 1951 United Nations Convention relating to the status of refugees defines a refugee as someone who:

owing to well-founded fear of being persecuted for reasons of race, religion, nationality, membership of a particular social group or political opinion, is outside the country of his nationality and is unable to, or owing to such fear, is unwilling to avail himself of the protection of that country; or who, not having a nationality and being outside the country of his former habitual residence as a result of such events, is unable or, owing to such fear, is unwilling to return to it

(UNHCR, 2007a, p. 16)

Worldwide, just over 11.4 million people were classified as either a refugee or asylum seeker (a person seeking to be recognised by the UNHCR as a refugee) at the end of 2007. This figure does not include 4.6 million Palestinian refugees or an estimated 51 million internally displaced persons, some of whom are receiving assistance or protection from the UNHCR, and many more who fall into these categories but who are not helped by the UNHCR (UNHCR, 2007b). In this chapter we will use a wider sense of the term 'refugee' as it is accepted more broadly to include all those who have fled their countries of origin to seek safety from harm (e.g., from war, violence, poverty and natural or man-made disasters).

Not surprisingly, most refugees come from countries experiencing conflict and or human rights abuses (see Table 8.1). You can find more information about the UNHCR and the plight of refugees on their website (www.unhcr.org).

Table 8.1: Top 10 countries of origin, 1 January 2007 (UNHCR, 2007b)

Country	Number of refugees
Afghanistan	2 108 000
Iraq	1 451 000
Sudan	686 000
Somalia	464 000
D R Congo	402 000
Burundi	397 000
Vietnam	374 000
Turkey	227 000
Angola	207 000
Myanmar	203 000

Australia's Refugee and Humanitarian Program

Australia has been accepting refugees since 1938 when it became a signatory to the Evian Conference that organised asylum for Jewish refugees fleeing from Nazi Germany (Richards, 2008). The signing of this document was controversial at the time and subsequent refugee policies have generated as much debate and controversy among Australians as this one did. If you are interested in knowing more about Australia's immigration history you may like to read *Destination Australia* (Richards, 2008). Australia provides humanitarian resettlement for refugees under the Humanitarian Program. Details of the visa categories for refugees are outlined in Box 8.1 (DIAC, 2009).

Box 8.1: Australian Humanitarian Program visa categories

Refugee category – for people who are subject to persecution in their home country and who are in need of resettlement. The majority of applicants who are considered under this category are identified by the United Nations High Commissioner for Refugees (UNHCR) and referred by UNHCR to Australia. The Refugee visa category includes Refugee, In-country Special Humanitarian, Emergency Rescue and Woman at Risk sub-categories.

Special Humanitarian Program (SHP) – for people outside their home country who are subject to substantial discrimination amounting to gross violation of human rights in their home country. A proposer (known as sponsor under the Migration Program) who is an Australian citizen, permanent resident or eligible New Zealand citizen, or an organisation that is based in Australia, must support applications for entry under the SHP.

Permanent Protection Visas (PPV) – granted to persons who enter Australia lawfully, who are then found to be refugees within the meaning of the 1953 *Convention on the Status of Refugees* ('the Convention') and who also satisfy health, character and security requirements.

Temporary Humanitarian and Protection Visas – two Temporary Humanitarian Visas and a three year Temporary Protection Visa were also available up until mid 2008. These visas allowed holders to remain in Australia on a temporary basis (visas extended to 30 months) and entitled holders to some but not all of the entitlements of PPV holders and other humanitarian entrants. However these temporary visas have since been abolished by the Rudd Government. Refugees currently holding these temporary visas now have access to a permanent visa called a 'Resolution of Status Visa' provided they meet health, character and security requirements.

The Department of Immigration and Citizenship's website (www.immi.gov.au) provides more detail about Australia's refugee and humanitarian program.

Resettlement in Australia

During the mid to late nineties the majority of refugees who resettled in Australia came largely from the Former Yugoslavia, the Middle East, South East Asia and Africa. Since 2003, the majority of humanitarian entrants have come from Africa with most of these people coming from the Sudan.

Many of these refugees would have spent some time in a refugee camp. For example, just over 48% of refugees resettling in Australia in 2005 had spent time in refugee camps. Of these people, nearly 92% had spent at least two years in refugee camps, 49% had spent over five years in camps, and just over 36% had spent more than ten years residing in camps (DIMIA, 2005).

In Australia, refugees are generally settled as close as possible to family members or friends, if they have any who are living in Australia. Where refugees have no extended family or social networks in Australia, settlement location is influenced by factors such as settlement needs, availability of settlement services and support from communities with a similar background, accessible health services and accommodation, and sustainable employment opportunities (DIMIA, 2005).

The refugee experience

> *Despite all the humiliation my mother went through she maintains her dignity. She is a dignified woman. She is a strong woman but my brother and I made her even stronger. She knew she had to be able to fight to protect us and some day, with or without our father, provide a stable home. The strength she had I've never seen. Seven days without eating, giving me and my brother the last crumbs she found in her pockets, drinking poisoned water and being beaten and still she managed to stay straight on her feet. It was admirable.*
>
> *(Zana Mujenovic, aged 17, in* Dark Dreams, *2004)*

For most refugees the process of migration to a new country has been a painful one involving stressful, and often traumatic pre-migration, transition and resettlement experiences (Fazel & Stein, 2002; Pine & Drachman, 2005). It is important to remember that during these experiences refugees have demonstrated incredible strength, determination, courage and resilience.

To be able to work effectively with clients from refugee backgrounds it is important to have an understanding of their ethnic, religious and cultural backgrounds. It is also important to have some knowledge of the experiences that refugees may have lived through (e.g., war, famine, time spent in refugee camps) and to be able to acknowledge and understand how these pre-migration and transition experiences together with post-migration challenges (e.g., mental health, grief and loss, adjusting to a new culture) may impact on parenting and child well-being in a new country. It is also important to recognise that some experiences that are normative for people born in Australia, such as receiving an education or gaining employment, may have been denied to refugees. By no means is this to imply that refugees are a homogeneous group, but rather to emphasise that developing knowledge and understanding of the range of experiences of this client group is essential to effective practice.

Pre-migration experiences

Exposure to torture, trauma and family separation

In their countries of origin, adults and children may have been exposed to or have experienced rape, killing of family members and friends, suicide attempts, concentration camp experiences, torture, brutality, starvation and displacement (Berk, 1998). In some cases, acts of violence may have been perpetrated by people known to them (Berk, 1998). Recent studies of the pre-migration experiences of refugees from a range of backgrounds settling in Australia report that in almost all instances, refugees describe experiencing or witnessing human rights violations, extreme deprivation, separation from or loss of family and friends, trauma and periods of lack of food and water (Allotey, 1998; Brough et al., 2003; Momartin et al., 2002; Momartin et al., 2006; Schweitzer et al., 2006; Silove & Ekblad, 2002; Sinnerbrink et al., 1997). In some cases, women and children are abducted and forced into servitude (e.g., as sex slaves or child soldiers) with their persecutors (Wessells, 2006).

Deciding to leave

The safety and well-being of children is a very significant factor for many families, if not most, seeking to flee their countries of origin and establishing new lives in other countries. Making the decision to leave can itself be a source of great stress. Individuals and families may have to abruptly flee their country of origin, or may be forced into exile. Others may choose to leave of their own volition. For some families, harrowing decisions must be made about who will leave and who will stay. Once the decision to leave is made, a long period of waiting may follow (Pine & Drachman, 2005).

Transition experiences

The journey from country of origin to a place of resettlement can be short for some and a long and perilous process for others, and may include multiple countries of resettlement (Pine & Drachman, 2005). Children and adolescents may be separated from their families either by accident or as a safety measure, and many are given to people smugglers to ensure escape (Fazel & Stein, 2002).

Some refugees spend many years in refugee camps or detention centres (Fazel & Stein, 2002; Millbank, Phillips & Bohm, 2006). Experiences in refugee camps have been shown to have a negative impact on the psychological well-being of children. This is particularly the case for children who have had traumatic experiences immediately prior to displacement, and children without parents or who have a parent or parents who are not coping well (Ajdukovic & Ajdukovic, 1998).

High levels of anxiety, depression and post-traumatic stress symptoms have been observed among adult asylum seekers who have been held in Australian detention centres (Keller et al., 2003; Procter, 2005; Steel & Silove, 2001). There is also evidence to suggest that asylum seekers held in detention may have suffered levels of trauma greater than those refugees who are not in detention (Procter, 2005).

Resettlement experiences

Currently, refugees coming to Australia face unemployment, language, housing and cultural barriers, and may experience anxiety about friends and loved ones left behind, racism and discrimination, lack of mainstream social networks, boredom and loneliness (Allotey, 1998; Brough et al., 2003; Chiswick & Lee, 2006; Keel & Drew, 2004; McMichael & Manderson, 2004; Momartin et al., 2006; Rosenthal, Ranieri, & Klimidis, 1996; Sinnerbrink et al., 1997). Refugees settling in regional areas may also be more susceptible to isolation, poverty and vilification (Millbank, Phillips & Bohm, 2006).

Health

Some refugees arrive with specific health needs (in some cases, for diseases that have never been present in Australia or which have not been present for a long time). Although people settling under the humanitarian programs have access to health services and trauma counselling, it has been argued that the level of understanding of those providing these services is inadequate or culturally inappropriate (Benson & Smith, 2007; Correa-Velez, Gifford & Bice, 2005; Harris & Zwar, 2005). Access to effective health care is also limited by cultural factors including distrust of government services, doctors or authority figures, having little or no English language skills, poor finances, and the low priority that is often given to health in the early period of resettlement (Kisely et al., 2002; Murray & Skull, 2003; Neale et al., 2007; Sheikh-Mohammed et al., 2006).

Unemployment

Unemployment is of particular concern to refugees who have been in Australia for less than five years. People who have recently arrived in Australia are often at a disadvantage when looking for work despite the settlement services available to them. A range of factors influence the likelihood of finding work (or finding work consistent with employees' skills and desires) including English language skills, non-recognition of qualifications, racial and cultural discrimination by employers, and a lack of mainstream social networks (Colic-Peisker & Tilbury, 2006). This is especially the case for those with Middle Eastern and African backgrounds (Millbank, Phillips & Bohm, 2006). Research indicates that refugees, regardless of their level of skills, are most often employed in low status, low paid jobs such as cleaning, aged care, meat processing, taxi driving and building and labouring (Colic-Peisker & Tilbury, 2006).

Changes in family roles

Changes in family roles resulting from the loss of family members or long periods of family separation significantly impact on refugee family well-being. Children and adolescents may be expected to take on the role of adults in the family because they have lost a parent or because a parent cannot fulfil their normal parenting role (Punamaki, Qouta & El Sarraj, 1997). Children may also become family advocates when they have greater English language skills than their parents. The expectations of these children may also reflect their roles and expectations of children as a part of traditional cultural practices (e.g., looking after younger children and contributing to family livelihoods). Family members may feel pressure to adopt 'non-traditional' roles, such as working outside of the home or doing tasks previously done by servants. Families who have been reunited after a long period of separation may find that family members have had very different experiences while separated from each other that may be accompanied by feelings of abandonment or betrayal. Cultural gaps may exist between family members, and some may need to rebuild their identities (especially for those who have been traumatised). Children who have been separated from their families, and who have grown up in refugee camps, may experience cultural dislocation due to a lack of role models (Centre for Multicultural Youth Issues, 2006; Gray & Elliott, 2001; Guerin et al., 2003; Rousseau et al., 2004).

Trauma and mental health

Refugees (and migrants, more broadly) show a U-shaped curve of adjustment after resettlement – after the initial relief and elation at finding safety in their host country, the 'honeymoon period' may then wear off as the realities and challenges of resettlement are faced, and as previous traumatic memories gradually resurface. This downward turn is then usually followed by periods of adjustment and readjustment as people settle into the new culture (Sims et al., 2008).

In addition to affecting individual mental health, the consequences of trauma can also affect family roles and obligations, communication (past experiences are not talked about), relationships between family members (e.g., survivor guilt and manifestations of trauma can place strains on relationships), language acquisition, and connections with local communities (Weine et al., 2004). Parents may be in need of help to deal with their own problems and those of their children after the experience of torture and trauma. Recently, concern has been expressed that Australia is not adequately prepared to cope with the special needs of refugees arriving from Africa who may have poor education, health and language skills, and a history of trauma and brutalisation (Millbank, Phillips & Bohm, 2006). It is also important to recognise that refugee children and adolescents may arrive unaccompanied (due to family separation or the death of both parents and other family members) that presents special challenges for practice as these children will need to be placed with families (usually from different cultural backgrounds). They are likely to have significant attachment and mental health problems due to the loss of their primary figures of attachment.

Acculturation

Acculturation refers to the process of adjusting to a foreign culture, and often involves changes in identity, values, behaviour, thoughts, attitudes and feelings (Chung, 2001). For many refugee families this means the difference between living in collectivist societies (i.e., societies that stress human interdependence and the importance of the group, rather than the importance of separate individuals) in their countries of origin and moving to societies that are highly individualistic such as Australia, the US, the UK and Canada. Making these changes can be a source of stress for many refugees, and highly urbanised Australian environments can be especially challenging to refugees from non-western and/or rural backgrounds (Chung, 2001; Colic-Peisker & Walker, 2003). Women may be more likely than their husbands to find jobs because of their willingness to work in low paid sectors (Snyder et al., 2005). Conflict within the family can occur when women obtain work outside the family and are exposed to the influences of Australian culture. In addition, men may feel acutely their loss of social status, and the ethnic and social boundaries that have thus far defined their role as fathers and husbands when women become the family breadwinners (Snyder et al., 2005).

Parent–child conflict is also likely to occur as children and young people rapidly acculturate to their new culture and their behaviour is no longer aligned with their culture of origin (Kagitcibasi, 2003). Added to this pressure, newly arrived refugee parents may find that parenting styles that were normative in their country of origin are not endorsed in their new society (Azar & Cote, 2002). For example, many Western cultures do not view multiple or communal parenting as a common way to raise children. A lack of validation of such parenting beliefs and practices can lead to additional stress for parents in a new culture (Ambert, 1994; Azar & Cote, 2002; Kotchik & Forehand, 2002; Multicultural Perinatal Network, 2000).

Working with refugee families

Morland et al., (2005, p. 793) highlight the:

> *potential for tragic consequences to newcomer refugee families when cultural differences, misunderstandings, language barriers, and a lack of cooperation exist between public child welfare, newcomer refugee families, and refugee-serving agencies.*

There is very little published literature about good practice when working with children and families from refugee backgrounds to strengthen family functioning. However, Pine and Drachman (2005, p. 538) argue that by understanding the experiences of refugee families, child welfare professionals are better placed to understand and assess the needs of these families and to provide effective prevention, protection, permanency and family preservation services.

> *Social workers who provide child welfare services must identify sources of support and stress in the relationships between families and their environment, and develop their intervention strategies accordingly. To provide effective services for immigrants that are family-centred and culturally competent, child welfare practitioners must understand the child and family's experiences in both emigration and immigration.*

Pine and Drachman contend that understanding the experiences of refugee families:

- Encourages awareness of the resilience and strengths of refugee families
- Makes more salient the mental health issues that can develop out of traumatic pre-migration experiences
- Allows examination of the social supports in the refugee service communities that can facilitate family preservation
- Encourages communication with the refugee communities that can inform child welfare workers on cultural issues such as gender roles, parenting practices, views on health and mental health, and help-seeking behaviour.

This last point is particularly important as some refugee families often do not seek help outside their communities and some do not seek help outside their families. Sometimes issues such as domestic violence can be hidden inside the family. Also, the Western concept of 'mental health' is unfamiliar to many refugees, as is the concept of counselling to address mental health concerns.

In 2006–07 the Australian Centre for Child Protection undertook a research project in collaboration with the South Australian Department for Families and Communities, to examine why refugee families were coming

into contact with the South Australian child protection system and to identify the best ways to support parenting needs in refugee families settling in
South Australia. Part of the project involved surveys and interviews with
child protection practitioners about challenges and strategies for working
with refugee families, and focus groups with refugee community members
to explore refugee parents' and community members' views on raising children in Australia and to identify strategies and resources that have supported them, or might support them, in their parenting role. The refugee
communities who took part in the focus groups came from Africa (Sudan,
Somalia, Democratic Republic of Congo, Liberia, Burundi) the Middle East
(Iran and Iraq) and Vietnam. The following sections will discuss the challenges of parenting in a new culture, the challenges practitioners face in
their work with refugee families, and strategies identified by practitioners
and community members for working successfully with refugee families in
child and family services. (The full report can be located at www.unisa.edu.
au/childprotection).

The challenges of parenting in a new culture

Refugee community members identified a number of challenges that they
face as parents in a new culture. The most significant of these included: the
changing expectations of their children in regard to their roles and responsibilities; understanding Australian laws and norms about parenting; the
perceived influence of schools and police on their children's behaviour and
attitudes; and changes in the sources and structure of social support.

Changes in children's roles and responsibilities

When refugee community members were asked about parenting in Australia
their overwhelming response was that Australian culture had significantly
challenged their traditional expectations about the role of children in family
and society (see Williams, 2008) for a more detailed exploration of role
expectations, parenting and filial piety in families from refugee backgrounds
being resettled in South Australia). In part this reflects the changes from
moving from collectivistic societies to individualistic societies and the differing rates of acculturation of children and adults, as described earlier. All of
the 130 community members who took part in the focus groups came from
cultural backgrounds where family roles (including expectations of children
to contribute to the family) are well-defined and reflect the traditional, economic, environmental and religious characteristics of their society. As one
Madi Sudanese man explained:

*We have a collective culture back home where we depend on each other.
So much relies on the extended family. Below six years of age, the children
are mostly attended to by older sisters and brothers and grandparents. The
men and grown up boys go hunting and dig around and the ladies, if strong
enough, do the weeding. The kids are surrounded by older sisters, brothers,
cousins, uncles and aunties.*

Refugee community members expressed that in their countries of origin
children are normally expected to remain in the family home until marriage,
unless they have to study or work away from home. According to community members, there are also well-defined rules and expectations between
boys and girls regarding dating and sexual relationships. Children are also
brought up to respect and obey their parents and to be respectful of other
community members. This means not answering back or challenging and
questioning parents' decisions. Most community members viewed children
as having obligatory roles to their parents.

*In Africa, we bring children up to be polite e.g., they need permission to go
out. The child is brought up to respect that. – Burundian and Congolese focus
group participant*

*In our country the children need to obey the adults, even women need to obey
their husbands. – Vietnamese focus group participant*

*The age of marriage is about 20–25 years for boys and girls. This depends
on schooling and refugee camp movements. Sex before marriage is not
allowed for girls (girls are severely punished, labelled, and this diminishes her
capability to find a partner). Boys are not labelled but severely punished. This
act can lead to a breakout of diseases. We talk about Toumi which is a local
shrine when a curse or misfortune befalls you. There might be an outbreak
of diseases … Toumi is a superstitious belief that instils fear in young people
not to have premarital sex. This prevents unwanted pregnancies. – Madi
Sudanese Men's focus group participant*

Parents and community members were very concerned about the independence that children have in Australia and about the impact that this was
having on their children, themselves and their community. Families may see
their children as leaving a cultural way of life.

*…. young men over there are just brought up in a kind of culture so they
are not preoccupied about when they are going to obtain independence so
they are not clashing with their parents there. In their mind they have been
scheduled to be very good persons. Even if they have left their home or get
married they will be in good contact with their parents. But here they are
already preoccupied that they can be independent later on, and they will not
need their parents. And the community tells them to do so, but in our culture,
the community on the reverse told them to stay with their parents rather
than to go out because they consider it a stigma. So it is quite different. Our
understanding is that it is happening here and some of the young men are*

totally independent from their family just because of the reality of the new situation here in Australia. – Iraqi focus group participant

I have experienced difficulty with young adults when they turn 18 years and become independent. In our culture, children are brought up to remain in the family. When married they still remain in the families and support them. In Australia, when you are 18 years old you are independent. Why is it that in Australia parents complain about their children not leaving home? Why are parents finding solutions for children to go away? That's not how we were brought up. With us, we want our children to stay home. The situation creates a problem for us because we do not want our kids to think that we want them to leave. – Madi Sudanese Women's focus group participant

Peer influence, the education system and Australian culture in general encourage children to be independent. Consequently children from refugee families are exposed to things they would not necessarily experience in their country of origin. This can make parenting difficult as parents are confronted with parenting situations that are unfamiliar and for which they are very likely to be unprepared.

With regards to the culture here… We love Australia, we love this country, the weather is beautiful but the culture is problematic for us. We see this especially for our children when they go to school. People ask a lot of questions – 'did you go out on the weekend? Who with?' In our culture, this is not appropriate. Dating, for example, is very different in both cultures. – Dinka/ Nuer-speaking Sudanese focus group participant

… Now in Australia, our social networks are already broken. We no longer have the extended family to help with disciplining the children. The new situation also exposes parents to confront children which wasn't done before. Children meld into society easier. It is much harder for older people. – Madi Sudanese Men's focus group participant

The perceived increased independence of adolescents from refugee backgrounds was closely linked with financial independence as some young people were eligible to receive youth allowance payments from the Australian Government. Many community members were angry or distressed that their children were able to receive financial support to live independently from their families. Parents were concerned that children did not know how to handle their financial independence and were worried about their safety and well-being. They felt that children were drifting away from the guidance of parents and those children who lived away from their families were more likely to encounter drugs and other negative influences. Some parents also expressed concern about how their children and families were being perceived in the mainstream community.

Teenagers leave home easily. [There is] no social support. In Vietnam, it is harder for our children to move out of the house. Here in Australia, the financial support creates difficulty for parents and removes their power. – Vietnamese Established Community focus group participant

I worry about drugs, alcohol, coming home late. I used to sleep on the floor near the front door, worried about her safety and where she is. – Iranian focus group participant

We want our children to grow up and develop the country! So that we can bring other people! The government don't allow our people to come now... If they see our children the way they dress. [Demonstration of how the youth dress and talk]. We want people to say he is a doctor, a lawyer, he is at university, he is a refugee child. They will be happy to help the community if they see this...! – Liberian focus group participant

However, Vietnamese focus group members, who had been in Australia for some time, acknowledged that their community has grown to accept their children's freedom to express themselves, although they did not always find it easy to do so.

The Australian way has influenced our own culture and we have adapted to this new way because of freedom that is available in this country. There is freedom for children to express themselves and school encourages them to do that. Sometimes, the kids don't respect their elders. We do agree with freedom to express themselves but still have to guide them using our culture and that can be difficult to do so. Freedom of speech is difficult to accept but we have to accept. – Vietnamese Established Community focus group participant

Parental perceptions about the rights given to children according to the Australian law and the broader Australian society were also raised. A large number of refugee parents articulated feelings of disempowerment, frustration and sadness by the rights, privileges and entitlements that had been granted to their children in Australia, and were unclear as to what their rights as parents were.

Parents feel disempowered. In Australia, being placed on the same level or table as kids (where there is equality between parents and children) and this puts parents in a very difficult position. In our society, there is a hierarchy. This causes the biggest trouble as it is difficult for parents who were initially the head of the household to be on the same level of negotiating with the children. – Madi Sudanese Men's focus group participant

But my heart is being broken more than in the war-zone – where we bring up children to respect us, grown ups. Parents have power. In Australia it is a different story. – Burundian and Congolese focus group participant

Understanding Australian laws and cultural norms regarding parenting

All refugee community members also believed that Australian law played a powerful role in how parents bring up their children in Australia, although there was confusion between what is perceived as being Australian law and what are Australian cultural practices. For all refugee groups the role of government in Australia was quite different from that of government in their country of origin.

> Coming from our country, we see the state or government as enemy. In our country, there is no role of state/government, no institution to take care of children. If something goes wrong, relatives take over. The Sudanese stakeholders are the relatives. If parents cannot look after children the relatives take over the role. In Australia the stakeholders are the government. This can sometimes be difficult for us as parents. – Dinka/Nuer-speaking Sudanese focus group participant

> A problem in Australia is the law, this is the main problem. In Iran, the government and the law support the parent and trust the parent. In Australia, a parent with a problem they don't trust. They don't trust the parent to do something good for their children. I don't think the government love my children more than me. When my children do something wrong, when children make big mistakes, they make a problem for the family. – Iranian focus group participant

Refugee community members spoke about the tensions that arose primarily as a result of different cultural practices in the disciplining of children. The majority of the focus group participants came from countries of origin where the use of physical discipline was accepted as an appropriate parenting practice and a reflection of parental authority (as it was in Australia until relatively recently). It is worth noting however, that while attitudes toward the physical discipline of children have changed; corporal punishment is still legal in Australia[1]. Parents felt not only powerless but also that their authority was challenged when they could no longer use such techniques to discipline their children.

> In Australia, for us Africans, there is a lot of freedom; we cannot punish children when they do bad. This is hard for parents as they cannot control children without punishing them. The Australian Government doesn't allow punishing and so children do what they want. Parents do not have power as it is automatically not allowed. – Madi Sudanese Men's focus group participant

> Here the government supports children not to listen to or respect their parents. We would like the government to let us bring up children the way we were doing it, for example, hitting a child – we don't hit to cause harm, it is a slighter hitting, we are not punishing them, it is a way for them to know what they did was wrong. – Burundian and Congolese focus group participant

---

1 Corporal punishment in the home is regulated at state level and is lawful throughout Australia under the right of 'reasonable chastisement' or similar (Australian Capital Territory under common law; *Northern Territory Criminal Code Act* s27; *Queensland Criminal Code Act 1899*, s280; *South Australia Criminal Law Consolidation Act 1935*, s20; *Tasmania Criminal Code Act 1924*, s50; *Western Australia Criminal Code 1913*, s257; *Victoria* under common law rule). For more information visit the following website: www.endcorporalpunishment.org

The perceived influence of schools and the police on children's behaviour and attitudes

Many refugee parents believed that their rights as parents were undermined by schools and that the schools encouraged their children to be independent and to challenge them. For some parents, the schools were seen as interfering with or challenging parental authority.

More important – in Iran, when children go to school from the first year they are taught to have respect for their elders and parents, to be kind and helpful. But in Australia they don't teach them this – the opposite – if your parent does this, call the police, if they do that, call the police. – Iranian focus group participant

Communication breaks down because of people in the schools – well intentioned people always asking the children how is their situation at home – triggering doubts on them as they feel they are so different – young people start questioning their tradition because of this. – Dinka/Nuer-speaking Sudanese focus group participant

The role of police was also of concern to refugee community members. A number of parents were horrified that their children would call or threaten to call the police if they felt that their rights were being challenged by their parents. Parents believed that the schools encouraged children to call the police and were concerned that teachers and the police did not confirm with them the version of events that had been told to them by their children. The threat of having a child taken away was seen as a real one and was understandably distressing to parents. It should be noted that the results of a case file analysis revealed child removal to be a relatively rare occurrence in families from the same countries of origin as those included in the focus groups (for more detail see the full report at www.unisa.edu.au/childprotection).

We are also finding it hard to communicate with our children. We feel like we cannot sit down and talk about what they have and have not done. Now, we don't know how to talk to the child because if they become upset and start saying 'You shouldn't say or do that, then we will call the police.' The police do not listen to the parents. – Burundian and Congolese focus group participant

But when a parent, for example, is used to having the last word inside the family and when his son or his daughter comes to him and says if you don't do what I want I will call the police, 000. He will come and talk to you and the police will come and take you away! This is, in our community, the worst thing that can happen to a parent. – Iraqi focus group participant

We have nine year old children ringing the police. Where does he get that from? The school? It feels like the authority is against us. – Dinka/Nuer-speaking Sudanese focus group participant

Changes in sources and structures of social support

The refugee communities who participated in the focus groups came from cultures where parenting ranged from being the responsibility of the biological parents through to being the responsibility of the wider community. All of the refugee groups had experienced diminished support, albeit to varying degrees, in their parenting roles since arriving in Australia.

> *Here in Australia, we don't have blood relatives but people who speak some of our own language become family. The kids come together and there is a lot of noise. The kids might be playing together and the neighbour construes it as noisy and them causing trouble. Kids won't associate freely…The teen boys come together as a group and they feel great all walking together and a passerby sees this and automatically thinks they are a gang, vandalising things and getting up to no good. This is a dilemma when kids cannot even play with family members. There are a lot of misunderstandings. We are easily misunderstood … – Madi Sudanese Women's focus group participant*

> *Back home there is family support – brother, sister, friend, neighbour – when they see a problem, they will talk to the child and the family straight away. People don't have support here. They are alone. It is bad to ask for support, bad for their reputation – it may be in a police report…and sometimes they will not know the law – their rights and children's rights. No information is given to people when they come to Australia about children's behaviour and the law. – Iranian focus group participant*

The absence of, and separation from, immediate and extended family members puts additional strains on parents adjusting to the new culture. This was particularly noted in cultures where family problems are kept within the family and help from outside agencies would not normally be sought. One Iraqi woman for example spoke of the shame that children's misbehaviour can bring to the community.

> *Parents will say okay, they will follow the law but they will never talk about the issue in front of any of the community. In front of the community, all things will continue normally as if nothing is happening. – Iraqi focus group participant*

Somali focus group participants spoke of the isolation of women, especially sole parents due to the religious practices of the Somali community. The Somali participants described how their religious beliefs do not allow single women to seek help from unrelated men within their own community and also from the broader community. Somali women spoke of the difficulty of obtaining a driver's licence because they could not find women to teach them. This meant that they found it difficult to take their children out on weekends and were often isolated at home with their children. Somali women also spoke of the difficulty in becoming involved in activities such as going swimming, to the gym and other sports because their religion does not allow them to mix with unrelated men.

Challenges in working with families from refugee backgrounds

Child protection practitioners related that they encountered a number of challenges in their work with refugee families including the following issues.

Cultural challenges

Differences in cultural practices and values between other cultures and the Australian culture presented considerable challenges to practitioners in their work with refugee families. This was particularly evident in the differing expectations of practitioners and families around parenting and family roles more generally. As discussed earlier in this chapter, the roles and expectations of children in refugee and other immigrant families can be quite different from those in Western cultures.

Language and communication issues

Practitioners and community members noted the difficulties that communication and language issues presented in working together to support refugee families. Practitioners commented that a lot of information is provided in written form and in English thus presenting a substantial barrier to non-English speaking refugees. Working with refugee individuals who had some English skills was also seen as challenging because it allowed room for misunderstandings and misinterpretations. These communication issues make the dissemination of information about alternative parenting practices and appropriate services difficult.

> And the way the information is provided may not be appropriate. A lot of the information is provided in written form and in English. And it is provided just once as well with no follow up. – Practitioner focus group participant

> Well, it's really frustrating when you've got someone who has limited English and we also use interpreter services. Trying to explain things, when if it had been delivered properly in the first place, is frustrating and not necessary. It's frustrating, it's embarrassing for the client and it's frustrating for us. So, it's about ensuring that the information provided is accurate and that the customer understands it. – Practitioner focus group participant

Refugee perceptions of government agencies

The perceived differing expectations of families compared with staff about the role of government agencies is an issue that practitioners found challenging. Some families from other cultures are not familiar with government agencies whose role is to support parents and families in their parenting roles. As described earlier, some families are suspicious and fearful of government agencies because of their previous experiences in their countries.

> *The barrier is that we're the government and so firstly people tend to shut down. Secondly, families have linked us as Families SA to child protection and you're the agency that takes children away from their families and thirdly, it's recognised that we're statutory which has sometimes turned against us and affects our ability to engage. – Practitioner focus group participant*

Organisational issues

A number of organisational issues were identified by practitioners as impeding their work with refugee families. These included lack of time in casework to become familiar with the cultural background of families; little time to engage and develop trust with refugee families; competing priorities; staff turnover and lack of cultural awareness, knowledge and training.

What helps practitioners in their work with refugee families?

Child protection practitioners were aware of the many issues facing the refugee families with whom they work. Practitioners reported on the previous experiences and histories of some of the refugee families such as mental health issues, alcohol misuse, financial difficulties, and highlighted the need for ongoing support. They recognised that the interplay of these challenges, in addition to cultural differences, all impact on the transition of refugee families to a new culture.

Practitioners and community members highlighted a range of strategies and approaches that would help individual practitioners in their work with refugee families. These included the personal and professional characteristics of practitioners, obtaining information about cultural and religious backgrounds, developing community links, using interpreters correctly and fostering internal and external collaboration. These will be discussed in more detail below. The strategies and principles of culturally sensitive practice with Aboriginal and Torres Strait Islander families described in Chapter 6 are also relevant to working with families from refugee backgrounds. It's also important that these strategies should be considered in line with what O'Hagan (1999, p. 273) has highlighted as the six sources needing to be considered in practice to promote cultural aspects of the families with whom they are working:

- New legislation
- Agency policies and guidelines derived from legislation

- Professional and/or ethical codes of the numerous professions involved (e.g., child and family health nurses, social workers, community mental health nurses, etc.)
- Training at both the pre-qualifying and in-service phases
- Employment and integration of family and child care staff from different cultural backgrounds and
- Pressure groups and community consensus within areas served by the agencies.

Personal and professional characteristics

In the Australian Centre for Child Protection's research, the personal and professional characteristics of practitioners identified as facilitating their work with families from refugee backgrounds, were consistent with the principles of relationship-based practice outlined in Chapter 1. Respect, adaptability, a sense of humour and determination to build and nurture trusting relationships were considered essential personal attributes for practitioners working with refugee families. In addition, meeting the client's needs, an ability to work with interpreters, increasing client's participation and negotiation skills, and building client's social support all contributed to developing effective working relationships with families from refugee backgrounds.

Developing trust with families was seen as key to being able to obtain information that could be used when working with, supporting and developing case plans for families.

> I mean a lot of these sole parents are not really sole parents. There's a father there and a mother because of the polygamy. So, you've got two parents with two separate lots of children and a brother that comes and stays overnight every now and then and they try to hide it and that's another barrier to us working with them because they feel they need to hide that. That's difficult because if they actually come out and tell me the truth then I'd be more able to assist. – Practitioner focus group participant

Being well-informed about clients' cultural and religious backgrounds

Practitioners reflected that it is important to be well-informed about the cultural and religious backgrounds of clients in order to understand their behaviour and respond in a sensitive and appropriate manner. At the same time practitioners emphasised the importance of not making assumptions about behaviour on the basis of this information. Practitioners discussed the importance of preparation and the recognition that each culture is different and that each family and individual come with their unique experiences.

Practitioners noted the importance of receiving up to date and regular feedback and education about the different histories and culture of refugees, and their previous experiences such as torture and trauma. Also, being able to consult with professionals with expertise in working with refugee families was considered a useful resource.

Developing community links

The development of community links, particularly with Elders and community leaders, was recognised as a key factor in supporting practitioners who work with refugee families and communities. With such support, practitioners were able to suggest techniques and services (e.g., counselling) that they might otherwise not have done for families from refugee backgrounds.

> When we access someone from community, we use leaders...and this worked well because it helped explain child protection concerns, appropriately and in not too shameful a manner where they can understand. For example, there were allegations of domestic violence and physical abuse in a community. There were concerns about dad's mental health, mum could not speak any English, the kids were school age and came to school with injuries. The kids told the teacher about the violence at home. Successful dealings with the department would include knowing about the culture and the genocide that went on. Given dad's mental health issues, we went around there with the cops (as we do with domestic violence issues) and dad became violent, threatening and we were not to talk to the kids. Dad eventually calmed down but we were disrespectful about parenting, [we] separated mum which was really wrong. We managed to get community leaders (man and wife) to explain why we were there, why you cannot commit assault, we're a statutory organisation concerned about supporting children and families and were not there to kill them. We were too threatening. – Practitioner focus group participant

Using interpreters correctly

Engaging appropriate interpreters and knowing how to work with interpreters were considered very important when working with refugee families.

> I think ... it's really important for workers to know how to work with an interpreter. You know, to actually speak to the clients themselves and let the interpreter do their job and develop the relationship with the client and the client–worker relationship. – Practitioner focus group participant

Practitioners highlighted some considerations when selecting interpreters:
- The first of these was being aware that interpreters may be members of the communities with whom they are working
- Another important consideration in engaging interpreters or bicultural workers, highlighted by practitioners, is that these workers can be placed in a difficult position and may be hesitant to intervene in families especially around sensitive topics such as child protection

- Interpreters who have knowledge of the area of child protection and are keen to engage these professional relationships were seen as particularly valuable.

The Women's Health Policy and Projects Unit (2007) suggests when using interpreters:

- Always use a trained interpreter. It is not appropriate to use partners or the client's children to interpret. A member of the client's community may also be inappropriate because of confidentiality.
- Use an interstate telephone interpreter if the client is concerned about confidentiality within his/her community group.
- Use short sentences and focus on one point at a time. Talk directly to the client, not the interpreter.

For an excellent reference on working with interpreters see Lisa Aronson Fontes' book, *Interviewing Clients Across Cultures: A Practitioner's Guide* (The Guilford Press, New York, 2008).

Internal and external collaboration

Practitioners identified the importance of both internal and external collaboration as strategies to improve their work with refugee families. The importance of strong inter-agency partnerships with key people and the need to develop networks with other agencies both inside and outside of their organisation were highlighted. In addition, external collaboration with settlement services and other support services such as the Migrant Resource Centre, Lutheran Community Care and the Australian Refugee Association were emphasised. Sims and colleagues (2008) provide an excellent summary of what mainstream and culturally specific services can do to work more effectively with families from culturally and linguistically diverse backgrounds, and to work well with each other.

Suggested strategies

A range of strategies was suggested by refugee community members to help address some of the challenges they were facing as parents in a new culture. These strategies involved a number of agencies including schools, police and child protection and family support services, as well as having implications for community members themselves. The proposed strategies included:

- Encouraging parents to communicate with their children (especially adolescents to open channels of communication between parents and children)
- Encouraging collaborative work between families, communities and schools to address problems between children and families in a consistent

manner (these included establishing parenting committees to resolve parenting issues)
- Providing information for newly arrived families about parenting in Australia at a time and in a manner that suits the needs and preferences of families (such information could include providing a consultative function in which parents can anonymously seek assistance as required to address parenting difficulties)
- Developing flexible and culturally responsive ways of working that allow for two-way interactions between government agencies and families – these ways of working include talking with parents *and* children when dealing with child protection concerns, and engaging with community leaders and elders; and
- Enhancing access to culturally responsive child care.

The ABCD Program

There are many promising programs being implemented across Australia that attempt to address some of the parenting issues encountered by refugee families. The ABCD Program, delivered by the Parenting Research Centre in Victoria, Australia, has shown some encouraging results. The program was designed for parents who have children between 10 and 14 years of age.

The program has a number of aims and objectives including:
- Strengthening parent–child relationships
- Improving family connectedness and
- Empowering parents to enhance their child's development and resilience by building their communication and problem-solving skills.

The program is designed as a weekly group program delivered in either a four or six week format. A range of topics are covered in the program from understanding adolescents, connecting and communicating with teenagers, setting effective limits and dealing with risky behaviour. In the group sessions a trained facilitator works with the parents to develop their skills and parenting strategies. The sessions last from two and a half to three hours and parents are encouraged to practise the strategies learnt in the groups at home between sessions. The program is available in five community languages: Arabic, Macedonian, Spanish, Turkish and Vietnamese. The ABCD Program has now been delivered to over 4000 families across Victoria, from English and non-English speaking backgrounds.

A group-based ABCD Program has also been delivered to parents of adolescents in Victoria's Somali community by trained Somali facilitators. Findings from the evaluation suggest the program is relevant, informative and enjoyable for Somali parents. Limited quantitative data obtained also indicated that parents found the program acceptable and gained some benefit in a reduction in disagreements with their adolescents (Burke, Ward & Clayton, 2007).

Reflective questions

If you were working with refugee families and newly arrived migrant families what type of problems and issues might they be experiencing? Consider: previous traumatic experiences related to their country of origin; the process of migration; settlement into Australia; and cultural differences. What kind of support is available for children, parents and families from refugee backgrounds? As a practitioner, what kind of attitudes/beliefs might you bring that impact on the way you work with refugee families? How might you address these? How can practitioners engage and support refugee families? What kinds of services already exist that work well – and how can we make them better?

Activity

Kaela's husband was killed in Somalia, as were her sister and mother. She has no relatives in Australia and has little social contact. Kaela has been suffering from depression since emigrating to Australia with her three children (aged three, five and nine). Kaela has a number of appointments during the week and leaves her nine year old daughter in charge of the younger children as she has no one else to care for the children. Kaela came into contact with the child protection system after reports were made concerning her three children being left alone for extended periods of time. A neighbour also reported that Kaela's two younger children have been found wandering the streets on a number of occasions and that they have asked for food a few times.

As a practitioner, discuss the issues you think you may encounter when working with this family. What approaches do you think might be most useful when working with this family/client?

What resources do you think might help you work with this family?

What other services and resources could be engaged to assist this family?

Conclusion

Refugee families experience a multitude of complex challenges as they start a new life in a new country. Drawing on the national and international literature, this chapter has attempted to provide a description of the experiences of refugee families during the pre-migration, transition and resettlement phases. In addition, this chapter has drawn upon the voices of refugee parents and communities about the challenges of raising children in Australia, and documented the challenges that child welfare practitioners encountered in their work. When refugee families come to a new country, they bring with them their own culture and way of life. As acculturation occurs for these families, tensions or problems emerge especially when there is a mismatch or clash between cultures and norms. A mismatch between norms related to roles of family members, parenting styles, disciplining of children, roles of government and support services can all impact on one's parenting ability. Furthermore, this is compounded by language and communication barriers and organisational restraints. There are promising approaches and strategies that have been found to be effective. For parents, these include improving communication with their children and actively seeking information about parenting in Australia. For practitioners these include forging trusting relationships and being well-informed about the cultural and religious backgrounds of the families with whom they are working, developing community links, and engaging in collaborative work with other services.

Useful websites

Bridging Refugee Youth & Children's Services: www.brycs.org

Parenting Between Cultures: The Primary School Years – A program for parents from culturally and linguistically diverse communities: www.marymead. org.au/files/Parenting%20Between%20Cultures%20Manual.pdf

Parenting in a New Culture Program – The Northern Migrant Resource Centre in Victoria: www.mrcne.org.au/Settlement-Family-Services5/ Parenting-in-a-New-Culture-Program

Foundation House – The Victorian Foundation for Survivors of Torture: www.foundationhouse.org.au/home/index.htm

Raising Children in a New Country: An Illustrated Handbook: www.brycs.org/ documents/RaisingChildren-Handbook.pdf

References

Ajdukovic, M. & Ajdukovic, D. (1998). Impact of displacement on the psychological well-being of refugee children. *International Review of Psychiatry. Special Issue: Childhood Trauma*, 10 (3), 186–95.

Allotey, P. (1998). Travelling with 'excess baggage': Health problems of refugee women in Western Australia. *Women & Health*, 28 (1), 63–81.

Ambert, A. (1994). An international perspective on parenting: Social change and social constructs. *Journal of Marriage and the Family*, 56, 529–43.

Azar, S. & Cote, L. (2002). Sociocultural issues in the evaluation of the needs of children in custody decision making: What do our current frameworks for evaluating parenting practices have to offer? *International Journal of Law and Psychiatry*, 25, 193–217.

Benson, J. & Smith, M. (2007). Early health assessment of refugees. *Australian Family Physician*, 36 (1–2), 41–3.

Berk, J. (1998). Trauma and resilience during war: A look at the children and humanitarian aid workers of Bosnia. *Psychoanalytic Review*, 85 (4), 640–58.

Brough, M., Gorman, D., Ramirez, E. & Westoby, P. (2003). Young refugees talk about well-being: A qualitative analysis of refugee youth mental health from three states. *Australian Journal of Social Issues*, 38 (2), 193–208.

Burke, K., Ward, J. & Clayton, O. (2007). *ABCD Somali: Translation of the ABCD Parenting Young Adolescents Program for the Somali Community*. Parenting Research Centre, Carlton, Victoria.

Centre for Community Child Health (2004). *Parenting Information Project. Volume 2: Literature Review*. Department of Family and Community Services, Canberra.

Centre for Multicultural Youth Issues (2006). 'Family and Community Issues'. Available online at: www.cmy.net.au/

Chiswick, B. R. & Lee, Y. L. (2006). Immigrants' language skills and visa category. *International Migration Review*, 40 (2), 419–50.

Chung, R. (2001). Psychosocial adjustment of Cambodian refugee women: Implications for mental health counseling. *Journal of Mental Health Counseling*, 23 (2), 115–26.

Colic-Peisker, V. & Tilbury, F. (2006). Employment niches for recent refugees: Segmented labour market in twenty-first century Australia. *Journal of Refugee Studies*, 19 (2), 203–29.

Colic-Peisker, V. & Walker, I. (2003). Human capital, acculturation and social identity: Bosnian refugees in Australia. *Journal of Community and Applied Social Psychology*, 13, 337–60.

Correa-Velez, I., Gifford, S. & Bice, S. (2005). Australian health policy on access to medical care for refugees and asylum seekers. *Australia and New Zealand Health Policy*, 2 (1), 23.

DIAC (2009). Department of Immigration and Citizenship Settlement Database. Available online at: www.immi.gov.au

DIMIA (2005). *Australia's Support for Humanitarian Entrants*. Department of Immigration and Multicultural and Indigenous Affairs, Canberra.

Fazel, M. & Stein, A. (2002). The mental health of refugee children. *Archives of Disease in Childhood*, 87 (5), 366–70.

Gonsalves, C. (1992). Psychological stages of the refugee process: A model for therapeutic interventions. *Professional Psychology: Research & Practice*, 23 (5), 382–9.

Gray, A. & Elliott, S. (2001). 'Refugee Resettlement Research Project Literature Review'. Available online at: www.immigration.govt.nz/

Guerin, B., Guerin, P., Abdi, A. & Diiriye, R. (2003). Identity and community: Somali children's adjustments to life in the western world. In J. Gao, R. Le Heron & J. Logie (eds), *Windows on a Changing World*, 184–8. New Zealand Geographical Society, Auckland.

Harris, M. & Zwar, N. (2005). Refugee health. *Australian Family Physician*, 34 (10), 825–9.

Kagitcibasi, C. (2003). Autonomy, embeddedness and adaptability in immigration contexts. *Human Development*, 46 (2–3), 145–50.

Keel, M. R. & Drew, N. M. (2004). The settlement experiences of refugees from the former Yugoslavia. *Community, Work and Family*, 7 (1), 95–115.

Keller, A., Ford, D., Sachs, E., Rosenfeld, B., Trinh-Shevrin, C., Meserve, C, et al. (2003). The impact of detention on the health of asylum seekers. *Journal of Ambulatory Care Management*, 26 (4), 383–5.

Kisely, S., Stevens, M., Hart, B. & Douglas, C. (2002). Health issues of asylum seekers and refugees. *Australian and New Zealand Journal of Public Health*, 26 (1), 8–10.

Kotchik, B. & Forehand, R. (2002). Putting parenting in perspective: A discussion of the contextual factors that shape parenting practices. *Journal of Child and Family Studies*, 11 (3), 225–69.

Lamberg, L. (1996). Nationwide study of health and coping among immigrant children and families. *Journal of the American Medical Association*, 276 (18), 1455–6.

McMichael, C. & Manderson, L. (2004). Somali women and well-being: Social networks and social capital among immigrant women in Australia. *Human Organization*, 63 (1), 88–99.

Millbank, A., Phillips, J. & Bohm, C. (2006). *Australia's Settlement Services for Refugees and Migrants*. Parliamentary Library, Parliament of Australia, Canberra.

Momartin, S., Silove, D., Manicavasagar, V. & Steel, Z. (2002). Range and dimensions of trauma experienced by Bosnian refugees resettled in Australia. *Australian Psychologist*, 37 (2), 149–55.

Momartin, S., Steel, Z., Coello, M., Aroche, J., Silove, D. M. & Brooks, R. (2006). A comparison of the mental health of refugees with temporary versus permanent protection visas. *Medical Journal of Australia*, 185 (7), 357–61.

Morland, L., Duncan, J., Hoebing, J., Kirschke, J. & Schmidt, L. (2005). Bridging refugee youth and children's services: A case of cross-service training. *Child Welfare*, 84 (5), 791–812.

Mujenovic, Z. (2004). Hope to survive. In S. Dechian, H. Millar & E. Sallis (eds), *Dark Dreams*. Wakefield Press, Kent Town, SA.

Multicultural Perinatal Network (2000). *Attachment Across Cultures*. Toronto Public Health, Toronto.

Murray, S. & Skull, S. (2003). Re-visioning refugee health: The Victorian Immigrant Health Programme. *Health Services Management Research*, 16 (3), 141–6.

Neale, A. N., Ngeow, J. Y. Y., Skull, S. A. & Biggs, B. (2007). Health services utilisation and barriers for settlers from the Horn of Africa. *Australian and New Zealand Journal of Public Health*, 31 (4), 333–5.

O'Hagan, K. (1999). Culture, cultural identity, and cultural sensitivity in child and family social work. *Child and Family Social Work*, 4 (4), 269–81.

Pine, B. A. & Drachman, D. (2005). Effective child welfare practice with immigrant and refugee children and their families. *Child Welfare*, 84 (5), 537–62.

Procter, N. G. (2005). Providing emergency mental health care to asylum seekers at a time when claims for permanent protection have been rejected. *International Journal of Mental Health Nursing*, 14 (1), 2–6.

Punamaki, R., Qouta, S. & El Sarraj, E. (1997). Models of traumatic experiences and children's psychological adjustment: The roles of perceived parenting and the children's own resources and activity. *Child Development*, 64 (4), 718–28.

Richards, E. (2008). *Destination Australia*. University of New South Wales Press, Sydney.

Rosenthal, D., Ranieri, N. & Klimidis, S. (1996). Vietnamese adolescents in Australia: Relationships between perceptions of self and parental values, intergenerational conflict, and gender dissatisfaction. *International Journal of Psychology*, 31 (2), 81–91.

Rousseau, C., Rufagari, M., Bagilishya, D. & Measham, T. (2004). Remaking family life: Strategies for re-establishing continuity among Congolese refugees during the family reunification process. *Social Science and Medicine*, 59 (5), 1095–108.

Schweitzer, R., Melville, F., Steel, Z. & Lacherez, P. (2006). Trauma, post-migration living difficulties, and social support as predictors of psychological adjustment in resettled Sudanese refugees. *Australian and New Zealand Journal of Psychiatry*, 40 (2), 179–87.

Sheikh-Mohammed, M., MacIntyre, C. R., Wood, N. J., Leask, J. & Isaacs, D. (2006). Barriers to access to health care for newly resettled sub-Saharan refugees in Australia. *Medical Journal Australia*, 185 (11/12), 594–7.

Silove, D. & Ekblad, S. (2002). How well do refugees adapt after resettlement in Western countries? *Acta Psychiatrica Scandinavica*, 106 (6), 401–2.

Sims, M., Guilfoyle, A., Kulisa, J., Targowska, A. & Teather, S. (2008). *Achieving Outcomes for Children and Families from Culturally and Linguistically Diverse Backgrounds*. Australian Research Alliance for Children and Youth, Perth.

Sinnerbrink, I., Silove, D., Field, A., Steel, Z. & Manicavasagar, V. (1997). Compounding of premigration trauma and postmigration stress in asylum seekers. *Journal of Psychology*, 131 (5), 463–70.

Snyder, C. S., May, J. D., Zulcic, N. N. & Gabbard, W. J. (2005). Social work with Bosnian Muslim refugee children and families: A review of the literature. *Child Welfare*, 84 (5), 607–30.

Steel, Z. & Silove, D. (2001). The mental health implications of detaining asylum seekers. *Medical Journal of Australia*, 175 (11–12), 596–9.

UNHCR (2007a). *Protecting Refugees and the Role of UNHCR.* United Nations High Commissioner for Refugees, Geneva.

UNHCR (2007b). *Convention and Protocol Relating to the Status of Refugees.* United Nations High Commissioner for Refugees, Geneva.

Weine, S., Muzurovic, N., Kulauzovic, Y., Besic, S., Lezic, A., Mujagic, A. et al. (2004). Family consequences of refugee trauma. *Family Process*, 43, 147–60.

Wessells, M. (2006). *Child Soldiers: From Violence to Protection.* Harvard University Press, Cambridge, MA.

Williams, N. (2008). Refugee participation in South Australian child protection research: Power, voice, and representation. *Family and Consumer Sciences Research Journal*, 37 (2), 191–209.

Women's Health Policy and Projects Unit (2007). *Guidelines for Responding to Family and Domestic Violence.* Women and Newborn Health Service, Perth.

Responding to parents with complex needs who are involved with statutory child protection services

Fiona Arney, Ruth Lange and Carole Zufferey

Learning goals

This chapter will enable you to:

1. Understand some of the characteristics of families who become involved with statutory child protection services
2. Understand some of the barriers to working collaboratively to assist families with complex problems who are involved with statutory child protection services
3. Recognise how intersectoral collaboration can support families with complex problems who are involved with statutory child protection services
4. Gain knowledge of how a program designed to work with families experiencing mental health problems and child protection concerns can overcome the barriers to collaborative work with families with complex needs.

Introduction

Inter-agency or inter-professional conflict is worse in bad cases, what happens is you see the other person as having the solution, you can't fix it, so you imagine they can fix it, so you blame them for not fixing it and then get angry... I could see that all over the place. – Staff member interviewed for the evaluation of the Mental Health Liaison Project

Mental health is one issue…child is another issue…issues bounce back and clash each other… [The child protection service] needs to take mental illness seriously, serious things could happen, [the child protection service] need to be more active in connecting people to services, get people's mental health stable because the concern is for the children. [The child protection service] need to take more steps to help families [in this situation]. – Parent interviewed for the evaluation of the Mental Health Liaison Project

All families will need support at some stage, but in families where disadvantage is chronic and ongoing (even across generations), children can be at a much greater risk of maltreatment, and particularly at risk of neglect (including medical, supervisory, educational and emotional forms of neglect) (Markoff et al., 2005; Spratt & Devaney, 2009).

Families with complex problems come into contact with services on either a voluntary or involuntary basis. They may present at community service organisations for assistance with housing, employment and finances, with other problems (e.g., drug and alcohol issues, mental health problems, family violence etc.) emerging as work progresses with the families (Hinton, 2008). Families may also be identified in universal service settings (e.g., in health care and education services) because of concerns about the welfare and well-being of children or other family members. Related to this, families may only come to the attention of services as a result of statutory interventions such as child protection or criminal justice related responses to concerns about the well-being or behaviour of family members and that may occur when the family is in crisis. It is this latter group of families that are the focus of this chapter.

Families in contact with child protection services

Research has found that up to 65% of maltreatment of children is chronic (Bromfield & Higgins, 2005, p. 44) and the most predictive warning signs of referral were that families experienced multiple interlinked problems such as psychiatric problems, drug and alcohol abuse, poverty and domestic violence (Bromfield & Higgins, 2005; Hamilton & Browne, 1999).

Figure 9.1 describes the child protection process in Australian states and territories. Intake and assessment systems vary from state to state, but in general, families come to the attention of the statutory child protection system through a notification, wherein someone (including parents) who has a concern about the well-being and safety of a child makes a report or referral to a centralised service or a non-government service provider. In families where there are child protection concerns it is usually as a result of an accumulation of risk factors (Schorr & Marchand, 2007).

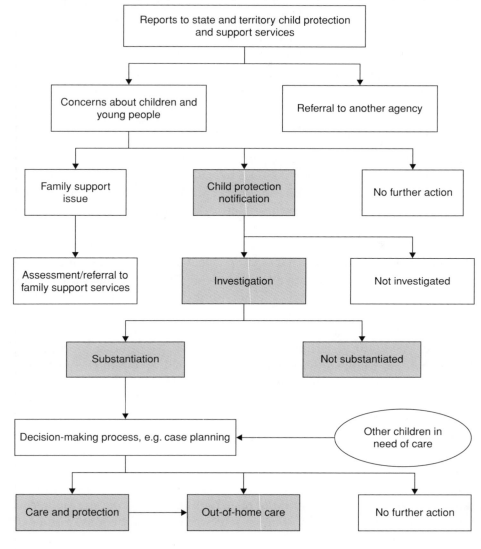

Notes

1. Family support services can be provided at any point in the process. A child may also be placed on a care and protection order or be taken into out-of-home care at any point.

2. This is a simplified representation of the key stages in the child protection process that are common across all states and territories. The actual process differs somewhat across the states and territories.

3. Shaded boxes are items for which data are collected nationally, however it should be noted that data may not be comparable across jurisdictions or within jurisdictions over time.

Figure 9.1: A simplified model of the child protection process (Australian Institute of Health and Welfare, 2009, p. 3)

Data from New South Wales about the characteristics of the notifications received by the Department of Community Services in 2005–06 highlights the significance of factors such as domestic violence (in 32% of notifications) and substance abuse (20% of notifications contained information about drug and alcohol issues combined, 12% drug issues only and 10% alcohol issues only) (Department of Community Services, 2007). It should be noted that these proportions may be underestimates as such issues may be unknown to notifiers or may not emerge until the notification has been investigated.

In families where the allegations of abuse and neglect have been investigated and substantiated, the incidence of parental risk factors increases. For example, data from Victoria show that in 2000–01 substantiated cases of child abuse and neglect were associated with domestic violence in 52% of cases, illicit drug abuse in 33%, alcohol abuse in 31% and psychiatric disability in 19% (Department of Human Services, 2002). Many parents had more than one characteristic.

Research has shown that circumstances in which parents lose custody of their children are commonly related to persistent severe mental illness, substance abuse, limited parenting knowledge and skills, being young at the birth of one's first child, having a larger number of live births, having a limited work history, living at or below the poverty level, being homeless, having fewer social supports and having difficulty coping with stressful situations (Hollingsworth, 2004; Jeffreys et al., 2009; Leek, Seneque & Ward, 2004; Millham et al., 1986; Odyssey Institute of Studies, 2004). In the past, poverty was a major factor contributing to children coming into state care but this has now been complicated by additional social vulnerabilities. Recent research has shown that 'parental substance misuse is associated with children's entry into care in South Australia in approximately 70% of all cases' (Jeffreys et al., 2009, p. 17). Alcohol was the predominant substance that was being misused (in 77% of families where there was parental substance misuse). Families for whom parental substance misuse was associated with child removal had complex profiles (e.g., high levels of domestic violence – 69% of cases, mental health problems – 65% of cases, and almost a third of families experienced financial difficulties, homelessness, and/or had parents in prison or engaged in other criminal activities), more so than in other families where child removal was not associated with substance misuse (Jeffreys et al., 2009). These factors not only influence the well-being of children and other family members, they also negatively influence clients' abilities to engage with services and take steps towards recovery (Hinton, 2008).

Parenting in stressful circumstances

While some cases of child abuse and neglect are intentional, the risk factors described above can also impact on parenting in ways that mean parents are not able to effectively meet the needs of their children despite their desire to do so. In some cases parents may not develop the skills and qualities necessary to meet their children's changing needs, in other cases, parents may 'lose' the effective parenting skills they have developed as life circumstances overtake them (Centre for Community Child Health, 2004). For example, parents who have come from situations of inter-generational hardship or who were placed in out-of-home care themselves as children may not have been exposed to positive parenting role models.

Similarly, isolated and unemployed parents may not have access to peers or professionals as sources of information about positive, proactive parenting techniques and may not have friends or colleagues they can approach for help in the parenting role (e.g., for advice, or support to meet the basic needs of their children) (Centre for Community Child Health, 2004). Social isolation may also mean that children are not identified as 'at risk' until abuse or neglect has occurred, because they have few other adults in their lives. Substance misuse and mental health problems may reduce motivation or self-confidence about being effective parents, and in the case of drug and alcohol misuse, may expose children to harmful situations involving other substance affected adults and/or dealers, low levels of parental supervision, and access to drug paraphernalia (Odyssey Institute of Studies, 2004).

Approaches to working with families in child protection services

Engaging families is vital to achieving outcomes for children and their families, however engaging families with multiple and complex needs can be very difficult. Such families are under great stress and may not know where to start or may feel they are unable to address the concerns about their children's safety and well-being. As a practitioner, building common ground between what your priorities are and what the family see as the issues that need to be addressed and in what order is vital to developing the family's engagement in the change process. However, this can be difficult at times, particularly if families have had poor experiences with other services. Relating the issues of concern to the children's safety and well-being is necessary. Incorporating a strengths- or resilience-based approach is also helpful (White, 2005; Social Exclusion Taskforce, 2007). The UK's 'Think Family' approach, and in particular their RESPECT Programme, an intensive working program for families with antisocial behaviour, has found that a mixture of challenging and supporting families has resulted in engagement with services (Social Exclusion Taskforce, 2007; Spratt & Devaney, 2009; Trotter, 2006).

Once families are engaged with the child protection system, they are likely to become involved with other services. The South Australian study by Jeffreys et al. (2009) showed that although a high proportion of families in which children were removed from their parents' care had drug and alcohol concerns, only 27% of these families had been connected with a drug and alcohol service before they came into contact with child protection services and that this contact was quite limited (e.g., drug and alcohol awareness sessions, methadone maintenance and/or one off assessments) (Jeffreys et al., 2009). For these families, child protection involvement was seen as a potential avenue for intervention from other services. However, it is important to remember how overwhelming having many services involved in a family's life can be, particularly in an already stressful situation. This further highlights the need for coordinated service delivery and for prioritising the work with the family. As one father recalls after child protection services intervened regarding concerns about the safety and well-being of his child/ren.

> *When we got home, once we were released on our supervision order, or whatever the orders they call them, we come home, we had nine workers here, in seven days…Sometimes we had two or three workers sitting at the kitchen table at the one time, from different places… See that even affects me now, what's happened. So if that's affecting me, what's it done to mum, what's it doing to bub… – Extract from the DVD resource,* Strengthening Every Family: Interviews with Parents with Learning Difficulties.

(Parenting Research Centre and Office of the Public Advocate, 2003)

Reflective questions

Imagine you are in a family where nine workers visit over seven days. As a parent how would this make you feel – about yourself, about the services, about your situation? How would it feel from the perspective of a worker? How would it feel from the perspective of a child in this situation?

Inter-sectoral collaboration

Using siloed approaches where the individual client or the individual problem (e.g., drug and alcohol, mental health) is the focus of treatment or a service response may not only overwhelm the client, but can cause tensions and conflicts between and within service providers (such as those outlined in Chapter 4). Focusing on all the individuals in the family rather than on one or two individuals to the exclusion of others can enhance collaborative practice (see Chapters 1 and 4). However, when individual family members' needs or rights may be seen to be in opposition with one another, as is often the case in child protection cases where child abuse and neglect is suspected or has been substantiated, this can make collaboration between adult-focused and child-focused services particularly difficult. In such cases, the child's needs should always be seen as paramount.

There has been an increasing demand for adult-focused and child-focused services to collaborate more effectively for the benefit of children at risk of child abuse and neglect. This is in response to recognition that multidisciplinary, inter-sectoral approaches to working with clients presenting with complex case histories can produce benefits not only economically, but also in terms of improved service flexibility and effectiveness, and enhanced communication and trust between practitioners from different agencies (Considine, 2005; Darlington, Feeney & Rixon, 2005a). For example, joint assessments with other professionals can provide a more comprehensive picture of the family's strengths and risk factors. An important finding when serious case reviews have been undertaken after children have been injured or killed is that no single agency had a complete picture of the family and the risk factors (Ofsted, 2008). Joint assessments can also help workers from different agencies to identify common treatment goals for the family members. For example, a common treatment goal for a family in which parental substance misuse is a concern could be reducing the impact of the parent's drug and alcohol use on their parenting.

While both policy makers and practitioners have positive attitudes towards inter-sectoral collaboration, in general, there are a number of systemic and professional barriers that have been identified in preventing collaboration between child protection and mental health services (Darlington, Feeney & Rixon, 2005a; 2005b). These barriers include issues to do with communication between practitioners in different sectors; knowledge and confidence around mental health problems; role conflict and problems with role clarity for common clients; resource issues; a lack of supportive structures and policies to facilitate inter-sectoral collaboration; confidentiality; and statutory requirements (Darlington & Feeney, 2008; Darlington, Feeney & Rixon, 2005b; Scott, 2005).

As described in Chapter 4, being able to effectively work with families with multiple and complex needs, requires specific knowledge, attitudes, skills and behaviours (see also Chris Trotter's 2006 work on working with involuntary families). This is a highly emotional area to work in. Having the ability to manage your own emotions, communicate well and develop relationships effectively is important in developing effective working relations and taking the lead in inter-agency management (Goleman, 2000). Cross-service and cross-discipline education strategies to improve knowledge, skills and confidence of workers in a range of services can be useful (Hinton, 2008). Adequate supervision that provides workers with a mix of support from different perspectives (e.g., mental health, child and family welfare, drug and alcohol) is also key.

While not necessarily targeted at the child protection context, a number of Australian initiatives exist that are designed to increase the knowledge and skills of practitioners working with clients with complex and multiple problems who are also parents, including:

- Children of Parents with Mental Illness (the COPMI Initiative: www.copmi.net.au; and the Child and Family Inclusive Practice Initiative for Mental Health Services, Cowling and Garrett, 2009)
- Parents with learning difficulties (the Healthy Start Initiative: www.healthystart.net.au), and
- Parents with drug and alcohol problems (the Parenting Under Pressure Program: www.pupprogram.net.au, Dawe and Harnett, 2007; and the Odyssey Institute of Studies (www.odyssey.org.au) that includes resources such as the Counting the Kids Program, the Brokerage Fund, and the Parenting Support Toolkit: www.health.vic.gov.au/drugservices/pubs/parenting-support.htm; UnitingCare Burnside's Moving Forward Program: see www.burnside.org.au/organisation and Chapter 13).

There are also a number of initiatives that have the aim of tertiary prevention of child abuse and neglect in families with complex needs where there are child protection concerns. Such programs include intensive family-based services to prevent child removal (see Chapter 13) and dyadic and group programs with therapeutic components, such as Parent and Child Therapy (PACT; Amos, Beal & Furber, 2007) and the New Parent–Infant Network (NEWPIN) Program (Mondy & Mondy, 2008 and see Chapter 13). The next section details another example of innovative practice to support families with complex problems in contact with child protection services – the Mental Health Liaison Project. In this section we discuss significant aspects of the background to and structure of the project, the approach and activities of the project that assisted in overcoming barriers to collaboration between adult mental health and child protection services, as well as the challenges and complexities faced by such a collaborative initiative.

The Mental Health Liaison Project

The Mental Health Liaison Project was initially proposed by child protection workers in response to barriers they identified regarding their clients' access to mental health services. These barriers included: waiting lists; strict eligibility criteria; clients' reluctance to follow up mental health assessment voluntarily or the inability to access services due to geographical location; client denial of mental health issues; and the focus of child protection services on the child rather than on the parents.

The Mental Health Liaison Project, which commenced in South Australia in April 2005, is a multidisciplinary approach that seeks to 'fast-track' referral to mental health services for parents and assists them to care safely for their children by improving collaboration between the mental health and child protection sectors. The Mental Health Liaison Project sites an experienced mental health nurse within the intake and assessment team in a statutory child protection service. The nurse uses a family-centred approach and assists with the assessment of parents and mobilisation of services appropriate to a family's level of need.

Broadly, the goals of the Mental Health Liaison Project are to improve outcomes for adults and children to prevent or reduce child removals; to improve communication across mental health and child protection services; and to develop collaborative processes and understanding across the service systems working with this client group.

The structure and activities of the Mental Health Liaison Project will be presented in the light of comments from practitioners and parents who were involved in an action research evaluation of the project conducted in 2006 by the Australian Centre for Child Protection (Zufferey, Arney & Lange, 2006). Key stakeholders in the research were the mental health Clinical Nurse Consultant (the mental health nurse) employed on the project (Ruth Lange), managers and staff in child protection and mental health services, and parents who were clients of child protection services. The research included qualitative semi-structured face-to-face interviews and focus groups with 25 workers (19 in child protection and six in mental health services) and eight semi-structured telephone interviews with parents (six parents who were clients of the project and, for comparative purposes, two parents who were clients of child protection services prior to the commencement of the Mental Health Liaison Project). The study aimed to identify what participants saw as working well with the project, what could be done differently and how, and if there was anything additional with which the project could assist.

Project structure

One role of the mental health nurse was to mediate between child protection and mental health services, using her networks, previous experience and credibility in the local mental health services. A complex but effective accountability network was established to enable the mental health nurse to be professionally and organisationally supported in her role (see Figure 9.2).

Broad support for the project at policy levels and local support from workers ensured that many individuals were committed to supporting parents with a mental illness and committed to agency partnerships. Workers emphasised the importance of the project being locally based and initiated by child protection workers in the field (in response to barriers in communication between mental health and child protection services).

Because the child protection service could not employ a nurse directly, a Memorandum of Understanding (MOU) was developed and signed by the mental health and child protection service. This allowed for the health service to employ the mental health nurse and second the position to the child protection service that reimbursed the health service from the project funds.

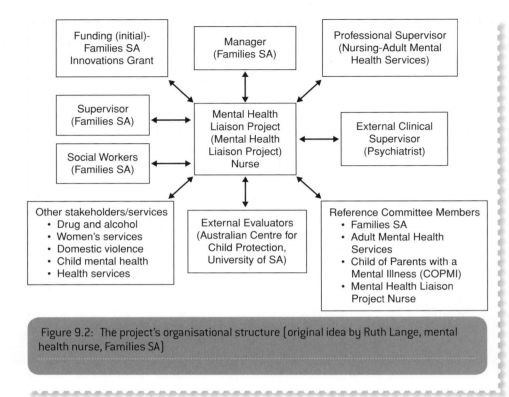

Figure 9.2: The project's organisational structure (original idea by Ruth Lange, mental health nurse, Families SA)

This structural partnership has benefited the project in many ways. It has allowed for a closer working relationship between adult mental health services and child protection through the mental health nurse, which allows for a freer exchange of information between the two agencies, and the use of community mental health assessment forms by the mental health nurse.

Reference committee

Terms of Reference were developed by the members of the reference committee and were agreed upon by the manager of the child protection service and the mental health nurse. The committee met monthly and members included representatives from the child protection service, the health service (including mental health and nursing) and the COPMI Initiative.

Supervision

Due to the innovative nature of employing an adult mental health worker in a child protection agency, the need for close supervision was recognised. It was felt that this would allow for closer monitoring of any problems and early problem solving. With this in mind the following supervision arrangement was agreed upon:

- Child protection intake supervisor for day-to-day management
- Child protection district centre manager for overall management, and
- The nursing director of the health service for professional supervision.

It was initially agreed that clinical discussion could be sought from an emergency mental health service if a referral was likely to take place. However, as the complexity of the issues for clients became apparent, formal clinical supervision was also arranged.

Linkage and exchange

In order to discuss the issue of information sharing and collaborative inter-agency work and to promote the project, an 'Advancing Agency Sharing' forum was held with senior staff and those working in clinical or field settings. A telephone conference discussing the consumer and carer views was also held. The forum and teleconference allowed linkages with other agencies to be developed early in the project, and was helpful in allowing for joint problem solving to develop closer inter-agency collaboration and to identify potential barriers and opportunities for collaboration. The mental health nurse liaised with a range of related initiatives in the same region as the Mental Health Liaison Project.

Project benefits

Workers and parents alike were overwhelmingly positive about the Mental Health Liaison Project's ability to enhance work with families with complex problems and to positively facilitate inter-sectoral collaboration, and recommended its continuation and expansion.

> *In almost five years now, it has been the one truly innovative project that I have seen that has worked. This is one of the best projects that I have actually seen in the department in terms of being viable, being accepted, being useful and working at a ground roots level…it has been a wonderful project. – Staff*

Many benefits of the project were reported. By improving collaboration between child protection and mental health services, workers reported that the Mental Health Liaison Project enabled clients to have a better understanding of what the roles of different agencies are; improved networking across services; provided on-going advocacy and support for parents with a mental illness within the child protection system; made for more efficient services; reinforced case plans for clients; offered a multidisciplinary mix of ideologies; enabled mental health and child protection workers to have fewer conversations that focused on child removal; enabled conversations between services to be more client focused and joint intervention resulted in different pathways for families.

I value her both as a colleague and for her professional skills and for her support for all the workers and her expertise on these cases and the way that she has been improving collaboration with a whole range of mental health services and that has been enormously helpful in the way we deal with our cases [resulting in] a much better outcome, a much better outcome. – Staff

Approach and activities

Characteristics of the mental health nurse

The personality, skills and experience of the mental health nurse employed in a partnership project and the ability to develop relationships with workers in diverse settings were seen by parents and staff as key factors that enabled successful cross agency collaboration. The availability and accessibility of the mental health nurse were also important to the success of the project. Personal and professional expertise such as displaying a calm manner, having a high profile, a good reputation, good mental health knowledge, the skills, knowledge and the ability to be supportive, being able to take a pragmatic approach, being receptive to ideas, having an inter-sectoral mindset and believing in a collaborative approach were all deemed important.

Her personal skills shine in the office – no matter how difficult the client or difficult the situation, it is her years of experience, she knows how to do that and she sees from our perspective now how difficult it is because each agency has fences up, gatekeeping to stop work flow. We are working on ours they are working on theirs, and trying to see how we can break down some of these fences and find some boards across and if we can co-work, rather than 'it is your responsibility', how about 'we do this together, this is my role, this is the information I can share with you' and trying to improve that general flow [of information]. – Staff

Parents saw the mental health nurse as easy to talk to, very helpful, respectful, polite, well mannered, able to listen to concerns and to work out what people did and didn't want, and parents felt confident in her ability to assist them. She referred parents to a range of diverse services including mental health services and also acknowledged client expertise about previous experiences with services. This positive relationship with and experiences of the Mental Health Liaison Project led to hopefulness and high expectations of services being able to assist.

Assessments

Families come to the attention of child protection services because of a range of underlying factors. The mental health nurse found that generally, these issues did not occur in isolation, and parents involved with the project experienced several issues. In particular, drug and alcohol issues and domestic violence were often present in such a way as to make it difficult to tease out which issue to deal with first or to reach agreement amongst services on how to prioritise them. The project worker aimed to increase the awareness of mental health workers when conducting risk assessments about the importance of the parenting responsibilities of clients who are parents and have a mental illness. In child protection services, the mental health nurse aimed to improve parenting assessments, which included developing the mental health knowledge and understanding of social workers working in child protection services to enable an improved response to parental mental health issues by child protection workers.

Close clinical partnerships were developed between the mental health nurse and some of the regional drug and alcohol counsellors. In order to extend this partnership to the intake and assessment team case conference meetings were set up.

Joint assessments (where opportunities were available) and the mental health nurse's involvement in family case conferences were reported to be effective at improving information sharing between mental health and child protection services. Joint client assessments were undertaken by the mental health nurse with both mental health services and child protection workers, which assisted in communication and information sharing across services.

In relation to child protection, the assessment and involvement of the Mental Health Liaison Project could serve to prevent child removal as indicated in the following quote:

> The [mental health nurse] was very good at coordinating everyone, put her foot down and really escalated through mental health services, we would have got to the point where [we] would have had to remove …I think for me we probably would have removed long ago because I would have got to the point where I would not have known where to go. She has been a great asset. – Staff

On the other hand, improved parenting assessments as a result of the mental health nurse's intervention may mean the child was placed in out-of-home care, which was also deemed a good outcome for the safety of the child, as indicated in the quote below:

> Mum and dad both have a mental health issue and a newborn… the assessment we got from three weeks [admission in a residential mental health service for parents and babies facilitated by project worker] really made us understand that these parents are really sick, they can't care for their child, so as a result the child was a lot safer, because we weren't going to put the child back into the parents' care as we once planned, in a way it is a good outcome because the child is safe. – Staff

Joint assessments were valued by clients and were seen as useful and helpful. Clients felt that it was worthwhile 'having a mental health nurse in [the child protection service] to assist parents with mental health issues', because it was 'like having two appointments in one' and prevented them having to repeat the same negative story.

> *It gets depressing telling the same thing over and over again, you start to think to yourself, 'God is it that bad?' and feel depressed, get more depressed, get judged by more people, feel more put down. – Parent*

Companion Agency Meetings

Companion Agency Meetings were developed as a mechanism to develop collaborative work between mental health services and the child protection services in the local region. This was prompted by a couple of clinical cases that had involved work between the agencies. The inter-agency case discussions had shown a great deal of mistrust and misunderstandings about how the other agencies worked, with the result that the families suffered a fractured case management service between the services or no service. It was thought that developing an on-going conversation with mental health services would contribute to building trust and increase each agency's understanding of how the other agency works, thus building up social capital between the services. Discussions focused around cases that were still open and that featured all (or most) of the services present. This was done to increase the relevance of the discussion for the participants and to highlight that inter-sectoral collaboration could occur on existing cases rather than being seen as generating more work and referrals.

Client's support needs

Parents reported positive effects from being able to talk about problems and being listened to respectfully by the mental health nurse, who made them feel that their concerns were important. The project was able to offer helpful practical assistance to both the parents and the children. The Mental Health Liaison Project enabled parents to have respite from parenting responsibilities and provided them with support by giving them access to more services. Participants stated that contact with the project assisted them to parent more effectively and helped them with their thought processes:

> *It is good to have a mental health nurse in [the child protection service] for people like me, to help me 'keep my mind straight', so I don't lose control at the children. – Parent*

The resourcefulness and resilience of parents were also evident. Although participants accessed a number of services, at times it was felt that not enough support services were available for their particular needs and they developed their own ways of coping. As one parent said:

> *Workers suggest strategies or guidelines about how to do things but it doesn't work… in the end you are on your own and find your own strategies.*

Another parent said:

> I've been to hell and back and I'm still standing, fighting all the way.

This indicates how personal barriers can be overcome by parental qualities such as client determination and resilience. Similar to observations made by Anderson et al. (2002), this finding indicates that it may be useful for service providers to move away from viewing themselves as 'experts' who implement interventions *to* people but instead develop partnerships *with* all stakeholders, including parents.

Identifying mental health resources and education

At a broad level, the project was able to improve the knowledge of staff in both services through initiating capacity building education and training activities such as information sharing forums involving a range of services, the dissemination of reference or resource materials as well as facilitating and organising training courses open to a range of services and staff involved with this client group.

The attitude of professional workers employed in both services, and understandings of the role and function of child protection and mental health services, were key hurdles that needed to be addressed. In order to develop a collaborative partnership between child protection and adult mental health services, staff on the ground in both services were being asked to broaden their horizons. Some enjoyed this and some resisted this. As one child protection worker states, the education initiatives implemented by the Mental Health Liaison Project were slowly working on these attitudes but changing them would take a long time:

> Attitudes that are so entrenched by lack of information and understanding of our respective roles. [In the cross agency forum, we] had such incredibly good conversations – that it is not our purpose, we want to see children in their families too but we have to work around issues of their safety, huge conversations and many more conversations needed will happen, but it was an incredibly good start in trying to breakdown barriers and fences that have been put up over probably many, many years. – Staff

The staff of the child protection service were receptive to the offer of education on mental health and how it can affect parenting and what resources are available in the area. Educational sessions were offered and taken up by all of the teams, for example staff representatives from all of the teams from the child protection service where the project was based were invited to attend the Advancing Agency Sharing Forum. In addition, Mental Health First Aid Training through Relationships Australia (a course developed by the Australian National University) was held for child protection district centres in southern Adelaide. The training received very positive feedback from participants.

The mental health nurse also liaised with UK lead nurses (mental health nurses working in the large health trusts, whose focus is child protection) and received resources, disseminating them to the Intake Team and senior staff at the child protection district centre and members of the project's reference committee. Other relevant electronic resources were obtained from various electronic mailing lists and networks.

Books on the area of child protection and mental health were identified and obtained for the project and the staff of the child protection district centre. A text on adult mental health was purchased as a reference for the child protection team. A series of fact sheets from Mental Illness Fellowship were also distributed to the staff.

For the first six months the mental health nurse worked two days per week for the COPMI Initiative, in assisting to develop a pilot training module on COPMI issues (on preventing illness and early intervention, enhancing and strengthening family well-being, promoting the care and protection of children and their families, and promoting multi-agency and multidisciplinary practice). The pilot training module 'Families In Mind' was successfully held in the southern region and a number of staff from the child protection district centre at which the Mental Health Liaison Project is run were able to attend (as well as a small number of mental health staff from the region).

Project challenges

Complexity of client problems including mental health issues

Seven out of the eight parents participating in the project evaluation were women and they discussed issues that interrelated with mental health and child protection or parenting concerns, which included experiencing domestic violence (discussed by half of the participants), children witnessing domestic violence, poverty, the stress of being a single parent (six out of eight were single parents), drug and alcohol use and abuse, living with a disability, grief, and loss, and trauma. Related to the complexity of the issues experienced by families, parents suggested a need for additional help with things such as accessing a psychiatrist and medication that suits them, practical assistance to help them care for their children, help with attending doctors' appointments, transport to the shops and to medical appointments, and assistance with the family court.

Parents reported that the project facilitated access to a range of services for themselves and their children, but recognised that their mental health concerns may have limited their use of the service.

> *I should have kept following her up. I've been thinking about her a lot lately. I might ring her to talk to her. She was good... If I was able to follow up suggestions, it may have worked better. – Parent*

Parents also reflected on the role that child protection can play in exacerbating mental health concerns (e.g., the fear of statutory intervention causing feelings of stress) and feelings of being under surveillance.

> It is like surveillance without the security camera, they can visit, ring, 'spot check' at any time…Every kid I have I am going to have welfare on my doorstep, I'm always looking over my shoulder, I can't have a happy life. – Parent

Systemic and resource considerations

Workers reported that although the Mental Health Liaison Project improved collaboration between mental health and child protection services, a number of structural and ideological barriers to collaboration continued to exist. Throughout the project it was noted that a strong 'us and them' culture still existed between child protection and mental health services, and that one person is not enough to change this systemically. This is compounded by different concerns about 'who is the client?' and confidentiality. For child protection services, the client is the child and for mental health services, the client is the adult, and each service has different legal responsibilities and accountabilities. A child protection worker comments on the limitations of one person:

> In the time she has been with us, certainly done a lot of work for us, in my opinion, there still is a lot of work that needs to be done [in] broader systems but also bringing on board the mental health field, to understand our role and somehow figure out how we can actually work together. We are slowly getting there, she is only one person and that one person is certainly getting her voice heard but I think we need time to establish and get something running. – Staff

Other barriers that staff identified to working collaboratively with families with complex problems in the child protection system included bureaucratic administrative processes that delayed the start of the project; the need for an ongoing commitment of dollars and resources; the need for bi-partisan support (advocating for joint child protection and mental health funding); and the need for political will to enable the project to continue. Systemic constraints such as having the resources to work on collaboration were key concerns because workers reported a lack of time to build collaborative relationships, high staff turnover and a high volume of work.

> It is important to be able to continue to have someone involved in that type of position, who can be vigilant in maintaining contact with mental health services and [child protection]… raising issues from both sides, child issues and mental health issues and keeping them prominent, so they are not being overlooked. – Mental health worker

Similarly, the most negative comments offered by parents were about systemic barriers, such as their experiences of accessing mental health services and child protection services. From the perspective of parents, the improvements needed in both services were related to the lack of communication with service users, staff turnover, access to appropriate services, limited support, the ability and capacity to follow up referrals, the parents' relationships with workers, how appointments were managed and the limited effectiveness of interventions or available services to assist in improving parenting skills.

> *They gave me too many social workers, they closed the case and I didn't know, they didn't ring me. – Parent*

> *The social worker went to another job and I've never heard from anyone since, nearly one year has passed and I have not met the new social worker or case manager. Don't know who it is and who the right person to talk to is. – Parent*

Conclusion

Working with families with multiple and complex problems in child protection contexts can be challenging, but it can also be very rewarding. The work in this field is growing, and increasingly family-based approaches to working with families in statutory settings are being adopted. In this chapter we have highlighted how professionals who are able to span the boundaries of different disciplines and different service sectors can act as a bridge between agencies and provide families with a more holistic and efficient service. Activities such as joint training, joint assessments and the development of resources were very helpful in promoting inter-sectoral ways of working across adult mental health and child protection services, and the support across all levels of the agencies involved was a key to this 'ground-up' approach becoming established and successfully implemented (Chapter 13 explores the factors involved in the successful development and spread of such innovative programs in more detail). The professional and personal characteristics of the mental health nurse, including flexibility in her role, a non-judgemental attitude, and extensive experience in the mental health sector, were driving forces of the success of the approach.

Activities

Read the autobiography: *Angela's Ashes* by Frank McCourt. This book describes growing up in Ireland and Brooklyn in the 1930s and 1940s. The book describes the experiences of a large family living in poverty through the eyes of the young Frank McCourt. Identify the risk and protective factors for each member of the family and for the family as a whole. What are the feelings that arise from reading Frank McCourt's story? How might those feelings impact on your work if you were to work with a family with similar issues? What are the ecological issues which affect this family?

See the film or read the biography *Romulus, My Father* by Raimond Gaita – a son's biography of his father that describes the experiences of a migrant family in which both parents experience mental illness. How did the author as a child make sense of his parents' mental illness? What might have been the signs and sources of his resilience? What were the strengths of the father–son relationship and in the fathering by Romulus? How might the experience by migration and settlement have affected the family?

Access the COPMI website (www.copmi.net.au/) and find one of the novels that describe the experience of children living with a parent who has a mental illness (e.g., *Helicopter Man* by Elizabeth Fensham, 2005; *Saving Francesca* by Melina Marchetta, 2003). Some are written for children so they are quite short in length. What difficulties did this present for the child? What strengths did the child display?

Useful websites

The Children of Parents with Mental Illness (COPMI) Initiative: www.copmi.net.au

Healthy Start – A National Strategy for Children of Parents with Learning Difficulties: www.healthystart.net.au

Odyssey House Victoria – Odyssey Institute of Studies: www.odyssey.org.au/institute/projects/index.asp

Parents Under Pressure (PUP) Program: www.pupprogram.net.au

Social Care Institute for Excellence (SCIE) Guide30:www.scie.org.uk/publications/guides/guide30/files/guide30.pdf

References

Amos, J., Beal, S. & Furber, G. (2007). Parent and Child Therapy (PACT) in action: An attachment-based intervention for a six-year-old with a dual diagnosis. *Australian and New Zealand Journal of Family Therapy*, 28 (2), 61–70.

Anderson, J., McIntyre, J., Rotto, K. & Robertson, D. (2002). Developing and maintaining collaboration in systems of care for children and youths with emotional and behavioral disabilities and their families. *American Journal of Orthopsychiatry*, 72 (4), 514–25.

Australian Institute of Health and Welfare (2009). *Child Protection Australia 2007–08*. Australian Institute of Health and Welfare, Canberra.

Bromfield, L. & Higgins, D. (2005). Chronic and isolated maltreatment in a child protection sample. *Family Matters*, 70, 38–45.

Centre for Community Child Health (2004). *Parenting Information Project, Volume One: Main Report*. Commonwealth of Australia, Canberra.

Considine, M. (2005). *Partnerships and Collaborative Advantage: Some Reflections on New Forms of Network Governance*. Centre for Public Policy, University of Melbourne, Melbourne.

Cowling, V. & Garrett, M. (2009). Child and family inclusive practice: A pilot program in a community adult mental service. *Australasian Psychiatry*, 17 (4), 279–82.

Darlington, Y. & Feeney, J. (2008). Collaboration between mental health and child protection services: Professionals' perceptions of best practice. *Children and Youth Services Review*, 30 (2), 187–98

Darlington, Y., Feeney, J. & Rixon, K. (2005a). Interagency collaboration between child protection and mental health services: Practices, attitudes and barriers. *Child Abuse and Neglect*, 29, 1085–98.

Darlington, Y., Feeney, J. & Rixon, K. (2005b). Practice challenges at the intersection of child protection and mental health. *Child and Family Social Work*, 10, 239–47.

Dawe, S. & Harnett, P. (2007). Reducing potential for child abuse among methadone-maintained parents: Results from a randomized controlled trial. *Journal of Substance Abuse Treatment*, 32, 381–90.

Department of Community Services (2007). *Annual Statistical Report 2005–06*. Department of Community Services, Sydney.

Department of Human Services (2002). *An Integrated Strategy for Child Protection and Placement Services*. Community Care Division, Melbourne.

Goleman, D. (2000). Leadership that gets results. *Harvard Business Review*, 78 (2), 78–90.

Hamilton, C. & Browne, K. (1999). Recurrent maltreatment during childhood: A survey of referrals to police child protection units in England. *Child Maltreatment*, 4 (4), 275–86.

Hinton, T. (2008). *'Just Another Manic Monday': The Challenge of Working with Clients with Alcohol and Other Drug Issues in Community Service Organisations*. Anglicare Tasmania, Hobart.

Hollingsworth, L. (2004). Child custody loss among women with persistent severe mental illness. *Social Work Research*, 28 (4), 199–209.

Jeffreys, H., Hirte, C., Rogers, N. & Wilson, R. (2009). *Parental Substance Misuse and Children's Entry into Alternative Care in South Australia*. Department for Families and Communities, Adelaide.

Leek, L., Seneque, D. & Ward, K. (2004). *Parental Drug and Alcohol Use as a Contributing Factor in Care and Protection Applications 2003*. Department for Community Development, Government of Western Australia, Perth.

Markoff, L., Reed, B., Fallot, R., Elliot, D. & Bjelajac, P. (2005). Implementing trauma-informed alcohol and other drug and mental health services for women: Lessons learned in a multisite demonstration project. *American Journal of Orthopsychiatry*, 75 (4), 525–39.

Millham, S., Bullock, R., Hosie, K. & Haak, M. (1986). *Lost in Care: The Problem of Maintaining Links between Children in Care and their Families*. Gower Publishing Company, Aldershot, UK.

Mondy, L. & Mondy, S. (eds) (2008). *NEWPIN: Courage to Change Together. Helping Families Achieve Generational Change*. UnitingCare Burnside, North Parramatta, NSW.

Odyssey Institute of Studies. (2004). *The Nobody's Clients Project: Identifying the Needs of Children with Substance Dependent Parents*. Odyssey Institute of Studies, Melbourne.

Ofsted (2008). *Safeguarding Children: The Third Joint Chief Inspectors' Report on Arrangements to Safeguard Children*. Ofsted. London.

Parenting Research Centre and Office of the Public Advocate (2003). *Strengthening Every Family: Interviews with Parents with Learning Difficulties* (DVD resource). Available online at: www.healthystart.net.au

Schorr, L. & Marchand, V. (2007). 'Pathway to the prevention of child abuse and neglect: California Department of Social Services'. Available online at: www. PathwaysToOutcomes.org

Scott, D. (2005). Inter-organisational collaboration in family-centred practice: A framework for analysis and action. *Australian Social Work*, 58 (2), 132–41.

Social Exclusion Taskforce (2007). *Reaching Out: Think Family*. UK Cabinet Office, London.

Spratt, T. & Devaney, J. (2009). Identifying families with multiple problems: Perspectives of practitioners and managers in three nations. *British Journal of Social Work*, 39, 418–34.

Trotter, C. (2006). *Working with Involuntary Clients: A Guide to Practice* (2nd edn). Allen & Unwin, Crows Nest, NSW.

White, A. (2005). *Assessment of Parenting Capacity: Literature Review*. Centre for Parenting & Research, NSW Department of Community Services, Ashfield, NSW.

Zufferey, C., Arney, F. & Lange, R. (2006). 'Evaluation of the Mental Health Liaison Project', Australian Centre for Child Protection. Available online at: unisa.edu. au/childprotection

Engaging family members in decision making in child welfare contexts

Marie Connolly

Learning goals

This chapter will enable you to:
1. Develop an understanding of the origins of family decision-making models of practice in child welfare
2. Place this development in the context of rights-based practice
3. Identify the key elements and knowledge base of family decision-making models of practice
4. Understand the key stages of the Family Group Conference as an example of family decision making
5. Reflect upon the possibilities of using family decision making in your own practice.

Introduction

Many services support the notion of involving families in decision making. The nature or extent of that family engagement in a child welfare context, however, creates a range of responses that are often influenced by societal pressures and competing demands (Connolly, 1999). Conceptualising family participation across levels of practitioner response is a useful way of understanding the extent of service commitment to meaningful family involvement (Connolly & Ward, 2008).

At the most basic level, families are consulted and their views taken into account. This requires that the practitioner listen to the family and consult over what may need to happen to resolve the concerns they may have. The next level will see families actively contributing to solutions. Here service providers demonstrate confidence in the family and trust family-led problem-solving. A higher level still of family participation might then see the proactive seeking of family feedback as a service user – and using that feedback to constructively improve services. But arguably the highest level of commitment with respect to family participation in service matters promotes the direct involvement of families in decision making and sharing responsibility for implementing those decisions. It is this level of family participation that we will explore in this chapter.

It is widely recognised that family decision making, and its innovative practice model the Family Group Conference, has originated in Aotearoa New Zealand. Introduced into New Zealand law in 1989, the Family Group Conference brings together professionals and the family, including the extended family, in a solution-focused meeting to sort out matters of care and safety. Parents, grandparents, aunts, uncles and members of the broader kinship system are entitled members of the Family Group Conference who come together at the meeting to support their child. Through a process of discussion and private family deliberation, family-led decisions and plans are made to strengthen the family and protect the child.

Whilst Family Group Conferencing is nested within New Zealand legislation and provides the key mechanism through which statutory decision making occurs, it has also been adopted and adapted as a practice model across international jurisdictions, including Australia (Harris, 2007). For example, in Victoria, the Victorian Aboriginal Child Care Agency Co-operative Ltd, in partnership with the Department of Human Services, provides an Aboriginal Family Decision Making Program called Dhum Djirri (Wurundjeri words meaning to gather and unite). Dhum Djirri has two convenors, an Aboriginal community convenor and a person from the statutory child protection service, and it aims to place culture and community at the heart of the decision-making process (www.vacca.org/01_program/afdmp.html).

This chapter will look at the motivation for involving families in decision making, and will examine both the practice and knowledge base of Family Group Conferencing. While this chapter explores the use of Family Group Conferencing in child welfare contexts, Chapter 13 describes how it has been more broadly applied in a range of practice settings (e.g., child care and parent–adolescent conflict resolution).

Why involve families in decision making?

Traditionally, Western systems of child welfare have a legacy of using systems of non-family care as a primary means of looking after children who could not live at home. In general, professionals made care decisions for children and many children in foster care lost touch with their family and their broader kinship network. Growing numbers of children were placed and spent extended periods of time in out-of-home care (Merkel-Holguin & Ribich, 2001). While some children remained in stable foster placements, many moved from one foster family to another, damaging attachment opportunities and resulting in a loss of family connectedness that other children take for granted. Children in care often missed out on being part of an extended family group who could be there for them as they grew into adulthood. This child welfare rescue model, with its heavy reliance on alternative care, also saw large numbers of Indigenous children in Australia and New Zealand being dislocated from both their families and their cultural heritage causing deep cultural losses (Connolly & Cashmore, 2009; Gilbert, 2009).

The increase in the numbers of children coming to the notice of protective services, the spiralling costs in providing out-of-home care, and the growing realisation that established professional processes of decision making and care were increasingly unable to address the care and protection needs of children sharply highlighted the limitations of the state as sole protector. A growing impetus for more family-centred approaches emerged from these insights: 'After 150 years of removing children from their homes in response to a wide range of family problems, the wisdom of this approach has been questioned. This questioning reflects at once a new understanding of the importance to children of family ties and a new tolerance for diverse family forms and family styles' (Nelson & Landsman, 1992, p. 202).

The New Zealand experience of introducing the Family Group Conference demonstrated that involving family in decision making provided the means through which families could be supported to resolve their own problems and care for their own children, with a consequential reduction of children being placed in out-of-home care. Across international child welfare systems there was pressure for change and many countries adopting the New Zealand model of Family Group Conferencing achieved notable success (Marsh, 2008).

Arguably, however, the key reason to involve families in decision making about their own life issues rests in its intrinsic association with their basic human rights. Families have a moral and human right to meaningful participation and self-determination (United Nations Conventions on the Rights of the Child, 2006). Further, a core principle of human rights that critically defends human autonomy, is the right to lead one's own life, and to 'evaluate, choose, deliberate, and plan' for one's self (Nickel, 2007, p. 63). Building on the work of Orend (2002), Connolly and Ward (2008, p. 24) argue that 'social recognition is essentially concerned with acknowledging the rights of individuals to direct the course of their own lives and to be treated in a dignified and respectful manner in accordance with their status as autonomous agents'. Once establishing a human rights justification for participation and self-determination, there is no option other than to embrace family engagement in decision making as a basic human right.

Of course, the issue of whether parents have their human rights curtailed when they are deemed to have failed in their responsibilities is an important one to consider. Professionals may struggle to reconcile that abusive or neglectful parents also have a right to 'evaluate, choose, deliberate, and plan' (Nickel, 2007, p. 63) for their children. Taking a rights-based approach helps to navigate a fair course through these ethical dilemmas. If parents who have hurt their children are nevertheless valued as fellow humans who deserve the opportunity to work with dignity toward positive solutions to keep their children safe, then there is no reason *not* to take a rights-based approach and involve them in decision making.

Taking this a step further it is also possible to argue group rights for extended families on the basis of a collective rather than individualistic rights perspective. While it is true that individuals are the actual holders of human rights, family members, as part of extended family groups, may see their individual rights given effect, collectively within a group setting.

In essence, on the basis of a human rights perspective engaging family in decision making, whilst having positive implications in the longer term for the child, is also the ethical and fair thing to do.

Reflective questions

What do you think are the key challenges in engaging families in decision-making in your practice? What do you think are the advantages and disadvantages of engaging families in decision making from the point of: parents; children; extended family members; practitioners; and services in general? What are some of the challenges for practices that are rights based?

Family Group Conferencing: an example of engaging families in decision making

The Family Group Conference as practised in New Zealand begins once a child is considered to be in need of care and protection. Firstly the family, including the extended family, and the professionals are brought together. The emphasis is clearly on building the problem-solving potential within the family. It is important to bring together as many family members as possible in a harnessing of family strengths. Considerable attempts are made therefore to engage people in the process. The 'family group' who are entitled to attend the Family Group Conference is broadly defined in New Zealand law to include people with whom the child has a biological or legal relationship, and people to whom the child has a significant psychological attachment.

The emphasis is on maximum family group attendance, minimal professional attendance, although professionals other than the referrer may be asked to come to the meeting if they have information that will be helpful to the family in their discussions.

Because attendance at the Family Group Conference is legally mandated, individuals, family members or otherwise, cannot place restrictions on who can attend the Family Group Conference. Only the coordinator of the meeting, a statutory position under the legislation, has the power to exclude a person with legal entitlement to attend. This action can be taken on the basis of the person's attendance being potentially detrimental to the interests of the child or undesirable for other reasons. Exclusion decisions are not made lightly, and if a person is excluded from the meeting the coordinator is required to record their views and present them to the Family Group Conference in their absence.

Preparing for the Family Group Conference

Preparing well for the meeting is very important to good outcomes. Families, and in particular extended families, will not necessarily be used to having an active role when working with professionals. Just as professionals have to make a shift from professional decision making to family decision making, so too the family needs to learn about the Family Group Conference and their essential role within it. Early discussions with the family may also reveal family tensions that require attention before decision making can occur during the Family Group Conference itself. Developing a comprehensive family genealogy is important, and can also help to identify potential areas of conflict. Using genograms and ecomaps in family work (Barker, 1986) can provide an enormous amount of important information very quickly, not only with respect to who is in the family, but also who is significant to the family and who is lost from it. Different family members can identify where the gaps are in the family information, and building the genealogy can provide support as the strengths within the family become more apparent.

Responding to the family's cultural needs is also an important part of the preparatory work. Appreciating family cultures broadly to include such things as religiosity and affectional preferences as well as ethnicity, will help to ensure that you have the right people at the conference and processes that are responsive to the family's needs. Culture plays a significant part in family dynamics and taking a strengths-based approach will help in achieving good outcomes.

Understanding issues of power within the family system and across family/worker systems will also help to anticipate and manage dynamics during the Family Group Conference. When bringing extended family members together it is critical that the interests of vulnerable members of the family are protected. It is important to know if violence characterises family dynamics, or if there is any likelihood of scapegoating as alliances develop. This depth of knowledge can influence decisions about meeting attendance – for example, whether support people need to be at the meeting, and how the meeting is managed on the day.

The purpose of the preliminary work is to prepare the ground for the effective coming together of family in a solution-focused process. As Saleebey (1997, p. 4) notes, focusing on strengths will shift attention to decisions that enhance possibilities: 'mobilise clients' strengths (talents, knowledge, capacities, resources) in the service of achieving their goals and visions and the clients will have a better quality of life on their terms'.

Getting people together

Whenever possible the Family Group Conference meeting is held in a child- and family-friendly place and typically begins by welcoming the family in ways that respond to their particular cultural needs. Marsh (2008, p. 170) notes the importance of thinking about what will help the family contribute positively to the Family Group Conference process, 'worry, hunger and other emotions can get in the way of engagement'. Managing child care matters sensitively so parents are not left worrying about stressed children might be another way of supporting their involvement. The meeting can take time and it is important that the workers do whatever they can to support full engagement with the process.

Once the family is warmly welcomed, the purpose of the meeting is explained in plain language and in ways that will further engage the family. The meeting then moves into its first phase: information sharing.

Information sharing

This phase of the meeting is important because it is critical to the development of safe decisions and plans for children. Information is shared relating to the nature of the concerns for the child and the assessments that have been undertaken. Mostly information is provided by the social worker who made the Family Group Conference referral, but sometimes the coordinator will bring other professionals to the meeting who have been working with the family, for example, medical or educational professionals. Rather than the information being read out in a report, professionals are encouraged to think creatively about ways of sharing information that will engage the family's interest and commitment to problem-solving. The information sharing phase of the meeting can be conflictual when information is disputed, and the coordinator needs to be skilled in the facilitation of group dynamics and able to refocus attention to the child's needs.

This time is also an opportunity for the family to clarify information and asking questions is encouraged. Once it is clear that the information is fully understood by the family the meeting moves to its second phase: private family discussion.

Private family discussion

This part of the meeting is probably the most innovative of the Family Group Conference process. Here professionals are required to withdraw from the meeting and leave the family to talk in private and make decisions and plans on what should happen next. It is clear that the intent of the New Zealand law is to ensure that the family have time to talk by themselves without professional pressure or influence. Whilst private family time is at the heart of the Family Group Conference and is seen to be of key importance to the process (Walton, McKenzie & Connolly, 2005), there are times when it also needs to be carefully managed by the coordinator when issues of safety may be present. This is where the preparation work before the conference is critical to successful Family Group Conference outcomes. Before bringing people together the coordinator needs to understand the family dynamics and, whenever possible, anticipate how these may impact on the Family Group Conference. Listening to family members will help the coordinator mediate difficult dynamics without compromising important elements of the Family Group Conference.

Once the family have had the opportunity to discuss the issues in private and come up with a plan for the way forward, the conference enters its third and final stage: reaching agreement on the decisions and plans.

Reaching agreement

It is the coordinator's role to bring the conference members back together and seek agreement to the family's decisions and plans. Often finer details of the family plan are negotiated during this phase and in the vast majority of situations agreement is reached. In situations where agreement is not able to be achieved, the matter can be presented to the family court for resolution.

Although originally developed in the context of child welfare, as Family Group Conference practice has spread across the world it has been used whenever issues of care or family support arise. By bringing extended family together practitioners have found that previously untapped resources and supports within the family can be found and positively engaged to help resolve family issues. The following case example illustrates how extended family, once alerted to concerns, can gather together in a circle of support for a troubled family.

A case example: the Jennings family

Mr and Mrs Jennings were referred to a family support service by a school counsellor concerned about the general care of their son Billy. The Jennings family had six children, aged from two to 12 years. Billy, aged 12, also had three siblings attending the school – John aged nine, and twin sisters Mary and Sarah aged seven. The children often came to school without breakfast and were poorly clothed. Over the years the school had expressed their concern to Mr and Mrs Jennings about the children's care but recently they had been found stealing food from shops in the area and scavenging for food in the rubbish bins located around the fast food outlets near the school. It was clear to the teaching staff that the children were becoming increasingly isolated from their peers and appeared lonely in class. In particular, Billy's behaviour was deteriorating and he was starting to become disruptive. Mr and Mrs Jennings indicated that they would welcome some support but nothing they had tried had worked in the past. Various services had tried to help and things had improved for a short time, but in the end everything went back to how it had been before when the workers withdrew.

The family support worker, Sue, found the family to be under financial strain. Mr Jennings worked in a factory and Mrs Jennings, who was limited intellectually, cared for the children at home. The couple also had two pre-school children, Ted aged four and Chantelle aged two. It was clear to Sue that Mrs Jennings had little control of things at home.

In talking with Mr and Mrs Jennings, Sue found that they had a large extended family, most living locally. This included a maternal aunt, two paternal aunts and paternal grandparents. Both maternal grandparents were deceased. Sue talked to the Jennings about the possibility of bringing the extended family together to see what could be done to help. Whilst Mrs Jennings seemed keen, Mr Jennings was initially uncertain as he had not seen his family for a number of years, despite living reasonably close by. They were not on bad terms with family members, however, and so he agreed to Sue bringing a Family Group Conference together.

Sue was delighted that all the available family agreed to attend the Family Group Conference. On the day of the meeting Sue encouraged them to share some family stories and catch up with what had happened since they had last seen each other. Then Sue talked about her work with Mr and Mrs Jennings, describing some of the difficulties in raising six children on a low income. Mr Jennings did not feel happy about the children being at the meeting and so Sue spent some time with them prior to the Family Group Conference so they would understand what the meeting was about and be able to contribute if they wanted to. The children agreed that Billy would represent them by writing a letter to the conference. Billy's school teacher was invited to the Family Group Conference and was given the responsibility of reading out the letter. Although the letter was not very long, it had quite an impact on the family. Billy talked about how much the children loved their parents and what it was like being in a big family. He also talked about school and how he worried about John, Mary and Sarah going to school hungry. He told his family how sad they were that other children didn't like them and how they had to stick together.

After the letter had been read out Sue asked the family if they needed any more information before moving into private family time. Sue reassured the family that the problems had been long-standing and that they would most likely take time to resolve. She did not want them to feel pressured to find solutions in the limited time of the meeting.

The family, in fact, took a long time to deliberate. They came up with a plan across a range of areas including greater supportive contact, respite care, a sharing of 'family clothes' (there were lots of children across the extended family and lots of opportunity for good quality hand-me-downs). One of the aunts – a nurse who worked part time at the local hospital – decided that she would come over every second day to see if they could, together, get the house on track. A subsequent review of the decisions revealed significant improvement in the home situation. For the first time in years the extended family spent Christmas together.

Activities

Identify what you think the tangible and intangible benefits of family engagement in decision making might be. Think about the ways in which professionals can positively influence the Family Group Conference process. How can they inhibit family engagement in decision making? Think of some ways Sue could help maintain family enthusiasm and momentum for change over time.

A case example: the Williams family

The following case study, drawn from Connolly (2006, p. 346) illustrates the way in which a Family Group Conference can also be used in complex situations where dispute between family members, in this case sexual abuse, is an aspect of the family dynamic.

Janice Williams lived at home with her parents and two younger siblings. She was 12 years of age when she first came to the notice of protective services following allegations that she had been sexually abused by her father. Subsequent to the abuse disclosure, Mr Williams admitted that he had abused Janice, although social workers were concerned that he minimised the extent of the abuse and the impact it had on his daughter. He moved away from the family home but had made it clear that he wanted to come back. He believed that the family should stick together.

Mrs Williams relied heavily on her husband for support, both in terms of the day-to-day running of the home and the emotional support he provided. When he left she struggled to cope and found even the most straightforward tasks impossibly difficult. She was feeling increasingly depressed, and while she was supportive of Janice, she missed her husband and wanted things back the way they were.

The Williams family had a reasonably large kinship network. Although both sets of grandparents were deceased, Mrs Williams had a brother who lived close by, and Mr Williams had two sisters living within driving distance. Only one member of the extended family was unable to attend the

Family Group Conference: Mrs Williams' older brother who was encouraged to send a letter to the meeting expressing his views. Janice was very fearful of seeing her father so soon after the abuse, and because of this, Mr Williams was excluded from the meeting. His views, however, were recorded and presented to the family group as part of the information sharing phase.

Prior to the Family Group Conference the Williams' extended family had largely lost touch with each other, and so the first part of the meeting provided an opportunity to rekindle links. Mrs Williams was uncertain how her husband's family may react to the problems raised in the Family Group Conference, particularly because her husband's letter to the Family Group Conference was so full of expressions of apology and distress. However, the coordinator encouraged the family to talk about the issues confronting them, and it was clear that family members on both sides wanted to support Janice and her mother.

The family took a long time to talk privately. When they finally returned to the meeting, they explained that they were troubled by Mr Williams' desire to return home and were concerned that Mrs Williams' reliance on her husband could create dangers for Janice. Their decisions reflected the need to both support Mrs Williams and protect Janice. They recognised the need to provide both emotional and practical support for Mrs Williams, and a plan of family support and child care was proposed. Additionally, the family requested that the social worker initiate court proceedings to secure a restraining order with respect to Mr Williams. It was acknowledged that he would find this a difficult family decision and that he would need support to understand the position taken by the family. One of the paternal aunts took responsibility for explaining this to him and to support him through the process and the criminal court proceedings that were to follow.

Activities

Consider yourself the coordinator bringing together the Williams family for the Family Group Conference. What would you do to prepare them for the meeting? What do you think the issues for each side of the family might have been in this situation and how might these have an impact on the Family Group Conference?

What do you think the implications were of Mr Williams being excluded from the meeting? What do you think will be important for this family into the future?

Knowledge for practice

As the practice of Family Group Conferencing has flourished internationally, researchers have been active in examining the functions and outcomes of family group decision making in practice. This research continues to strengthen the knowledge base and increases our capacity to learn from different systems as they adapt and use the model.

The Family Group Conference is about finding safe solutions for children and maintaining them within their kinship system if that is possible. It is important, therefore, to understand the ways in which the Family Group Conference supports child safety and the child's connection with their family network. With respect to child safety, researchers have found a reduction in child maltreatment and resubstantiation of abuse following the Family Group Conference (Pennell & Burford, 2000; Titcomb & LeCroy, 2005). Supporting the retention of the child within the kinship network, a key aim of Family Group Conferencing, several studies have reported increased rates of relative care for children at risk (Edwards et al., 2007; Gunderson, Cahn & Wirth, 2003; Koch et al., 2006; Morris, 2007; Titcomb & LeCroy, 2003; Walker, 2005). Greater placement stability has been noted (Gunderson, Cahn & Wirth, 2003; Pennell & Burford, 2000) and shorter periods of time in care for children (Wheeler & Johnson, 2003). Importantly, increased kin support has also been identified (Kiely & Bussey, 2001; Morris, 2007); with Horowitz (2008) finding increased emotional support (75%), increased help with transportation (44%) and increased respite care for the family (35%). Not surprisingly family relationships have strengthened, and the relationship between the young person's home and school have also improved (Crow, Marsh & Holton, 2004; Staples, 2007). Although the Family Group Conference is not a therapeutic process, researchers have found potential for the Family Group Conference to have a therapeutic or healing effect for family members (Holland & Rivett, 2008).

As with most practice models that have been adopted across international systems, some Family Group Conference research has presented challenging findings. Sundell and Vinnerljung (2004) undertook a Swedish three year follow-up study that found 69% of their Family Group Conference group sample had at least one new child abuse notification, and 60% were substantiated. It was noted, however, that the Family Group Conference group presented with increased histories of investigation and more serious problems than the comparison group which may be relevant to this finding. Worryingly, however, both the Family Group Conference group and the comparison group had low levels of re-reporting by members of the extended family. Given that the Swedish study contradicts other positive research it is necessary to take care when making international comparisons. It may be that notions of extended family involvement in child protection decision making may find a more sympathetic fit in societies supporting a greater collective responsibility for children (Burford et al., 2009). Countries that have a nuclear family focus may find processes involving extended families more challenging, raising issues relating to cross-cultural application. That said, the Family Group Conference has been found to have supported successful outcomes across international jurisdictions (Kiely & Bussey, 2001; Marsh & Walsh, 2007; Pennell & Burford, 2000) and successful cultural adaptations of the Family Group Conference have been promoted (Desmeules, 2003; Glode & Wien, 2007). This reinforces the need to appreciate the context within which the Family Group Conference is developed and the ways in which it is implemented.

Interesting findings have been reported relating to private family time during the Family Group Conference. Whilst some research suggests that private family time promotes 'within-family challenge and self-regulation' (Connolly 2006, p. 355) and is seen as an empowering process by professionals, one study has indicated mixed responses from families (Holland et al., 2005). Some families have also indicated a reluctance to involve wider family in their own family matters (Terry Stanford Institute of Public Policy, 2006). Notwithstanding this, a significant number of studies have found high levels of family satisfaction with the Family Group Conference process (Crow, Marsh & Holton, 2004; Falck, 2008; Holland, Aziz & Robinson, 2007; Titcomb & LeCroy, 2003; Titcomb & LeCroy, 2005) with increased father involvement (Falck, 2008; Holland et al., 2005) and importantly, increased involvement with the paternal family (Koch et al., 2006).

Whilst research will continue to support and challenge the development of practice, it is nevertheless clear that a growing body of international research supports the use of family group decision making. 'Collectively, the results of the studies reinforce and realise many of the hopes held for Family Group Conference in child welfare. They undermine myths that have persisted to exclude families from planning processes… The evidence… offers considerable support for the advancement of Family Group Conference and good reasons to further mainstream its practice' (Merkel-Holguin, Nixon & Burford, 2003, p. 11).

Voices of participants

With the spread of Family Group Conferencing, every day across the world families and professionals come together to work through complex family matters. Here some of the participants talk about their Family Group Conference experience:

> I liked the way people talked about me. They didn't make me seem like an angel or a bad guy at the conference, people were neutral. They told the story the way it is but also talked about what I do well.
>
> (Young person quoted in Dawson & Yancey, 2006, p. 3)

> Before the conference, I hadn't seen my dad for 5 years, but after the conference I see him like once a week.
>
> (Young person quoted in Dawson & Yancey, 2006, p. 2)

Really bad at first. They made me so mad. But it … really turned out good. We are talking now.

> *(Mother quoted in Pennell, 2005, p. 28)*

I wasn't sure at first… I know how our attitudes can be… When we get on each other's nerves, we are awful. …We accomplished a lot. We're doing great – we talk to each other every day.

> *(Father quoted in Pennell, 2005, p. 28)*

My most abiding memory when I leave this job will be the courage of people, the courage of parents having to front up to that process. I'm always amazed and impressed at their courage – defending themselves, sitting here and hearing all that history about them and how their children came to notice. It's really hard. I suppose its like going to confession.

> *(Coordinator quoted in Connolly, 2006, p. 350)*

There was non-agreement, nothing. Not because we didn't do a good job but there was going to be non-agreement because of the dynamics. But at the end of that they all hugged each other, kissed each other, and exchanged phone numbers and to me that was success because they hadn't been talking before the conference.

> *(Coordinator quoted in Connolly, 2006, p. 353).*

Reflective questions

What do you think it would be like being a participant at a Family Group Conference? What would a Family Group Conference involving your family be like, and how might the dynamics impact on the process? What do you think marks a successful Family Group Conference?

Barriers to mainstreaming family decision making

Over the past two decades, despite promising research and the enthusiasm of strong advocates of family decision-making practices, the Family Group Conference's mainstream potential has not been realised (among other programs, Chapter 13 examines the spread of family group conferencing across Australia). Across Western jurisdictions, a heightened awareness of child abuse has resulted in greater numbers of children being referred to child protection services, which has put pressure upon the responsive capacity of statutory systems. Increased negative media exposure of high-profile cases and growing expectations that services will never fail a child at risk has created risk averse systems of response (Scott, 2006). It is within this environment that family empowerment and participation must compete with risk discourses and the forensic application of procedure and law. When practice is shaped more conservatively by external pressures, then it is more likely that we will also see shifts toward more professionally driven processes. And the more professionally driven practice becomes, the harder it is for systems to embrace notions of family decision-making in practice.

Even in New Zealand where Family Group Conferencing is deeply embedded in the child welfare system, there are indications that practice is not immune to this increasingly forensic response. Professionally driven elements can easily creep into an essentially family-led process (Connolly, 2004). As practice develops, even when practitioners identify strongly with the principles of family-led practice, professional power dynamics can be very influential and can critically shape practice pathways by encouraging a greater dependency of the family on 'expert' solutions.

Assumptions about the efficacy of family decision making have also impacted upon the greater use of family decision making in generalist or mainstream practice. Whilst research has increasingly been supportive of the practice, it is nevertheless erroneous to assume that one or two meetings alone can change the way families function in the longer term. The Family Group Conference is merely a mechanism through which families can be brought together, and needs to be understood in the context of good supportive practice with families. The follow-up work is critical to the success of Family Group Conference plans. Good services need to be provided that will support and motivate families to achieve enduring change. In this sense the Family Group Conference can be seen as one piece of a practice package that supports family rights and enables the development of family-led solutions.

Reflective questions

In what way might professional processes and behaviour influence practice away from the principles of family decision making? If a worker wants to uphold the principles of family decision making, how might they withstand these pressures? How can we rekindle the family's strengths-based potential when practice slips into more professionally driven processes?

Conclusion

Despite the undoubted challenges confronting child welfare systems, practised with integrity it is clear that family group decision making has the potential to provide a 'beacon of hope' for families and workers involved with child welfare systems. Resolving issues of child care and safety is a complex endeavour and workers will always need to carefully navigate child safety and family support imperatives. That said, building ethical and fair decision-making processes that support work with families is likely to be more effective for children and families in the longer term.

Useful websites and resources

The American Humane Association has demonstrated leadership in the promotion of family group decision making in child welfare and their website is an important resource for practitioners wanting information on the Family Group Conference. This is available at: www.americanhumane. org/protecting-children

Burford et al. (2009), have recently completed an annotated bibliography on engaging the family group in child welfare decision making. This is available at: www.americanhumane.org/protecting-children/programs/ family-group-decision-making/re_annotated_bibliography/literature-reviews.html

The Family Rights Group – the following UK training video is aimed at people wanting to know more about family group conferences. It shows two fictional Family Group Conferences with comments from participants: *Taking Care of the Children: A Video about Family Group Conferences.* A training video (2001). White, John (dir.) and Surgenor, Gael (prod.). Family Rights Group, Mental Health Media, London.

The Victorian Aboriginal Child Care Agency Co-operative Ltd provides a broad range of services for Aboriginal children and their families. Descriptions of their programs, including the Aboriginal Family Decision Making Program, can be found on the following website: www.vacca. org/01_program/afdmp.html

References

Barker, P. (1986). *Basic Family Therapy*. Collins, London.

Burford, G., Connolly, M., Morris, K, & Pennell, J. (2009). 'Annotated bibliography on engaging the family group in child welfare decision making', American Humane Association. Available online at: www.americanhumane.org/protecting-children/programs/family-group-decision-making/re_annotated_bibliography/

Connolly, M. (1999). *Effective Participatory Practice: Family Group Conferencing in Child Protection*. Aldine de Gruyter, New York.

Connolly, M. (2004). *Child and Family Welfare: Statutory Responses to Children at Risk*. Te Awatea Press, Christchurch.

Connolly, M. (2006). Upfront and personal: Confronting dynamics in the family group conference. *Family Process*, 45 (3), 345–57.

Connolly, M. & Cashmore, J. (2009). Child welfare practice. In M. Connolly & L. Harms (eds), *Social Work: Contexts and Practice*, 275–90. Oxford University Press, Melbourne.

Connolly, M. & Ward, T. (2008). *Morals, Rights and Practice in the Human Services: Effective and Fair Decision-making in Health, Social Care and Criminal Justice*. Jessica Kingsley Publishers, London.

Crow, G., Marsh, P. & Holton, E. (2004). *Supporting Pupils, Schools and Families: An Evaluation of the Hampshire Family Group Conferences in Education Project*. University of Sheffield and Hampshire County Council, Sheffield, UK.

Dawson, A. & Yancey, B. (2006). 'Youth participants speak about their family group conference', American Humane FGDM Issues in Brief. Available online at: www.americanhumane.org/assets/docs/protecting-children/PC-fgdm-ib-youth-participants.pdf

Desmeules, G. H. (2003). 'Family group conferencing: a decolonization journey for aboriginal children and families in child protection services'. Unpublished Master's thesis. Royal Roads University, Victoria, British Columbia, Canada.

Edwards, M., Tinworth, K., Burford, G. & Pennell, J. (2007). *Family Team Meeting (FTM) Process, Outcome, and Impact Evaluation Phase II Report*. American Humane Association, Englewood, CO.

Falck, S. (2008). *Do Family Group Conferences Lead to a Better Situation for the Children Involved?* NOVA (Norwegian Social Research), Ministry of Education and Research, Oslo.

Gilbert, S. (2009). Aboriginal issues in context. In M. Connolly & L. Harms (eds) *Social Work: Contexts and Practice*, 94–106. Oxford University Press, Melbourne.

Glode, J. & Wien, F. (2007). Evaluating the family group conferencing approach in a First Nations context. In C. Chamberland, S. Léveillé & N. Trocmé (eds), *Enfants à proteger, parents à aider, des univers à rapprocher*, 264–76. Presses de l'Université de Québec, Quebec City, Canada.

Gunderson, K., Cahn, K. & Wirth, J. (2003). The Washington State long-term outcome study. *Protecting Children*, 18 (1 & 2), 42–7.

Harris, N. (2007). 'Mapping the adoption of Family Group Conferencing in Australian states and territories'. Available online at: www.unisa.edu.au/childprotection/documents/FGCHarrisN.pdf

Holland, S., Aziz, Q. & Robinson, A. (2007). *The Development of an All-Wales Evaluation Tool for Family Group Conferences: Final Research Report*. Cardiff University, Cardiff.

Holland, S. & Rivett, M. (2008). 'Everyone started shouting': Making connections between the process of family group conferences and family therapy practice. *British Journal of Social Work*, 38 (1), 21–38.

Holland, S., Scourfield, J., O'Neill, S. & Pithouse, A. (2005). Democratising the family and the state? The case of family group conferences in child welfare. *Journal of Social Policy*, 34 (1), 59–77.

Horowitz, M. (2008). 'Family conferencing as core child protection practice'. Unpublished manuscript.

Kiely, P. & Bussey, K. (2001). *Family Group Conferencing: A Longitudinal Evaluation*. Australia: Macquarie University, Sydney.

Koch, M., Hilt, L., Jenkins, L. & Dunn, T. (2006). 'Family Group Conferencing: 45 children a 12 month study'. Paper presented at the World Forum: Future Directions in Child Welfare, Vancouver, British Columbia, Canada, November 2006.

Marsh, P. (2008). Engaging children, young people and their families via family group conferences. In C. Calder (ed.), *The Carrot or the Stick: Towards Effective Practice with Involuntary Clients in Safeguarding Children Work*, 165–72. Russell House Publishers, Dorset, UK.

Marsh, P. & Walsh, D. (2007). *Outcomes of Family Group Conferences: More than Just the Plan?* Department of Sociological Studies, Sheffield University, Sheffield.

Merkel-Holguin, L., Nixon, P. & Burford, G. (2003). Learning with families: A synopsis of FGDM research and evaluation in child welfare. *Protecting Children*, 18 (1 & 2), 2–11.

Merkel-Holguin, L. & Ribich, K. (2001). Family group conferencing: An 'extended family' process to safeguard children and strengthen family well-being. In E. Walton, P. Sandau-Beckler & M. Mannes (eds), *Balancing Family-Centered Services and Child Well-Being: Exploring Issues in Policy, Practice, Theory and Research*, 197–218. Columbia University Press, New York.

Morris, K. (2007). 'Camden Family Group Conference Service: An evaluation of service use and outcomes'. Available online at: www.frg.org.uk/pdfs/Camden%20 FGC%20Service.pdf

Nelson, K. & Landsman, M. (1992). *Alternative Models of Family Preservation: Family-Based Services in Context*. Charles C. Thomas, Springfield, IL.

Nickel, J. W. (2007). *Making Sense of Human Rights* (2nd edn). Blackwell, Oxford.

Orend, B. (2002). *Human Rights: Concept and Context.* Broadview Press, Ontario, ON.

Pennell, J. (2005). Before the conference – promoting family leadership. In J. Pennell & G. Anderson (eds), *Widening the Circle: The Practice and Evaluation of Family Group Conferencing with Children, Youths, and their Families,* 13–32. NASW Press, Baltimore, MD.

Pennell, J. & Burford, G. (2000). Family group decision making: Protecting children and women. *Child Welfare,* 79 (2), 131–58.

Saleebey, D. (ed.) (1997). *The Strengths Perspective in Social Work Practice* (2nd edn). Longman, New York.

Scott, D. (2006). 'Sowing the seeds of innovation in child protection.' Paper presented at the Tenth Australasian Conference on Child Abuse and Neglect, Wellington, NZ. 14–16 February 2006.

Staples, J. (2007). *Knowle West Family Group Conference Project: Evaluation Report.* Barnardo's/Knowle West Neighborhood Renewal, Bristol, UK.

Sundell, K. & Vinnerljung, B. (2004). Outcomes of family group conferencing in Sweden: A 3-year follow-up. *Child Abuse & Neglect,* 28 (3), 267–87.

Terry Stanford Institute of Public Policy (2006). 'Multiple Response System (MRS) Evaluation Report to the North Carolina Division of Social Services (NCDSS)', Duke University Center for Child and Family Policy, Durham, NC. Available online at: www.eric.ed.gov/ERICDocs/data/ericdocs2sql/content_storage_01/0000019b/80/1b/d6/3a.pdf

Titcomb, A. & LeCroy, C. (2003). Evaluation of Arizona's family group decision making program. *Protecting Children,* 18 (1 & 2), 58–64.

Titcomb, A. & LeCroy, C. (2005). Outcomes of Arizona's family group decision making program. *Protecting Children,* 19 (4), 47–53.

United Nations (2006). 'Convention on the Rights of the Child (2006)'. Available online at: www2.ohchr.org/english/law/crc.htm

Walker, L. (2005). A cohort study of Hawaii's Ohana conferencing in child abuse and neglect cases. *Protecting Children,* 19 (4), 36–46.

Walton, E., McKenzie, M. & Connolly, M. (2005). Private family time: The heart of family group conferencing. *Protecting Children,* 19 (4), 17–24.

Wheeler, C. E. & Johnson, S. (2003). Evaluating family group decision making: The Santa Clara example. *Protecting Children,* 18 (1 & 2), 65–9.

Supporting parents whose children are in out-of-home care

Mary Salveron, Kerry Lewig and Fiona Arney

Learning goals

This chapter will enable you to:

1. Understand the role of out-of-home care in keeping children safe from harm
2. Identify the advantages and disadvantages of maintaining contact between natural parents and their children in out-of-home care
3. Develop awareness of the experiences of parents whose children have been placed in out-of-home care
4. Recognise the potential of child welfare practitioners to engage parents involved with the child protection system in ways that will enhance their ability to interact with their children in out-of-home care
5. Identify the characteristics of parenting programs that promote engagement of parents whose children are in out-of-home care.

Introduction

The last decade has witnessed a doubling in the rates of children living in out-of-home care in Australia from approximately 3.1 per thousand children (14 470 children) to 6.2 per thousand children (31 166 children) on 30 June 2008 (Australian Institute of Health and Welfare, 2009). Similar increases in the rates of children taken into care are also evident in other developed countries like England, the Republic of Ireland and the US (Department for Education and Skills, 2006; Health Social Services and Public Safety, 2006).

Disturbingly, the growing number of children requiring out-of-home care, the need to secure permanent placements for many of these children thereby reducing the capacity of existing carers to take on new children entering the system, and a reduction in the number of people willing to become foster parents has meant that only children with the most serious needs are placed in care (Bromfield et al., 2007). Children currently entering out-of-home care are therefore likely to have more complex needs than previous cohorts of children entering care because of prolonged exposure to maltreatment and family disruption prior to entering care (Bromfield & Osborn, 2007).

The lack of alternative placements for children has significant implications for practitioners working in child protection and child and family services. There is increasing pressure to provide services to families involved in the child protection system that will enable children at risk of child abuse to remain safely at home or to be reunified with their natural families when they have been placed in out-of-home care (Australian Institute of Health and Welfare, 2009; Bromfield & Osborn, 2007). This is a challenging task as many of these families are difficult to engage because of complex and chronic underlying issues such as substance abuse, mental health issues and domestic violence (Australian Institute of Health and Welfare, 2009).

This chapter will provide a brief overview of out-of-home care in Australia; describe some of the characteristics of parents of whose children are in care; discuss the issue of maintaining contact between natural parents and their children who are in care; explore parents' experiences when their children have been placed in care; and discuss the characteristics of group programs that have been shown to be successful in engaging parents whose children have been placed in out-of-home care.

Contextual setting

In Australia, children who are unable to live at home because of substantiated child abuse and neglect or because their parent/s cannot adequately care for them (e.g., because of illness or family conflict) are provided out-of-home care, by each of the states and territories. Out-of-home care may be foster care, placement with relatives or kin, or residential care. Most children are either placed in foster care (48%, June 2008) or with relatives or kin (45%, June 2008). Residential care is provided primarily for children with complex needs or where attempts are being made to keep siblings together. Some children removed from their parents' care return home but many also remain in out-of-home care and become wards of the state or territory until they are 18 years old (Australian Institute of Health and Welfare, 2009).

The current trend in child protection policy and practice is to enable children to remain at home with their families wherever possible. Where children are placed in out-of-home care emphasis is given to reuniting children with their families. These goals are facilitated through the provision of intensive family support programs. Where reunification is not possible, emphasis is placed on securing permanent placements for the children concerned. In these cases, and particularly with Aboriginal and Torres Strait Islander children, the preferred placement option is home-based care either with a foster parent or with relatives or kin (Australian Institute of Health and Welfare, 2009).

Characteristics of families whose children are placed in out-of-home care

There are no national data as to why children are placed in out-of-home care (Australian Institute of Health and Welfare, 2009). However, the circumstances of the families involved in the child protection system show that many of these families are coping with a constellation of complex issues that impact on their ability to provide adequate parenting, including poverty, drug and alcohol abuse, mental health issues, family violence and the stressors of sole parenting (Australian Institute of Health and Welfare, 2009), as outlined in greater detail in Chapter 9. It is believed that the steady upward trajectory of children entering out-of-home care is due in part to increases in the numbers of families with complex and multiple needs as well as greater complexity of needs (Bromfield & Osborn, 2007).

Aboriginal and Torres Strait Islander children, who are over-represented in the child protection system, are almost nine times more likely to be placed in out-of-home care than non-Aboriginal and Torres Strait Islander children (Australian Institute of Health and Welfare, 2009). The reasons for this are complex and are believed to relate to 'the legacy of past policies of the forced removal of some Aboriginal children from their families; inter-generational effects of previous separations from family and culture; poor socio-economic status and; perceptions arising from cultural differences in childrearing practices' (Australian Institute of Health and Welfare, 2009, p. 31 and see Chapter 6).

Natural family contact for children placed in out-of-home care

Maintaining children's contact with their natural families forms an important component of case planning for children in out-of-home care. However the degree and reasons for maintaining contact differ according to their placement goals. If the goal of the placement is eventual reunification of a child with their family, frequent family contact is considered an important means for promoting and preparing for this outcome. If, on the other hand, a child is to remain in permanent out-of-home care, increasingly less frequent contact is generally encouraged. In the latter case the aim of contact is predominantly to preserve a child's links with their biological and/or cultural heritage (Panozzo, Osborn & Bromfield, 2007; Scott, O'Neill & Minge, 2005).

Promoting contact between children in long-term care and their natural parents has only relatively recently been encouraged and there is little research on the effect of contact on children in foster care (Taplin, 2005). The primary arguments put forward for maintaining contact between children and their natural families are that contact: promotes reunification and or attachment; helps preserve links and cultural identity, and; enhances children's psychological well-being. Evidence for and against these arguments are discussed briefly below. For a detailed discussion of the advantages and disadvantages of contact between parents and their children who are in care refer to the reviews by Panozzo, Osborn and Bromfield (2007), Scott, O'Neill and Minge (2005) and Taplin (2005), listed in the references.

Does contact promote reunification?

Research shows that a number of children need and want to see their parents and that upon leaving foster care (at either age 18 or 21), 57% return home (McCoy, McMillen & Spitznagel, 2008; Shirk & Stangler, 2004). According to Millham et al., (1986, p. 218) parental contact emphasises the 'emotional bond and pattern of belonging between child, parent and other significant relatives'. Parent–child visits are considered a primary means for maintaining and supporting parent–child relationships and have been considered by many authors as necessary for successful reunification (Haight et al., 2001; Loar, 1998; Wulczyn, 2004). However, recent research also shows that while contact is related to reunification, the relationship is not causal because factors likely to lead to more frequent and better quality contact between parents and children are also more likely to lead to family reunification (Barber & Delfabbro, 2004; Jenkins & Norman, 1972; Leathers, 2002; Loar, 1998; Mapp, 2002; Millham et al., 1986). A South Australian longitudinal study of children in out-of-home care found that children were more likely to be reunified with their families if their parent was incapacitated in some way (e.g., by physical or mental illness) or if there had been improvements in their mothers' capacity to cope. On the other hand, reunification was less likely for children living in rural areas, Aboriginal children, and children who were victims of neglect (Delfabbro, Barber & Cooper, 2003).

Does family contact have a positive or negative impact on children?

It is also argued that contact between children in out-of-home care and their natural parents can positively contribute to child well-being by enhancing adjustment to placements, and promoting a stronger sense of identity and personal history. According to Wright (2001, p. 15): 'visitation is the primary mechanism for healing the parent–child breach caused by both the maltreatment and the separation, and for building or restoring a home for the child that provides safety, permanency and well-being'. Children who are visited by their parents should be less likely to feel that they have been abandoned, will have a better sense of 'who they are' and will be reminded that their families are safe and well (Hess, 1988). However parent–child contact may not always be a positive experience. Research shows that this is particularly the case for children whose parents' have substance misuse problems or serious mental illness. Children in these situations may find that their contact visits are undermined by parent unreliability, rejection, parent intoxication, and children may also be re-abused (Taplin, 2005). Further, children can become distressed at the separation that accompanies the end of each contact visit, may not wish to see their parents and may demonstrate behaviour problems upon return to their care placements after a contact visit (McMahon, 1998; Wilson & Sinclair, 2004).

Recent research has highlighted the impact of infant visitation plans on systems, carers and child protection workers and volunteers (Humphreys & Kiraly, 2009). Frequent visitation (e.g., more than four times per week) may be part of the case plan for infants because of the perceived importance of contact for parent–child attachment (as described in Chapter 1). Staff and carers noted that such frequent visits can involve complex travel arrangements for the infants, handling by multiple strangers, and can disrupt their sleeping and feeding routines. The report suggested that improving the quality rather than the quantity of parent–infant contact visits is more likely to lead to better experiences of contact visits for all parties (infants, parents, carers, staff and volunteers).

It is important to note that Taplin (2005, p. 10), in her review of this research, highlights that: 'the evidence suffers because few studies have measured children's psychosocial adjustment or intellectual development beyond social workers' opinions. Furthermore, prior measurement of the level of functioning, essential before differences relating to contact can be understood, is usually unavailable'.

Support for parents whose children are in out-of-home care

Engaging and supporting parents whose children have been placed in out-of-home care can be an important component in enhancing contact between children and their natural parents (Panozzo, Osborn & Bromfield, 2007). Retaining a sense of being a parent after children have been placed in care is very difficult, particularly if parents had very little confidence in their parenting role before their children were removed. Assisting parents to make personal changes and to improve their parenting and problem-solving skills can therefore be especially helpful in enhancing contact (Panozzo, Osborn & Bromfield, 2007).

In addition to contact visits, where modelling of positive parental behaviour can occur (Haight et al., 2001), parents may be encouraged to attend parenting groups while their children are in out-of-home care. However, there are limitations to mainstream groups for parents whose children are in care. The complex lives of parents in the child protection system contribute to their poor engagement with services generally (Kovalesky, 2001; Scott, O'Neill & Minge, 2005). When children are placed into out-of-home care, parents have to contend with the problems that brought their children into care, and deal with the after effects of removal. While more research is needed in this area, the available literature tells us that parents whose children have been removed from their care may experience feelings of despair, grief, loss, powerlessness, helplessness and intimidation, as well as isolation, low self-esteem and limited access to resources (Burgheim, 2005). As a consequence, post-removal issues may exacerbate the circumstances that contributed to child removal in the first place. Parents whose children have been placed in care may resort to taking drugs and alcohol to 'numb the pain' of having children taken away from them (Quinton & Rutter, 1984a; 1984b). Parents may also have more children to replace the children they have had removed from their care (Quinton & Rutter, 1984a; 1984b).

> *You never get over the services jumping into your life. Every child now that I have, I don't know how to feel about. I don't know whether the services are gonna be jumping in. I don't know whether I'll be able to bond with this child properly, or be able to actually spend time with that child as much as I'd like ... – Extract from the DVD resource, Strengthening Every Family: Interviews with Parents with Learning Difficulties,*

> *(Parenting Research Centre and Office of the Public Advocate, 2003)*

Further, for parents who would like to attend a parenting group the stigma associated with having children in care and the contributing circumstances (e.g., substance abuse and mental health issues) together with the lack of opportunity to practise the skills learnt in parenting education sessions with their children, present significant barriers to successful participation. Research also shows that children who are in care have higher levels of behavioural problems compared with children in the general population (Sawyer et al., 2007), and therefore require greater levels of parenting knowledge and adaptability (Centre for Community Child Health, 2004; and as described in Chapters 1 and 9).

Parenting groups designed specifically for parents whose children have been placed in care offer a promising alternative to mainstream parenting groups, providing parents with the opportunity to develop their parenting skills and improve the quality of contact with their children (Thomson & Thorpe, 2004). However, parenting groups incorporating parental contact with their children in-out-of-home care will not be suitable for all parents, for the reasons outlined earlier in this chapter.

Parenting groups for parents whose children are in out-of-home care

The literature on group-based work with parents whose children are in out-of-home care is quite limited and the majority of programs discussed in the literature have not been evaluated. A recent systematic review of this literature (Salveron, Lewig & Arney, 2009) identified the following characteristics of groups as being successful in engaging parents whose children are in care:

- A neutral, supportive and non-judgemental environment where a sense of trust among group members can be built
- Involvement of parents in shaping and providing input into the direction of the group
- Group facilitators who were non-judgemental and accepting of parents
- Opportunities for parents to talk about emotions related to the removal of their children and towards child protection services, parenting capacity and social problems such as domestic violence, housing problems, drug and alcohol misuse and mental health issues.

However, of the programs identified in the literature, only one included structured parenting sessions where parents where were able to practise newly acquired parenting skills with their children (Simms & Bolden, 1991). Unfortunately this program was not formally evaluated.

Parents Plus Playgroups – an innovative example of a parenting group for parents whose children are in out-of-home care

The Parents Plus Playgroups Program began as a joint initiative of Families SA (which includes the statutory child protection service in South Australia) and Good Beginnings Australia, a non-profit organisation that delivers early intervention programs to families with young children. Parents Plus Playgroups is a voluntary parenting program for parents who have a child or children in out-of-home care. The aim of the program is to provide an environment where parents whose children are in out-of-home can learn and apply much of the essential parenting knowledge that they have not been exposed to previously. Parents are referred to the program by Families SA staff. The playgroups are not designed to replace contact visits, do not guarantee parent–child reunification, and include parents whose children have been placed in care on shorter term orders as well as those whose children are under the guardianship of the Minister for Families and Communities until they are 18 years old. Parents who have sexually abused their children, or whose drug and alcohol use will affect their attendance at the group, and/or who pose a violent threat to the child and family are not eligible for the program.

The program involves weekly group sessions that are structured into three parts beginning with a one hour parenting education session, followed by a one and a half hour supervised children's playgroup where parents have the opportunity to practise the skills they have learnt in the parenting education session, finishing with a one hour education and debriefing session. The playgroups run one morning per week, are delivered in a group setting across three sites, and are held in a community setting such as a school or community centre.

In 2006, the Australian Centre for Child Protection was invited to undertake an evaluation of the Parents Plus Playgroups Program. The aims of the evaluation were to assess the process, perceived outcomes and acceptability of the playgroups. For a copy of the report see Salveron, Arney and Lewig (2006).

Parents', staff and volunteers' views about the Parents Plus Playgroups

The evaluation involved 17 parents (12 mothers and five fathers), representing 14 families, and included two parents who had previously attended the playgroups and were no longer attending. Three parent focus groups and 10 individual parent interviews were conducted to gather parents' views about the program. Parents also completed four short questionnaires assessing playgroup acceptability, parenting confidence and satisfaction, social support and perceptions of individual feelings, at two time periods during the evaluation. This chapter includes the voices of parents and staff from the qualitative component of the study. Fifteen telephone interviews and/or face-to-face interviews were conducted with staff and volunteers from Good Beginnings Australia, Families SA and the community centres and schools where the playgroups were operating. Eighteen children (11 girls and seven boys) attended the playgroup sessions ranging in age from five months to nine years. The children had been in care between one to eight years.

All but one of the families reported a history of substance use and domestic violence when referred to the Parents Plus Playgroups. The majority of families came from low socio-economic backgrounds and possessed low literacy skills, and only one family had paid employment. Other issues for some of the families included previous criminal history, poor physical health and mental health issues.

The program

The program was welcomed by Families SA staff and parents as a much needed alternative to mainstream parenting groups.

> *It gives us a place to tell parents where they can go. This type of service is needed desperately as most of the [mainstream] parenting education sessions are targeted at middle class families. – Families SA staff*

> *Because you know what…when people find out that you've had your kids taken from you, they look at you different…like you're some kind of leper or something. That happened to me the other week. A nurse came out to check on my baby at home and when I told her that I had a kid who was in care she virtually ran out the door. People can be so judgemental. Here, everybody is in the same boat and can relate to each other. – Parent*

Setting

The Parents Plus Playgroups are held in a safe, parent- and child-friendly environment (e.g., schools, community centres) where parents can share their life experiences with other parents and build happy memories together with their children. Several aspects of the program environment were important to the groups' success and included: having a safe and fun place for children to play; holding the playgroup in a community-based centre where the focus is on children (and separate to child protection offices); having a playground attached to the playgroup room; providing good equipment and lots of toys; being close to public transport; and having an open space for play.

> *The atmosphere of this place really makes the playgroup work. It's friendly, not stuffy, open space, with a good variety of play things. – Staff/volunteer*

> *The playgroups are good because I get to see the kids. We all have good fun. There are lots of toys which keeps the children amused because there is lots of stuff and [the children] feel comfortable here. – Parent*

> *Playgroups provide a soothing environment for parent interaction, having the smaller environment allows for the kids to be closer, [we] have an opportunity to watch the children and see their development (the Families SA office was too small). – Parent*

Information

The program provides parents with information for discussion in the group sessions on a variety of topics including positive parenting, anger management, developing self-esteem, grief and loss, learning through play, building children's trust and confidence, and budgeting and finances. Parents consistently identified nutrition, hygiene and behaviour management as useful topics in the group discussions.

> *An hour and a half before the kids come we learn about different parenting strategies, how to cope with stressful situations, behaviour management, safety, healthy eating (preparing healthy meals), confidence building that is about working on your self-esteem and also encouraging your kids to have more confidence in themselves. – Parent*

> *I've learnt about nutrition, proper discipline not punishment, healthy eating, teaching kids to get along, to be independent (encourage them to do things for themselves), play with other kids. I've got a lot out of this group and I love it. I have learnt to become a better parent. – Parent*

However, parents and staff identified the need for a larger number of families to participate in the groups to promote discussion and to allow for fluctuating group size due to parents and children not being able to attend. Discussions with parents and workers also revealed that because parents learn at different rates, a buddy system could be implemented where a parent (who may have done the parenting session topic before or was more confident on the topic) be paired up with another parent (who may not be at the same stage) and they mentor each other through the parenting sessions.

The children's playgroups

A key focus of the program is on building parent–child attachment through play and interaction in a positive learning environment. The Parents Plus Program uses role modelling as part of its parenting education and the children's playgroup allows staff to demonstrate appropriate behaviour to parents as well as giving parents the opportunity to practise skills learned in the parent group sessions. The use of role modelling was appreciated by several parents and staff and was seen to be a very effective component of the playgroups. Parents emphasised that working through techniques for dealing with potentially difficult situations was particularly helpful. Enabling parents to spend one-on-one time with their children in a supportive, fun-filled environment was one of the most valued aspects of the playgroups for parents and workers.

> *I really like the play-oriented focus, it's very play based, the child's capacity and need to play is central to the learning of the child … and supporting the parents to become engaged in that and to see how the families are now with their play with their children today compared to some less caring and gentle ways of engaging with their children … that's been significant. But also they include an activity which is a very tangible form of engagement for adults … because the play can be tangible for parents. – Staff/volunteer*

> *I am given ideas and learn through role modelling. This is the best way for me because I can practise what I learnt with my child and see what works and what doesn't. Seeing the workers with the children also helped. They're so*

good with the kids. They know how to talk to them and get through to them and the kids love them. – Parent

This group gives parents one-to-one time with our child. My daughter loves this group. She plays with the other kids and I've made lots of friends too. I can now sit down and play with the tea set with her and that's not something that I did before. We can have fun together. – Parent

I am closer with my son and he is happy to see me now. Its better that there is one-on-one time for me and him. – Parent

Flexibility

The program is designed to be flexible and responsive to needs of parents. The flexibility of the program around discussion topics and method of delivery of the content for discussion were seen as key features to the success of the groups. This made the sessions highly relevant to parents, giving them the chance to deal with aspects of their lives that may have been presenting barriers to their engagement around parenting issues and to full participation in the groups.

It is flexible so the parents don't have to come in, and something is going on in their lives like domestic violence, but they have to sit there and listen to us telling them how much sugar is in a can of Coke. You need to be flexible with people, especially where there is so much going on in someone's life. – Staff/ volunteer

Talking about it is easier, [than] reading. We don't sit on the same subject every week and get bored with it. We jump from one subject to another but then we go back over it and we write it up on the whiteboard and start to remember what we actually learnt the week beforehand and it all comes sinking back into our heads. – Parent

The group

Parents expressed a genuine sense of ownership of the group because they were able to contribute to the direction of the sessions. Parents also appreciated that the group allowed them to talk with and relate to other parents in similar circumstances, in a non-judgemental way. This allowed parents to feel listened to and to listen to others, to learn strategies to deal with their emotions, to feel accepted, and to address their emotional issues before interacting with their children.

I don't feel alone here. I am still learning about other parents but so far I feel comfortable which normally takes time for me to do. – Parent

I have become more open and I don't feel so alone any more. These people understand what I am going through. – Parent

I was really, really down before coming here because of things happening in my personal life but now I can face the bad stuff that life throws me. – Parent

The rules and routines (e.g., ensuring group members were on time, and having mutual respect amongst all group members) were also regarded highly by parents as was the trust and reciprocity among parents and between parents and the program team. Comments were also made about the potential for angry parents and/or parents who do not follow the rules to disrupt the playgroup sessions. This concern was expressed by parents and workers from all three sites in the evaluation.

Barriers to participation

A number of potential barriers to participating in the program were also identified. Families SA staff identified aspects of the current referral process such as delayed response times and confusion about whether the process should be written or verbal, as potential barriers to program participation. One worker suggested that regular team meetings that include the playgroup team and representatives from Families SA could improve communication and enhance child protection workers' understanding of the aims and structure of the playgroups (e.g., to convey the message that participation in the playgroups is voluntary rather than mandatory).

Lack of transport was also mentioned by a number of parents as a potential barrier to participation in the program. Although, as identified by a staff member, parents' motivation to attend the groups helped them overcome this barrier, it was unknown to what extent transportation difficulties could have prevented other parents from attending the groups.

> *Some of the families…it just shows their dedication, some of them are travelling for an hour and a half to get to this group and an hour and a half to get home again and that – really three hours travel to a three and a half hour group – takes a real lot of commitment especially on their part when their lives are quite often subject to other factors that influence how often they can get out or mental health issues or depression, some of them are in domestic violence situations where that can make it really difficult for them. Some of them have physical disabilities and still take two buses to get to here, and when groups start at 9.30 that's getting up fairly early in the morning, and I just think that proves their commitment to their children… – Staff/volunteer*

The staff

The playgroups use a strengths-based approach that focuses on the positive strengths of the parents to facilitate positive parenting (see Chapter 7). Empowering parents and building on their strengths, skills and suggestions is believed to be essential in parent engagement (Mather, Barber & the parents of the Connect Parenting/Playgroup, 2004; Thomson & Thorpe, 2003). The playgroup facilitators are trained in early childhood development and are supported by volunteers who work with the parents to supervise the parenting and playgroup sessions and help guide the parents to implement the things they have learnt (e.g., behaviour management techniques, initiating play). Learning is tailored to meet the needs of the parents and the children and occurs in a non-judgemental and non-threatening environment.

As with the themes of relationship-based practice identified in earlier chapters (Chapters 1, 6 and 9), in this study, parents identified the personal and professional characteristics of the playgroup facilitators and volunteers as vital to their positive experiences of the playgroups. In particular, the non-judgemental and positive approach of playgroup workers, their honesty, 'down-to-earth' natures, sense of fun, creativity, and love of the children in the playgroups, were outstanding characteristics identified by parents and other workers. The facilitators' extensive knowledge of parenting and child development and their interaction with the children were also seen as crucial.

> The volunteers are wonderful and they come here every week and take us for who we are. They don't judge us either and there are a lot of judgemental people out there. – Parent

> The parents were constantly told to be positive…you don't get the recognition you deserve and here you get that and you know what, you eventually start to believe it. You forget the negatives and concentrate on the positives. – Parent

> But to me compassion is empathy and looking at another individual and saying 'Wow, you know I really see you for who you really are' rather than actually forming a judgement in that same comparison – loving them for who they are and acknowledging that, that their presence is just as important as anyone else. – Staff/volunteer

In addition, the majority of parents reported trusting the facilitators and volunteers and appreciated how up front they were about their notification responsibilities (e.g., if facilitators and volunteers came across any suspicion of child abuse and neglect, they were to report it). Facilitators also commented on the importance of ensuring transparencies of report writing (e.g., reporting to Families SA) with the parents. This in turn built trusting relationships between parents and the workers involved.

Perceived benefits from participation in the program

Increased parenting confidence

Parents reported an improvement in their parenting knowledge, skills and confidence as a result of participating in the program. Parents related that learning a range of strategies when managing the behaviour of their children helped increase their strength and confidence in parenting and decreased their anxiety about the parenting role (a sense of becoming a 'better parent'). Confidence was further enhanced by the opportunity to interact with the children of other parents in the group. These changes in parenting approaches and confidence were also noted by all of the interviewed workers, including Families SA social workers whose clients were attending the playgroups.

I am a stronger person, with more confidence and knowledge about parenting. I know now that I can do things, I know about where to go for help like ringing up Parent Helpline. I have also learnt about the different ways to deal with the different problems that come up. – Parent

I asked myself am I worthy? Am I good enough [as a parent]?... The groups helped me bond with my girls and do what's best for them because at first I was scared to see them. – Parent

I feel like I am more capable as a dad. This group has taught me more, my knowledge on parenting is broader and about bringing them [children] up. – Parent

For children and families, the parents have definitely more confidence in themselves. They have a better understanding of their roles as a parent and knowing that discipline is about guiding behaviour and not smacking the child. It's about learning different techniques and learning to play with children. – Staff/volunteer

Parents and their caseworkers commonly reported an increase in parents' understanding of children's development, needs and reasons for behaviour, as a benefit of the playgroups. In addition, parents and workers reported that the child-focused perspective of the playgroups increased parents' abilities to consider that 'the kids' best interests are most important'. A key area in which greater understanding of child development was demonstrated was in parents' recognition of the importance of play in the early years.

You learn to play with kids...what's appropriate and what's not. They taught us about motor skills and by doing things. It's certainly helping with their development. – Parent

Parents also highlighted the benefits of the groups in terms of improving their sense of emotional well-being and resilience, which in turn had positive outcomes for their children.

Being part of this group puts me on a natural high. I feel good about myself and the children are also more relaxed. – Parent

Improved relationships and social networks

The benefits of the playgroups for parents were not limited to the interactions that occurred on site. Parents noted that their relationships with other family members improved as a result of their learning in the group and their greater confidence in themselves. In addition, parents' involvement in the playgroups also developed their social networks and links with other community services. Families SA staff also commented that in some cases increased parental confidence had improved the communication between parents and caseworkers. Parents were better able to articulate their needs in a more appropriate way. For some parents, attending the group had softened their attitudes towards child protection services, allowing them a greater understanding of the aims of such services.

Although not a key objective of the program, workers and parents reported that the groups provided informal supports for families and decreased social isolation. In particular the playgroups provided parents with new friendships, a sense of acceptance and belonging (with people from similar backgrounds), practical assistance (e.g., borrowing lawn mowers and obtaining employment for each other), opportunities for social interaction and support for each other that was maintained outside the groups. The groups also provided parents with valued information and resources about services and courses that would be suitable for their circumstances.

> *I have more confidence and actually have a reason to get out of the house. I am slowly building friendships and this group will keep me up to date with parenting because I am going on past knowledge (e.g., about discipline). I am getting to know about what is going on out there for me to access. – Parent*

Benefits for children

Parents and workers commented that there were also benefits for the children who took part in the playgroups, however it should be noted that no formal evaluation of the outcomes of the playgroups for children was undertaken. Perceived benefits for children included having fun, meeting new friends, improved attachment to parents, sense of routines, a sense of safety and the benefits of effective parenting and positive interactions with their parents (e.g., play).

> *At first, [child] was always in the corner and so shy. He has come out of his shell, he plays properly now, sings songs. The kids definitely get a lot out of it. – Parent*

> *For the children definitely this group has been so helpful. They come here now and they know the routine and they know when it's pack up time to go when they sing the goodbye song and they know mum or dad or both are going to be here. – Staff/volunteer*

Activity

Imagine you are attending a parenting group for parents whose children are in out-of-home care. Discuss with a colleague what your experiences might be from the perspective of a parent, worker and a child attending the playgroup. How do you feel about participating in the group? What expectations do you have? What might motivate you to take part? What would stop you from attending?

Conclusion

Parents whose children have been placed in out-of-home care experience complex life problems that are unlikely to be ameliorated without appropriate and thoughtful intervention. With the continuing trend toward greater numbers of children entering out-of-home care, it is important that statutory services recognise the specific needs of parents who have longer term involvement in the child protection system and tailor responses accordingly.

Parenting education groups designed specifically for parents whose children are in out-of-home care offer one promising approach to encouraging appropriate parenting practices among this group of parents. In this chapter we have touched upon some of the characteristics of parenting groups that may help to engage this often difficult to connect group. The most important of these is a respectful and non-judgemental environment that has the flexibility to respond to the complex lives of parents. Of equal salience is the opportunity for parents to improve their parenting knowledge and skills through modelling and practical supervised engagement with their children. Improved parental understanding of child development and children's physical, emotional and psychological needs, the ability to manage adverse emotions and having access to appropriate strategies for managing children's behaviour can improve parenting confidence and contribute to more satisfying contact for parents and their children who are in out-of-home care.

Useful websites

Bromfield, L. M. & Osborn, A. (2007). *'Getting the Big Picture': A Synopsis and Critique of Australian Out-of-home Care Research.* National Child Protection Clearinghouse: www.aifs.gov.au/nch/pubs/issues/issues26/issues26.html

The Family Inclusion Network: www.finwa.org.au/ and www.micah.merivale.org.au/library/items/298017-upload-00001.pdf

Scott, D., O'Neill, C. & Minge, A. (2005). *Contact Between Children in Out-of-home Care and Their Birth Families:* www.community.nsw.gov.au/docswr/_assets/main/documents/oohc_research.pdf

Taplin, S. (2005). *Is All Contact Between Children in Care and Their Birth Parents 'Good' Contact? A Discussion Paper.* Centre for Parenting & Research. NSW Department of Community Services: www.community.nsw.gov.au/docswr/_assets/main/documents/research_good_contact.pdf

References

Australian Institute of Health and Welfare (2009). *Child Protection Australia 2007–08.* Australian Institute of Health and Welfare, Canberra.

Barber, J. G. & Delfabbro, P. H. (2004). *Children in Foster Care.* Routledge, New York.

Bromfield, L. M., Higgins, J. R., Higgins, D. J, & Richardson, N. (2007). Why is there a shortage of Aboriginal and Torres Strait Islander carers? *Promising Practices in Out-of-Home Care for Aboriginal and Torres Strait Islander Carers and Young People: Strengths and Barriers. Paper 1.* Australian Institute of Family Studies, Melbourne.

Bromfield, L. M. & Osborn, A. (2007). 'Getting the big picture': A synopsis and critique of Australian out-of-home care research. *Child Abuse Prevention Issues*, 26, National Child Protection Clearinghouse, Australian Institute of Family Studies, Melbourne.

Burgheim, T. (2005). The grief of birth parents whose children have been removed: Implications for practice in out of home care. *Developing Practice*, 13, 57–61.

Centre for Community Child Health (2004). *Parenting Information Project: Volume 2: Literature Review.* Department of Family and Community Services, Canberra.

Delfabbro, P. H., Barber, J. G. & Cooper, L. (2003). Predictors of short-term reunification in South Australian substitute care. *Child Welfare*, 82 (1), 27–51.

Department for Education and Skills (2006). 'Children Looked After in England (Including Adoption and Care Leavers), 2005–2006'. Available online at: www.dcsf.gov.uk/rsgateway/DB/SFR/s000691/index.shtml

Haight, W., Black, J., Workman, C. & Tata, L. (2001). Parent–child interaction during foster care visits. *Social Work*, 46 (4), 325–38.

Health Social Services and Public Safety (2006). 'Children Order Statistical Bulletin 2006'. Available online at: www.dhsspsni.gov.uk/stats-cib-cobulletindec06-2.pdf

Hess, P. (1988). Case and context: Determinants of planned visit frequency in foster family care. *Child Welfare*, 67 (4), 311–26.

Humphreys, C. & Kiraly, M. (2009). *Baby on Board. Report of the Infants in Care and Family Contact Research Project.* Alfred Felton Research Program, School of Nursing and Social Work, University of Melbourne, Melbourne.

Jenkins, S. & Norman, E. (1972). *Filial Deprivation and Foster Care.* Columbia University Press, New York.

Kovalesky, A. (2001). Factors affecting mother–child visiting identified by women with histories of substance abuse and child custody loss. *Child Welfare* 80 (6), 749–68.

Leathers, S. J. (2002). Parental visiting and family reunification: Could inclusive practice make a difference? *Child Welfare League of America*, 4, 595–616.

Loar, L. (1998). Making visits work. *Child Welfare*, 77 (1), 41–58.

Mapp, S. C. (2002). A framework for family visiting for children in long-term foster care. Families in Society. *The Journal of Contemporary Human Services*, 83 (2), 175–82.

Mather, L., Barber, L. & the parents of the Connect Parenting/Playgroup (2004). Climbing the mountain: The experience of parents whose children are in care. *International Journal of Narrative Therapy and Community Work*, 4, 13–22.

McCoy, H., McMillen, J., C. & Spitznagel, E. (2008). Older youth leaving the foster care system: Who, what, when, where and why? *Children & Youth Services Review*, 30 (7), 735–45.

McMahon, A. (1998). *Damned if You Do, Damned if You Don't: Working in Child Welfare*. Ashgate Publishing Ltd, UK.

Millham, S., Bullock, R., Hosie, K. & Haak, M. (1986). *Lost in Care: The Problem of Maintaining Links between Children in Care and their Families*. Gower Publishing Company, Aldershot, UK.

Panozzo, S., Osborn, A. & Bromfield, L. M. (2007). 'Issues relating to reunification', Research Brief No. 5. Available online at: www.aifs.gov.au/nch/pubs/brief/rb5/rb5.html

Parenting Research Centre and Office of the Public Advocate (2003). *Strengthening Every Family: Interviews with Parents with Learning Difficulties* (DVD resource). Available online at: www.healthystart.net.au

Quinton, D. & Rutter, M. (1984a). Parents with children in care. I. Current circumstances and parenting. *Journal of Child Psychology and Psychiatry and Allied Disciplines*, 25 (2), 211–29.

Quinton, D. & Rutter, M. (1984b). Parents with children in care. II. Intergenerational continuities. *Journal of Child Psychology and Psychiatry and Allied Disciplines*, 25 (2), 231–50.

Salveron, M., Arney, F. & Lewig, K. (2006). *Evaluation of the Parents Plus Playgroups. Final Report and Recommendations: Parent and Worker Perspectives*. Australian Centre for Child Protection, University of South Australia, Adelaide.

Salveron, M., Lewig, K. & Arney, F. (2009). Parenting groups for parents whose children are in care. *Child Abuse Review*, 18 (4), 267–88.

Sawyer, M. G., Carbone, J. A., Searle, A. K. & Robinson, P. (2007). The mental health and wellbeing of children and adolescents in home-based foster care. *Medical Journal of Australia*, 186 (4), 181–4.

Scott, D., O'Neill, C. & Minge, A. (2005). 'Contact between children in out-of-home care and their birth families'. Available online at: www.community.nsw.gov.au/docswr/_assets/main/documents/oohc_research.pdf

Shirk, M. & Stangler, G. (2004). *On Their Own: What Happens to Kids When They Age Out of the Foster Care System?* Westview Press, Boulder, CO.

Simms, M. D. & Bolden, B. J. (1991). The family reunification project: Facilitating regular contact among foster children, biological families, and foster families. *Child Welfare*, 70 (6), 679–90.

Taplin, S. (2005). 'Is all contact between children in care and their birth parents good contact?' Discussion paper. NSW Centre for Parenting & Research, Dept of Community Services, Ashfield, NSW. Available online at: www.community.nsw.gov.au/docswr/_assets/main/documents/research_good_contact.pdf

Thomson, J. & Thorpe, R. (2003). The importance of parents in the lives of children in the care system. *Children Australia*, 28 (2), 25–31.

Thomson, J. & Thorpe, R. (2004). Powerful partnerships in social work: Group work with parents of children in care. *Australian Social Work*, 57 (1), 46–56.

Wilson, K. & Sinclair, I. (2004). Contact in foster care: Some dilemmas and opportunities. In E. Neil & D. Howe (eds), *Contact in Adoption and Permanent Foster Care*, 165–85. British Association for Adoption & Fostering, London.

Wright, L. E. (2001). *Using Visitation to Support Permanency: Toolboxes for Permanency*. Child Welfare League of America, Washington, DC.

Wulczyn, F. (2004). 'Family reunification', the future of children. *Children, Families and Foster Care*, 14 (1), 95–113.

Using evidence-informed practice to support vulnerable families

Fiona Arney, Kerry Lewig, Leah Bromfield and Prue Holzer

Learning goals

This chapter will enable you to:
1. Recognise the role that research can play in improving the lives of vulnerable families and their children
2. Be aware of contemporary views of research-informed child and family welfare practice
3. Understand how research is used by policy makers and practitioners and what factors influence their use of research
4. Understand the types of knowledge that are important in decision making for policy and practice, and
5. Think about how you might use research to inform your practice with vulnerable families and their children.

Introduction

Those who are enamored of practice without science are like a pilot who goes into a ship without rudder or compass and never has any certainty where he is going.

(Leonardo da Vinci, 1452–1519)

The National Framework for Protecting Australia's Children 2009–2020 identifies 'supporting a national research agenda' as an action for the first three years of its implementation in order to support the improvement of and consistency in child protection services (Commonwealth of Australia, 2009, p. 27). A high quality evidence base has the potential to inform decision making in policy and practice (Bromfield & Arney, 2008). It can play an important role in the development and delivery of interventions (Lochman, 2006). It can also assist in screening children and families who are in need of services; provide frameworks and models for intervention; aid in assessing, refining and maximising the effectiveness of interventions; and help to identify why programs do and don't work (Lochman, 2006).

Research can support a public health approach (described in the Introduction) by providing child protection policy makers and practitioners, researchers and communities with information about:

- The classification, diagnosis, prevalence and incidence of child abuse and neglect – what is defined as child abuse and neglect, how it can be recognised, to what extent it occurs in the community, and to what extent is it being reported and responded to by services
- The aetiology of child abuse and neglect – what are the risk and protective factors, what are the outcomes, and what are the causal mechanisms
- Intervention and evaluation data – what works for whom in what settings and to what extent
- Implementation and policy research – what helps and what hinders the adoption and implementation of what works (Bromfield & Arney, 2008).

This is in line with the increasing call for child and family practitioners to adopt practices and interventions that are underpinned by sound knowledge and quality evidence about 'what works for whom, when and why' (Little, Kohm & Thompson, 2005, p. 207). This chapter explores the role of research evidence in child and family welfare practice; what helps and what hinders the use of research evidence in practice; and identifies strategies that can aid in using many types of evidence.

What is evidence-based practice?

Evidence-*based* practice is the 'conscientious, explicit and judicious use of current best evidence in making decisions about individual patients' (Sackett et al., 1996, p. 71). Evidence-*informed* practice is informed by the best available evidence of what is effective (i.e., research and evaluation findings), but also recognises the knowledge and experience of practitioners and the views and experiences of service users in the current operating environment (e.g., with the resources and practitioners available at the given time) (Petch, 2009). Evidence-informed policy making applies the same principles to larger groups, populations, organisations and service systems.

The concept of evidence-based practice is not new and has its earliest manifestations in evidence-based medicine (Walshe & Rundall, 2001). The logic of evidence-based medicine has since spread beyond acute medicine into allied health, social work and human services (Marston & Watts, 2003).

Why is evidence-based practice important?

How many plans have been adopted on the assumption that certain procedures would bring desirable results! How few have been tested to see how far the assumptions on which they are based have been verified! This is perhaps the most important job before the social work profession at the present time: to undertake the measurement of effectiveness of social treatment and the study of causes of success and failure.

(Claghorn, 1927, p. 181 as cited in Briggs & McBeath, 2009)

While calls for evidence-based action have been made for decades, it is only more recently that the push for implementing evidence-based practices and policies across a wide variety of fields including health care, criminal justice, education and management has been formally recognised in service agreements (Briggs & McBeath, 2009; Dopson et al., 2003) and has received greater emphasis as a key platform of policy development by governments (e.g., see Banks, 2009).

Primarily, the imperative for evidence-based practice is to ensure the best interventions are provided to improve outcomes for the client, and to safeguard against treatments or interventions that could cause harm (Bromfield & Arney, 2008; Kessler, Gira & Poertner, 2005; Lewig, Arney & Scott, 2006). Evidence-based practice can justify funding for the implementation and/or continuation of programs and initiatives; can inform quality improvement through efficiency and effectiveness; and ensures public money is expended upon interventions that we know work. The requirement for practical evidence of what works in policy environments and service delivery organisations in turn requires resources to be directed into research that meets these information needs (Davies, Nutley & Walter, 2005; Kessler, Gira & Poertner, 2005; Lewig, Arney & Scott, 2006; Walshe & Rundall, 2001). More recently, research has suggested that the implementation of evidence-based practices, with external support to retain fidelity to the original model, can potentially increase rates of staff retention when compared with implementation without such external support and also when compared with usual practice (Aarons et al., 2009).

When there is little or no knowledge of the efficacy or effectiveness of programs and practices designed to help vulnerable children and their families, there is a good likelihood that there will be *overuse* of ineffective interventions; *underuse* of effective interventions; and *misuse* of interventions especially when evidence of effectiveness is unclear or ambiguous (Walshe & Rundall, 2001). This can mean that interventions are unhelpful, or worse, harmful to children and families. This was evident in the field of 'infant health' when parents were advised, against available evidence from clinical research, to place babies on their stomachs to sleep, which contributed to Sudden Infant Death Syndrome (SIDS) (Gilbert et al., 2005). In the field of juvenile justice, as outlined below, there have also been examples of interventions that have been ineffective or harmful to participants.

Example: Scared Straight

The 'Scared Straight Program' was developed in the US in the 1970s, to deter juvenile offenders and at-risk children from future offending. The program was started by life serving inmates in a New Jersey prison and involved organised visits to the prison where participants were exposed to the more violent aspects of prison life in an effort to scare them away from a life of crime.

Following a television documentary about the program in 1979, in which a 94% success rate for the program was claimed, Scared Straight was rapidly replicated across the US. Since then Scared Straight type programs (that is programs that use deterrence as their underlying theory) have become a popular method of crime prevention in the US and to a lesser degree internationally. It has been argued that these programs are popular because they fit with common beliefs about 'getting tough on crime', they are inexpensive, and they provide a means for prisoners to contribute to society.

However, research conducted over the past two decades, including randomised control trials and a well publicised review of over 500 crime prevention evaluations undertaken by the University of Maryland in the 1990s, has shown these programs to be ineffective and in some cases harmful. Indeed, a recent systematic review of this research, undertaken by the Cochrane Collaboration in 2009 concluded that 'programmes like Scared Straight are likely to have a harmful effect and increase delinquency relative to doing nothing at all to the same youths. Given these results, agencies that permit such programmes must rigorously evaluate them not only to ensure that they are doing what they purport to do (prevent crime) – but at the very least they do not cause more harm than good' (Petrosino, Turpin-Petrosino & Buehler, 2009, p. 2).

Different approaches to practice

Chaffin and Friedrich (2004, p. 1101) have contrasted traditional (non-evidence-based) approaches to practice in child and family welfare with what an evidence-based approach would look like. Table 12.1 outlines the differences in these approaches. These are archetypes used to aid comparison of the two approaches, in reality there is likely to be varying degrees of both approaches evident in service delivery.

Table 12.1: Contrasting evidence-based practice with traditional practice

	Traditional practice	Evidence-based practice
Source of knowledge	Accumulated subjective experience with individual cases. Opinion about practice outcomes emphasised. 'In my experience…'	Well-designed, randomised trials and other controlled clinical research. Facts about practice outcomes emphasised. 'The data show that…'
Knowledge location and access	Hierarchical. Knowledge is possessed by opinion leaders and gurus. Charismatic, expert driven	Democratic. Knowledge is available to anyone willing to read the published scientific research or research reviews. Information technology driven
Method of achieving progress	Haphazard, fortuitous, based on changing values, fads, fashions and leaders	Systematic, predictable, based on incremental and cumulative programs of outcome research
Practitioner expertise	Quasi-mystical personal qualities and intuition	Specific, teachable, learnable skills and behaviours
View of practice	Art. Creative artistic process with fluid boundaries	Craftsmanship. Creativity within the boundaries of the supported models and protocols
Research→practice link	Indirect. Inferential	Direct. Integral and fundamental to practice
How is research summarised and applied to practice? ⌐	Individual subjective practitioner synthesis of whatever literature is consumed	Best practices work group or collaborative summary based on exhaustive reviews of the outcome research and meta-analysis
Program evaluation	Inputs (credentials of practitioners) and outputs (number of clients served, number of service units delivered)	Outcomes (measurable 'bottom-line' client benefits)

(Cont.)

Table 12.1: (*Cont.*)

	Traditional practice	Evidence-based practice
Location of research	Mostly in laboratory settings and divorced from actual practice	Field clients routinely enrolled in trials in order to test benefits and refine services
Quality control	Focuses on how well service rationales are conceptualised and the credentials of who provides them	Focuses on how well services are behaviourally delivered vis-à-vis a descriptive protocol
Practice visibility	Actual practice is seldom observed by anyone other than the practitioner and the client	Direct peer or consultant observation of actual practice, and specific feedback is common
Assumptions about outcomes	Faith. Service programs in general are seen as good and are assumed to be beneficial	Scepticism. Knowledge that interventions may be inert or even harmful. Benefit must be empirically demonstrated, not assumed

While there are sound reasons for using research to inform practice and policy, it is important not to presume research is intrinsically good, when research can be poor quality, costly, mistaken in its conclusions or implications, and used to justify rather than inform a decision or action (Gough, 2004). In order to balance the potential positives and negatives of research, it is important that researchers and research users are clear about the purpose of research, the quality and robustness of its findings, and whom or what a particular research project serves (Gough & Elbourne, 2002).

Reflective questions

Looking at Table 12.1 above, where would you say your practice lies – in the domain of traditional practice, or of evidence-based practice, or is it somewhere in between? Why? What would be some of the difficulties and possible disadvantages of taking an evidence-based approach to practice in your field? What would be some of the benefits of such an approach?

'Evidence-informed' practice in child and family welfare

If evidence-based practice is seen to be effective for children, families, staff and organisations, why is it not done to a large extent? For example, it has been estimated that in the US between 80–90% of child-serving systems do not use evidence-based interventions, and if they are implemented, they are often quickly adapted or changed, which may result in the program or intervention losing the key ingredients that were critical to its effectiveness (Forman et al., 2009; Palinkas et al., and see Chapter 13). As mentioned in Chapter 1, evidence-based practice and policy presents certain challenges to the field of child and family services, and for the following reasons it may be more useful to refer to 'evidence-informed' rather than 'evidence-based' policy and practice in this sector. One of the major challenges is that the vulnerable families who are at risk of child abuse and neglect have very complex needs (e.g., drug and alcohol misuse, mental health problems, domestic violence, poverty). There are ethical and practical reasons why certain methodologies such as randomised control trials cannot always be employed with these families. Moreover, the complexity of cases and the multiple pathways to child abuse and neglect make it difficult to examine causal relationships, and predictive models only account for a small proportion of the variance. On the other hand, the complex nature of child and family welfare offers the opportunity to develop and/or implement a range of methodologies to examine research questions and to be creative in the development of such questions. For example, by examining families at risk but in which child abuse and neglect is not an issue, we can examine factors associated with resilience that can then be used to guide interventions with those families experiencing child abuse and neglect (Bromfield & Arney, 2008).

The complexity of the challenges confronting at-risk families often means that it is necessary to aggregate and conduct research across multiple disciplines. This provides the opportunity for collaboration across research questions to gain multiple perspectives and to provide messages for practice that can transcend traditional research and sectoral boundaries.

For these reasons the knowledge base in child and family welfare, and child protection in particular, may be less established than in other human service sectors (e.g., health and education). As described earlier in this chapter, there is a strong need for research in this field to be coordinated (e.g., under the *National Framework for Protecting Australia's Children*) and for those who believe they have examples of effective practice to rigorously evaluate and widely disseminate such practice and programs (also see Chapter 13 for more detail).

A further challenge to evidence-based practice is the need for evidence to compete with other information sources (e.g., practice wisdom, emulating similar systems, use of expert advice and professional guidelines), making it hard to define 'best practice' in the complex decision-making environment of child and family services (Gira, Kessler & Poertner, 2004; Kessler, Gira & Poertner, 2005, p. 245). See *Multidimensional Evidence-Based Practice*, edited by Christopher Petr (2009), for ways to reconcile complementary and conflicting sources of information for evidence-based practice that incorporates knowledge, research and values.

It is important to recognise that research and researchers are not always the most powerful voice competing for attention in the policy and practice decision-making arenas, and nor should they necessarily be. It can also be difficult to disentangle the implications of research findings for policy and practice when they are complex, unclear or when they conflict with other sources of information. *Lies, Damned Lies and Science* by Sherry Seethaler (2009) is a useful resource for people trying to interpret and critically appraise research findings in highly politicised contexts.

Moreover, it has been argued that the experiential rather than empirical-based culture within the social services has led to a greater emphasis on decision making based on practice experience rather than research evidence (Barratt, 2003). In some areas of health there have been recent critiques of evidence-based practice and the assumption that 'knowledge transfer' from research to professional practice is a one-way process (Fowler & Lee, 2007). Practice experience and research evidence have the potential to inform each other, with insights from practice being a rich source of hypotheses and propositions that might be tested in research (Scott, 2001; 2002). Again, these challenges also present opportunities. For example, research questions may be less constrained by a particular view of evidence, and may also be of greater relevance to practitioners when they arise from, or are informed by, practice wisdom. Research-informed practitioners and practice-informed researchers have much to offer each other. For more information on the practitioner–researcher you may like to read 'The Practice Sensitive Researcher' by Scott in *Professional Practice in Health, Education and the Creative Arts* (2001), Joy Higgs and Angie Titchen (eds). Also more recently, interactive models with researchers and practitioners co-producing evidence-based practice have been proposed in which the 'global' research knowledge is adapted to fit the local context using practitioner and client wisdom for a more applied approach (see Brocklehurst & Liabo, 2004; Palinkas et al., 2009 for more details).

Given the vast number of research publications, in peer-reviewed journals and 'grey literature' (e.g., sources of information such as scientific and technical reports, theses, government publications, conference papers that are distributed outside of the normal channels of publication), systems have been developed to construct hierarchies of evidence to inform policy and practice (Leigh, 2009). Shonkoff (2000) has suggested that one step towards building agreement around what constitutes evidence is to use a simple taxonomy to refer to knowledge. This taxonomy includes three categories: *established knowledge* (defined by the scientific community and governed by strict criteria for evidence); *reasonable hypotheses* (generated by researchers, practitioners or policy makers, these are assertions informed by established knowledge (i.e., theory and research); and *unwarranted assertions* (generated by anyone, these are assertions that are not linked to established knowledge, or are distortions of it, and do not guide responsible policy making or service delivery).

Reflective questions

What are your thoughts on Shonkoff's taxonomy of knowledge? Do you agree with the distinctions he makes? Why or why not? What steps might you take to check you are making reasonable hypotheses versus unwarranted assertions?

The idea of three cultures

Shonkoff (2000), among other authors, has sought to explain the use and non-use of research with reference to the cultural differences that exist between the research, practice and policy communities. Specifically the three communities are conceptualised as three separate cultures, defined by unique characteristics (see Figure 12.1) yet sharing similar goals. These

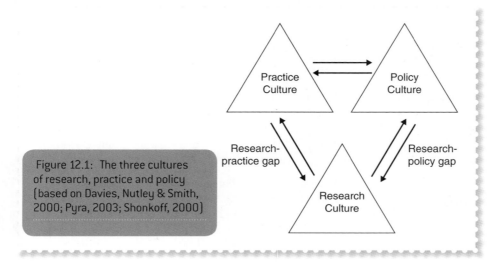

Figure 12.1: The three cultures of research, practice and policy (based on Davies, Nutley & Smith, 2000; Pyra, 2003; Shonkoff, 2000)

cultural characteristics create 'gaps' which then act as barriers to using research evidence to inform practice interventions and policy decisions that could more effectively benefit children and families. It is hypothesised that research is unlikely to be used in a significant way unless people from the different communities of research, policy and practice are able to establish on-going communication with each other.

The policy, practice and research cultures differ with respect to: time frames; communication styles; priorities; and work environments (see Table 12.2). For example, practitioners usually have short time frames as they need to work in the 'here and now' with their clients, and at times, decision making needs to take place immediately. Policy makers who are developing strategies in response to areas of need, work in an environment with short-to-medium time frames. In contrast, researchers may have more lengthy time frames in developing, undertaking and analysing research information. The Three Cultures Model does not suggest that any one culture has precedence, rather the players in the research, policy and practice communities bring different types of knowledge to bear in their respective areas (Head, 2008). The model suggests that a greater awareness of the characteristics of the different cultures, and a sense that all players are working together with the same goal in mind (e.g., the promotion of child safety and well-being), will help facilitate communication and the flow of knowledge between cultures.

Table 12.2: **Differences between policy, practice and research cultures** (Davies, Nutley & Smith, 2000; Pyra, 2003; Shonkoff, 2000)

Cultural factors	Practice	Policy	Research
Time frames for results	Usually short	Usually short or medium	Usually long
Languages for communication	Guidelines and protocols	Issue briefs, government reports, media	Highly technical, expert language
Priorities for knowledge	Efficiency and effectiveness	Feasibility, implementation	Theory, methodology, scientifically answerable questions
Work environments	Immediacy of service delivery	Multiple decision makers, political, economic and social forces	Research rigour, pressure to publish, academic reputation

Consistent with the Three Cultures Model, Palinkas and colleagues (2009) have identified the following as important to the cultural exchange process between research and practice in their examination of efforts to embed evidence-based practice in a range of settings:

- Possession of similar goals (e.g., the well-being of the child versus protection of 'turf' or academic advancement)
- A sense of teamwork and shared control in the evidence-based practice implementation (e.g., scheduling, training, monitoring of performance, adaptation to suit the needs of specific groups of clients)
- Perceived reciprocity (i.e., do we both get something desirable out of the interaction?)
- Frequency of communication with one another (Palinkas et al., 2009, p. 9).

The Three Cultures Model is very useful in highlighting the different pressures and professional imperatives of research, policy and practice. More recently, the Three Cultures perspective has been augmented (including by the authors of this chapter) with additional information about wider influences on the use of evidence in policy and practice, which acknowledges the alternate sources of information and different pressures that influence decision making. This is especially important in fields such as child and family welfare where contextual influences (such as the law, community values, and the social and political context) play a very significant role.

What helps and what hinders the use of research?

The literature investigating the use of research by practitioners and policy makers, derived in most part from the field of health, has identified many factors (barriers and facilitators) that influence research use. The most significant of these factors concern the individual practitioner/policy maker, the environmental context (the characteristics of the organisation, system, political and economic climate), the nature of the research evidence and methods of communicating research findings (dissemination).

The literature shows that some individuals are more receptive to research use than others, and policy makers in particular often need to consider competing influences such as the political and social context, the views of interested stakeholders and the institutional arrangements for policy making. The capacity of an organisation to implement and sustain change will also influence the extent to which research use is taken up by its employees.

While little attention has been given to the clients of services as research users, they are ultimately the most important stakeholders, as they stand to gain and lose most as a result of effective and ineffective services (an example of a research to consumer initiative is the Australian Government's 'Raising Children Network: The Australian Parenting website': http://raisingchildren. net.au). There may be factors other than effectiveness that are of importance to children and families including the cultural acceptability of interventions and the stigma that may be associated with receiving some services. That is why, as discussed in the previous chapters describing promising innovations, the views of clients are important to consider when implementing evidence-based interventions.

A study of research use by Australian child and family welfare professionals

In 2007, the Australian Centre for Child Protection at the University of South Australia and the National Child Protection Clearinghouse at the Australian Institute of Family Studies undertook a research project that aimed to understand how child and family welfare professionals use research. As described above, many factors influence the use of research in a range of fields and this study aimed to identify which of these factors were and were not relevant in the field of child and family welfare. The study comprised telephone interviews with 59 professionals (28 child protection practitioners, 13 child protection policy makers, and 18 'other' professionals in the child welfare field including non-statutory child and family welfare professionals who were working primarily in non-government organisations) (Holzer et al., 2008).

Child and family welfare professionals who participated in this study identified various factors, many of which were similar to those identified in the broader health and social science literature, which helped or hindered their use of research. These included: resources; external influences; support for research use within their organisations; workload; individual factors; the need to consider other sources of information; and opportunities to talk with researchers or undertake research projects, each of which are discussed in greater detail below. Not surprisingly, the relevance and presentation of research findings also played an important role in the use of research, and will be discussed in more detail later in this chapter.

The findings from this research, together with a review of the literature on research utilisation were used to expand the Three Cultures Model. The resulting 'Cultures in Context Model' (Figure 12.2) attempts to draw together: (a) research regarding the barriers and facilitators of research use and (b) the theories within the three cultures perspective in order to clearly articulate the context in which policy and practice decisions are made and the alternate influences and imperatives against which research competes.

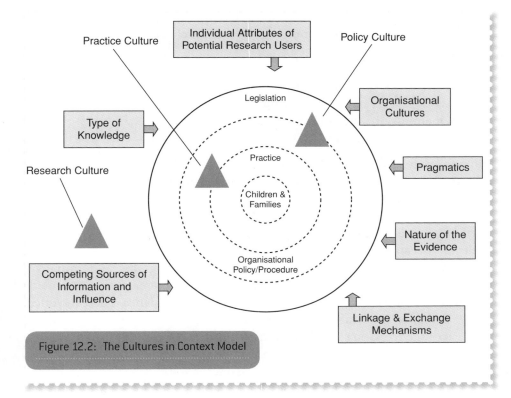

Figure 12.2: The Cultures in Context Model

The model shows the proximal and distal influences on children and families of different types of knowledge in the child and family welfare system by placing the key actors and settings within concentric circles, situating children and families at the centre, and then moving outwards to include practice (service provision), policy and legislation. The Cultures in Context Model places the three cultures of research, policy and practice within the wider socio-political context, and represents empirical research as just one source of knowledge to be considered together with knowledge from other sources including practitioners, the policy community, the organisation and the service users (Arney et al., 2009, p. 180–1; Petr, 2009).

Each of the contextual influences on research use in policy and practice presented in the model are described below, along with pertinent research findings from the study described in Holzer et al. (2008).

Organisational culture or climate

The culture or climate of an organisation is often defined as the norms, values and rituals present in the workplace. These features essentially establish 'the way things are done' in a given workplace (Hemmelgarn, Glisson & James, 2006). In relation to research use, norms, values and rituals are thought to be influential in providing circumstances that are, or are not, conducive to accessing and applying research, such as:

- Clarity of mission and goals
- Leadership
- Staff cohesiveness and autonomy
- Work-related stress and burnout
- Openness of communication, and
- Openness to change.

In our study, the formal recognition of research use as a priority within an organisation was seen as an important facilitator of research use. For example, professionals emphasised the importance of their workplace endorsing research-related activities and making the value of research apparent by offering research-based student placements; seeking partnerships with other relevant organisations; and providing appropriate training.

Professionals provided examples of different programs and initiatives designed to raise staff awareness of the importance of research and to provide information and advice based on the latest research evidence. These included:

- Research publications and resources including electronic 'Research to Practice Updates', 'Research to Practice Notes', 'Research Papers', 'Seminar Notes', and 'Research Guidelines'
- Seminars/workshops on specific issues for staff
- Two-way forums/practice sessions enabling staff to identify research needs and assist in the development of evidence-based resources, and
- A Research to Practice network made up of credible and enthusiastic staff who act as catalysts for promoting the use of research in policy and practice.

Professionals were more readily able to access and apply research where colleagues, supervisors and managers supported the use of research. This type of support was one of the most frequently identified facilitators to the use of research. On the other hand, research use was hampered when it was not supported and endorsed by the wider organisation, managers, supervisors or colleagues (e.g., where learning and career development plans did not have time allocated to knowledge development including research use).

Pragmatics

The term 'pragmatics' describes those factors unlikely to change in the short to medium term and over which practitioners, policy makers, and – to some extent – even their respective organisations have little influence. Pragmatic factors include:

- The economic and political climate
- Community attitudes and mass media

- The status of an organisation (e.g., whether statutory or non-government/charitable organisation)
- Decision-making processes (centralised, decentralised, hybrid)
- Organisational and systems capacity
- Resources
- Work role
- Time frames, and
- Funding.

Participants in the research reported that having access to the internet, email facilities, departmental libraries and research services were important factors aiding research use. On the other hand, a lack of access to these facilities, especially the internet, was seen as a major barrier to research use. Staff shortages were also reported as having an adverse impact on research use, primarily because this reduced the amount of time employees had to read research and apply it. Having a lack of time to access and apply research due to day-to-day demands of the job, large case loads, competing priorities within cases and staff shortages emerged as one of the greatest barriers to research use for professionals in the study. Conversely, research use was facilitated where workloads were more 'manageable' and where there was time for reflection and consultation.

Professionals from non-government and not-for-profit organisations reported that an inability to afford journal subscriptions or to obtain funds to attend conferences, workshops and training sessions also hindered their access to research. Time release to attend conferences, workshops and training sessions was a particular concern for rural workers.

Nature and extent of the evidence

The term 'nature and extent of the evidence' refers to the extent to which there is a high quality and robust research base to inform any single area of policy or practice and the qualities and characteristics of research that promote its dissemination and use (e.g., the ease with which it can be readily understood, and its practical application or relevance to the user). Reviews and systematic audits of the Australian child abuse prevention, child protection and out-of-home care research base have concluded that there was a shortage of Australian research to inform sound policy and practice. Further that, while the quality of the research was largely good, there was an over-reliance on qualitative techniques such that there was an evidence base rich in detail, but with limited capacity to be generalised (Bromfield & Arney, 2008).

Where evidence is available, the nature or characteristics of the research and the way in which it is presented and disseminated impact on whether it is used in policy and practice. Characteristics include, for example:

- Ease of understanding
- Relevance
- Complexity
- Relative advantage over another policy or practice
- Effectiveness
- Efficiency
- Practicality, and
- Being non-controversial or equivocal.

The content of research findings and how they are communicated can strongly influence whether they will be used. Because practitioners have heavy work-loads and tight time lines, and because the volume of research is ever expanding, professionals must be selective in the research that they seek to help them in their decision making. The types of research particularly useful to child and family welfare professionals in the study included comprehensive literature reviews, secondary analyses of research specific to particular practice topics, and articles that provide a critical analysis of relevant issues.

Overwhelmingly, participants were more likely to see research as useful when it had a potential practical application, such as:

- Offering solutions that could be easily implemented into practice
- Providing a framework or foundation from which to work
- Improving understanding of practice and policy issues, or
- Validating or affirming current practice.

Research conducted in the culture and context in which service delivery occurred (e.g., Australian versus international research) was preferred. Large sample sizes and longitudinal studies were also seen as contributing to the value and significance of a particular research project. On the other hand, research that was dated, too theoretical, or employed a poor or inappropriate methodology was likely to be overlooked by practitioners and policy makers.

Research also needs to be clearly written, easy to understand and have a practical application. Factors identified by the professionals in our study that make research easy to understand and thereby increase the likelihood of research being used are shown in Box 12.1.

Box 12.1: Characteristics of research reports relevant to child and family welfare that make them easier to understand

- Use plain English and provide definitions
- Have informative abstracts or research summaries
- Have a logical format (e.g., historical overview, research evidence, arguments, critical review, overall conclusions, questions to be considered, practice implications)

- Have a good summary of the rationale and make the context clear
- Have clear research aims that are stated up front
- Avoid unnecessary detail
- Place less emphasis on background theory and details of analysis
- Don't try to answer too many questions
- Have a clear methodology
- Don't overemphasise statistics
- Present data in charts, graphs and tables
- Use case studies and examples to illustrate findings and important points
- Compare their findings with other studies
- Place emphasis on outcomes and implications for practice and policy
- Clearly explain the limitations of the study

Conferences and workshops are another way in which research is disseminated. Professionals in our study described a number of features of a conference or workshop that they had attended that made the conference or workshop stand out for them. These features are shown in Box 12.2.

Box 12.2: Characteristics of conferences or workshops that are seen as more useful to child and family welfare practitioners

- Have practical application
- Use practical examples
- Provide materials, handouts, information packages to take back to the workplace
- Present up to date/cutting edge research
- Include local content
- Enable 'hands on' involvement/active participation
- Include international speakers and a range of expert presenters
- Present a range of viewpoints
- Provide opportunities to network
- Have presentations that are polished, clear, succinct, relevant and use visual aids
- Are held in appropriate venues (small preferred)

Linkage and exchange mechanisms

The term 'linkage and exchange' was coined by Jonathan Lomas (2000) to refer to partnerships between researchers and policy makers. The 'Cultures in

Context Model' uses the term 'linkage and exchange mechanisms' to describe the ways in which researchers and research users might come into contact with one another. These mechanisms are believed to facilitate research use, for example through:

- Shared networks
- Opportunities for practitioners and policy makers to be involved over the life course of a research project, and
- The use of 'knowledge brokers'.

Opportunities to liaise with researchers/experts, including partnerships with universities belonging to relevant networks and associations, and forming relationships with research bodies, were seen as important facilitators to research use by the participants in the study. Support and funding to establish local research (e.g., research conducted in the workplace or region in which the respondents were working) were seen as an important facilitator of research use – especially to applying research findings to practice. On the other hand, funding bodies that did not give opportunities to staff to update their skills and knowledge, and issues concerning control and dissemination of research within organisations, were viewed as barriers to research use. The political context in which child protection is delivered, public opinion, and a lack of recognition of research by the courts were also identified as barriers to research use.

Competing sources of information and influence

The term 'competing sources of information and influence' refers to the various avenues (e.g., researchers, lobby groups, and the media) through which professionals in the child and family welfare sector access information – intentionally or otherwise – regarding the provision of services to children and families. Informants may include:

- Researchers
- Lobby groups
- Media
- Networks, and
- Service users.

The need to consider other sources of information (e.g., media, interest and lobby groups, formalised procedures) apart from research findings was the most frequently endorsed barrier to the use of research in the study.

Individual factors

Individual factors refer to a person's own values, beliefs and assumptions. In relation to the work of child and family welfare, people typically possess different views as to the value of empirical evidence compared to 'hands-on' practice knowledge and experience. Individual factors that may impact on research include:

- Mistrust of research findings
- Lack of motivation to use research
- Lack of knowledge and skills to evaluate or assimilate research, and
- Research that contradicts existing experience, knowledge, values, beliefs and interests.

Participants in the study spoke of previous work experience involving research and a personal commitment to research (e.g., preparedness to seek out and read research in one's own time, and a desire to maintain professional networks that facilitate research awareness) as individual attributes facilitating research use. Individual factors that were viewed as barriers to research use included past unsatisfactory research experiences (e.g., while studying); lack of knowledge or experience in accessing and using research; and a lack of trust and/or interest in research (e.g., preferring to stick with familiar approaches).

Reflective questions

With the Cultures in Context Model in mind, which of the factors do you think might influence your ability to use research in a particular organisational context? What could be changed to increase your opportunities to access and apply research in this setting? Can you think of any other factors that might be important in helping you translate research into action?

Applying the Cultures in Context Model

The model demonstrates that each of the players in the three cultures perspective have different opportunities, roles and responsibilities in translating research into action (even though some of the factors at play in the model might influence all of the players). While researchers can make efforts to enhance the likelihood of their research being used (e.g., by presenting their research in the ways described in Boxes 12.1 and 12.2, and by involving research users in the research process), they are just one source of information that is considered for policy and practice.

Policy makers and practitioners ultimately determine whether the benefits of research-informed policy and practice are passed on to families – practitioners by the decisions they make at the 'coal face' of practice, and policy makers by whether or not they consult evidence in developing new policies and programs that are then put into practice. (Although not discussed in this chapter, the gap between policy and practice also influences the extent to which research-informed policy is translated into practice – see Fixsen et al. (2005) for a review of implementation science examining this point.) In this section, we discuss how researchers, research disseminators, policy makers and practitioners in government and service delivery agencies need to work in partnership across the child welfare sector to succeed in getting research in practice.

No one agency can address all of the factors identified in the Cultures in Context Model that influence research use. Each organisation or individual needs to address those areas within the Cultures in Context Model over which they have control (e.g., researchers can enhance the nature of the evidence) and to promote and encourage others to address those areas over which they have control (e.g., researchers can work with service delivery agencies to assist and encourage them to create a 'research ready' organisational culture). The following is an excerpt of a paper by Arney et al. (2009) in which the authors explore the role and opportunities for academics, research disseminators and service delivery organisations to enhance evidence-informed policy and practice profiling five different Australian-based organisations.[1]

The National Child Protection and the Australian Domestic and Family Violence Clearinghouses

The Australian Institute of Family Studies' National Child Protection Clearinghouse[2] is a research, information and advisory body for child abuse prevention, child protection and out-of-home care. Similarly, the Australian Domestic and Family Violence Clearinghouse is a national organisation, providing high quality information about domestic and family violence issues and practice. Both clearinghouses are funded by the Australian Government, Department of Families, Housing, Community Services and Indigenous Affairs.

In terms of the Cultures in Context Model (Figure 12.2), clearinghouses are a conduit for information from researchers. Primarily the type of knowledge that is disseminated through clearinghouses is research, although policy knowledge (e.g., national comparison of child protection systems) and organisational/

---

1 Representatives from the five organisations profiled attended a 2008 UK-based workshop entitled 'Beyond the Rhetoric: International Perspectives on Evidence-Informed Practice' hosted by Research In Practice and Research In Practice for Adults. The aim of the workshop was to extend the knowledge, skills, and learning of 'knowledge brokers' from around the world.

2 The National Child Protection Clearinghouse is one of five clearinghouses based at the Australian Institute of Family Studies. Other clearinghouses at the institute include the Australian Centre for the Study of Sexual Assault, the Communities and Families Clearinghouse Australia, the Australian Family Relationships Clearinghouse and Closing the Gap: The Indigenous Clearinghouse (operated by the Australian Institute of Family Studies in partnership with the Australian Institute of Health and Welfare).

practice knowledge (e.g., 'Domestic and Family Violence Clearinghouse Good Practice' database) may also be collated and disseminated.

The clearinghouses provide resources and supports for policy makers and practitioners in government agencies, and in specialist and generalist services, and for other stakeholders including researchers, advocates and activists. The clearinghouses aim to prevent child maltreatment, and domestic and family violence, and to enhance quality service provision through:

- Publications: issues papers, topic papers, research and practice briefs, resource sheets, stakeholder papers, newsletters, occasional research reports and papers for external publications including other newsletters and academic journals
- Research and information repositories: library repository, database and online catalogue (Child Protection Clearinghouse), research, good practice, and resource databases (Domestic and Family Violence Clearinghouse)
- Oral dissemination: conference papers, workshops, seminars, teaching, a phone-based research 'help desk', and podcasts of various forums
- News and current events: newsletters, 'What's new' web page, *childprotect* email discussion list
- Websites: all clearinghouse resources and links to other useful information and advice are provided on the websites (Child Protection Clearinghouse www.aifs.gov.au/nch/; Domestic and Family Violence Clearinghouse www.austdvclearinghouse.unsw.edu.au/); and
- Research: the clearinghouses also undertake new research (self-initiated and commissioned).

Strategies that are used to enhance the accessibility of research (the nature of the evidence) include providing shorter papers that are written in plain, jargon-free language, are relevant to policy and practice, using case studies and examples, clearly highlighting key messages and identifing the implications of findings for policy makers and practitioners.

Recent evaluations have shown that the clearinghouses have been successful in facilitating *access* to research. The *Australian Institute of Family Studies 2006–07 Annual Report* (2007) showed that the National Child Protection Clearinghouse website was well used during the year with 1 532 373 hits and 767 735 downloads (including 287 265 downloads of clearinghouse publications). The Australian Domestic and Family Violence Clearinghouse reports an average of 22 000 unique users of their website each quarter (Edwards, 2004). Independent evaluations of both clearinghouses indicated a high level of uptake by a range of stakeholders, including instances in which the clearinghouses had a direct influence on policy or practice (Edwards, 2004; Delfabbro & Borgas, 2007).

A further key strategy for clearinghouses are linkage and exchange mechanisms targeted primarily through oral dissemination strategies and sector events and by pursuing opportunities for collaboration. Clearinghouses must also attend, to – and where possible take advantage of – organisational culture/climate and pragmatic factors: for example, the political climate and personal interests of decision makers.

The Australian Centre for Child Protection and the Alfred Felton Chair in Child and Family Welfare

The Australian Centre for Child Protection is funded by the Department of Innovation, Industry, Science and Research, and is based at the University of South Australia. Established in 2005 and with approximately 20 staff and PhD students, the centre's purpose is to enhance the lives of children by providing policy makers and practitioners with evidence-informed professional education initiatives and consultation. It aims to add to the evidence base around three key areas: the use of research in policy and practice; the evaluation and diffusion of promising practices in child and family services; and ways of working with disadvantaged children and their families, including Aboriginal and Torres Strait Islander children and families from refugee backgrounds. The Alfred Felton Chair in Child and Family Welfare is a research chair based at the University of Melbourne and is a joint initiative of the university and the Centre for Excellence in Child and Family Welfare (the peak body of child welfare non-government organisations in Victoria). The chair undertakes policy and practice-relevant research to ensure that projects are embedded in the needs of the sector, and includes a knowledge brokerage component to actively create links and disseminate information to the sector, as required.

Regarding the Cultures in Context Model, the work of the Australian Centre for Child Protection and the Alfred Felton Chair focus research-to-practice initiatives in two key domains: linkage and exchange mechanisms; and types of knowledge.

Key linkage and exchange mechanisms employed by the two organisations include knowledge brokers who provide policy makers, practitioners and other researchers with evidence to inform policy and practice. This includes: providing advice on policy development; reviewing child protection legislation in a range of jurisdictions; acting as advocates for children (e.g., as members of ministerial advisory bodies); giving a large number of keynote presentations at national and international conferences; consultancies and evidence-informed training for service organisations; community education through media comment; and board memberships of organisations involved in the delivery of services to children and families.

Staff from the Australian Centre for Child Protection and the Alfred Felton Chair in Child and Family Welfare are also key members of a range of networks across Australia, including the Australian Research Alliance for Children and Youth, which focus on bringing together researchers, policy makers and practitioners (and, at times, service recipients) to set research agendas, identify research questions and design and implement research projects. Opportunities for linkage and exchange are also provided by engaging policy makers and practitioners in all stages of collaborative research projects, including agenda setting, research design, data collection, analysis and dissemination. This includes situating research staff in service delivery organisations (e.g. health and child protection) and hosting policy makers and practitioners within the research organisations as partners in the research process.

Recognising that research is only one type of knowledge that influences practice, it is important to view it as a complementary form of knowledge rather than as a 'competitor'. For example, the Australian Centre for Child Protection and the Alfred Felton Chair aim to embed research in practitioner knowledge through informing undergraduate and postgraduate training and workforce development. By the same token, they aim to inform their research using practice wisdom in setting the research agenda, identifying the theoretical models to be examined and involving practitioners (and their clients) as informants in the research and as researchers themselves.

The Benevolent Society

The Benevolent Society is a New South Wales and Queensland based non-profit organisation comprising 1700 staff and volunteers and offering services to families and communities across the lifespan. The society's purpose is 'to create caring and inclusive communities and a just society' (www.bensoc.org.au) and it is involved in several promising evidence-into-practice strategies that directly address organisational culture and pragmatic barriers to research use.

Rather than seeing themselves as passive recipients of research evidence, services are striving to become 'learning organisations' (Argyris & Schon, 1996), which has meant rethinking traditional approaches to knowledge. This shift does not come easily and requires resources and organisational changes, which are only just starting to be understood. For example, the Benevolent Society is making efforts to create a receptive organisational *culture*, with the right *leadership* and a clear *strategy* to implement the evidence. The senior team members, including the CEO, are involved in knowledge brokering activities (e.g., challenging the traditional boundaries between sectors) and act as champions of evidence-into-practice, for example by lobbying externally to try and build evidence-in-practice and evaluation into service-funding models.

In addition, a staged approach to practice change has been identified that involves *access* to evidence, *engagement* with the knowledge and putting the evidence into *use*. For example, staff took part in a workshop facilitated by staff from the Parenting Research Centre[3] on evidence-based parenting programs (*access*), key staff were then involved in selecting the 'Incredible Years' as the program they perceived as most likely to lead to positive child outcomes (*engagement*). 'Incredible Years' facilitators then ran workshops for practitioners who are now in the process of being accredited to provide the program (*use*). The Benevolent Society has striven to create a learning culture, and the recent results of a large employee climate survey provide promising evidence that a learning culture is developing.

With so many competing demands on practitioners, there is a need for dedicated research or professional development time and resources to be allocated to practitioners to enable them to overcome pragmatic constraints on the use of evidence. The Benevolent Society has attempted to communicate clear messages that evidence-in-practice is central to purpose and organisational strategy, and has sought to embed these messages through practical mechanisms such as work plans, supervision sessions, team meetings and performance reviews.

Activities

Investigate some of the websites and resources described below – maybe you have already heard of some of them. Find out how they are trying to enhance the use of research in practice. Write down what you think about these strategies. Describe what appeals to you and what you think could be done differently. Share some of the strategies you find most useful with your colleagues.

Conclusion

Practice and policy efforts need to be informed by research that details what works for whom, when and in what context. While we work to build this evidence base, increasing efforts are being made to translate what is currently known into effective practice with children, young people and their families. This chapter outlined some of the barriers to research translation, and presented strategies that individuals and agencies can use to help them implement evidence-informed practice. In summary, the translation of research into action is highly achievable in settings where: research summaries are widely available and accessible; time and resources are available to

---

3 The Parenting Research Centre engages in a range of research activities to help parents raise children well and to translate their research into practical strategies, programs and solutions (www.parentingrc.org.au)

practitioners to apply research; organisations explicitly aim to use research to inform policy and practice; and frequent opportunities are available for practitioners and policy makers to engage with research and researchers.

Useful websites

Australian Research Alliance for Children and Youth (ARACY): www.aracy.org.au

Building Capacity in Evaluating Outcomes – Program Development and Evaluation, University of Wisconsin – Extension: www.uwex.edu/ces/pdande/evaluation/bceo/index.html

The Campbell Collaboration: www.campbellcollaboration.org

The Cochrane Collaboration: www.cochrane.org

Nutley, S., Davis, H. and Walter, I (2002). Conceptual synthesis 1: Learning from the Diffusion of Innovations: www.ruru.ac.uk/PDFs/Learning%20from%20the%20Diffusion%20of%20Innovations.pdf

Research Unit for Research Utilisation: www.ruru.ac.uk/

What Works for Children?: www.whatworksforchildren.org.uk/

References

Aarons, G. A., Sommerfield, D. H., Hecht, D. B., Silovsky, J. F. & Chaffin, M. J. (2009). The impact of evidence-based practice implementation and fidelity monitoring on staff turnover: Evidence for a protective effect. *Journal of Consulting and Clinical Psychology*, 77 (2), 270–80.

Argyris, C. & Schon, D. (1996) *Organisational Learning II: Theory, Method and Practice*. Addison-Wesley, Reading, MA.

Arney, F., Bromfield, L., Lewig, K. & Holzer, P. (2009). Integrating strategies for delivering evidence-informed practice. *Evidence & Policy*, 5 (2), 179–91.

Australian Institute of Family Studies (2007). *Australian Institute of Family Studies Annual Report 2006–2007*. Australian Institute of Family Studies, Melbourne.

Banks, G. (2009). 'Evidence-based policy-making: What is it? How do we get it?' Paper presented at the ANZSOG/ANU Public Lecture Series 2009, Canberra, 4 February.

Barratt, M. (2003). Organizational support for evidence-based practice within child and family social work: A collaborative study. *Child & Family Social Work*, 8 (2), 143–50.

Briggs, H. & McBeath, B. (2009) Evidence-based management: Origins, challenges, and implications for social service administration. *Administration in Social Work*, 33, 242–61.

Brocklehurst, N. & Liabo, K. (2004). Evidence nuggets: Promoting evidence-based practice. *Community Practitioner*, 77 (10), 371–5.

Bromfield, L. & Arney, F. (2008). Developing a road map for research: Identifying the priorities for a national child protection research agenda. *Australian Institute of Family Studies, Issues Paper No 28*. Australian Institute of Family Studies, Melbourne.

Chaffin, M. & Friedrich, B. (2004). Evidence-based treatments in child abuse and neglect. *Children and Youth Services Review*, 26 (11), 1097–113.

Commonwealth of Australia (2009). *Protecting Children is Everyone's Business: National Framework for Protecting Australia's Children, 2009–2020*. Commonwealth of Australia, Canberra.

Davies, H., Nutley, S. & Smith, P. (2000). Introducing evidence-based policy and practice in public services. In H. T. O. Davies, S. M. Nutley & P. C. Smith (eds), *Evidence-Based Policy and Practice in Public Services*. The Policy Press, University of Bristol, UK.

Davies, H., Nutley, S. & Walter, I. (2005). 'Assessing the impact of social science research: Conceptual, methodological and practical issues. A background discussion paper for ESRC symposium on Assessing Non-academic Impact of Research'. Research Unit for Research Utilisation, School of Management, University of St Andrews, St Andrews, UK.

Delfabbro, P.H. and Borgas, M. (2007) *National Child Protection Clearinghouse: Evaluation Report*, Australian Institute of Family Studies, Melbourne.

Dopson, S., Locock, L., Gabbay, J., Ferlie, E. & Fitzgerald, L. (2003). Evidence-based medicine and the implementation gap. *Health*, 7 (3), 311–30.

Edwards, R. (2004) *Staying Home Leaving Violence: Promoting Choices for Women Leaving Abusive Partners*. Australian Domestic and Family Violence Clearinghouse, Sydney.

Fixsen, D. L., Naoom, S. F., Blase, K. A., Friedman, R. M. & Wallace, F. (2005). *Implementation Research: A Synthesis of the Literature*. University of South Florida, Louis de la Parte Florida Mental Health Institute, The National Implementation Research Network (FMHI Publication #231), Tampa, FL.

Forman, S. G., Olin, S. S., Hoagwood, K. E., Crowe, M. & Saka, N. (2009). Evidence-based interventions in schools: Developers' views of implementation barriers and facilitators. *School Mental Health*, 1, 26–36.

Fowler, C. & Lee, A. (2007). Knowing how to know: Questioning 'knowledge transfer' as a model for knowing and learning in health. *Studies in Continuing Education*, 29 (2), 181–93.

Gilbert, R., Salanti, G., Harden, M. & See, S. (2005). Infant sleeping position and the sudden infant death syndrome: Systematic review of observational studies and historical review of recommendations from 1940 to 2002. *International Journal of Epidemiology*, 34 (4), 874–87.

Gira, E. C., Kessler, M. L. & Poertner, J. (2004). Influencing social workers to use research evidence in practice: Lessons from medicine and the allied health professions. *Research on Social Work Practice*, 14 (2), 68–79.

Gough, D. (2004). Research for practice in child neglect. In J. D. B. Taylor (ed.), *Neglect: Practice Issues for Health and Social Care*, 43–56. Jessica Kingsley, London.

Gough, D. & Elbourne, D. (2002). Systematic research synthesis to inform policy, practice and democratic debate. *Social Policy and Society*, 1 (3), 225–36.

Head, B. W. (2008). Research and evaluation: Three lenses of evidence-based policy. *The Australian Journal of Public Adminstration*, 67 (1), 1–11.

Hemmelgarn, A. L., Glisson, C. & James, L. R. (2006). Organizational culture and climate: Implications for services and interventions research. *Clinical Psychology: Science and Practice*, 13 (1), 73–89.

Holzer, P., Lewig, K., Bromfield, L. M. & Arney, F. (2008). *Research Use in the Australian Child and Family Welfare Sector*. Australian Institute of Family Studies, Melbourne.

Kessler, M. L., Gira, E. & Poertner, J. (2005). Moving best practice to evidence-based practice in child welfare. *Families in Society*, 86 (2), 244–50.

Leigh, A. (2009). What evidence should social policymakers use? *Economic Roundup*, 1, 27–43.

Lewig, K., Arney, F. & Scott, D. (2006). Closing the research-policy, research-practice gaps: Ideas for child and family services. *Family Matters*, 74, 12–19.

Little, M., Kohm, A. & Thompson, R. (2005). The impact of residential placement on child development: Research and policy implications. *International Journal of Social Welfare*, 14 (3), 200–9.

Lochman, J. E. (2006). Translation of research into interventions. *International Journal of Behavioural Development*, 30 (1), 31–8.

Lomas, J. (2000). Connecting research and policy. *Printemps* (Spring), 140–4.

Marston, G., & Watts, T. (2003). Tampering with the evidence: A critical appraisal of evidence-based policy-making. *An Australian Review of Public Affairs*, 3 (3), 143–63.

Palinkas, L. A., Aarons, G. A., Chorpita, B. F., Hoagwood, K., Landsverk, J. & Weisz, J. R. (2009). Cultural exchange and the implementation of evidence-based practices. *Research on Social Work Practice*, 19 (5), 602–12.

Petch, A. (2009). Guest editorial. *Evidence & Policy*, 5 (2), 117–26.

Petr, C. G. (ed.) (2009). *Multidimensional Evidence-Based Practice: Synthesizing Knowledge, Research and Values*. Routledge, New York.

Petrosino, A., Turpin-Petrosino, C. & Buehler, J. (2009). "Scared Straight' and other juvenile awareness programs for preventing juvenile delinquency (Review)', The Cochrane Library. Available online at: /mrw.interscience.wiley.com/cochrane/clsysrev/articles/CD002796/pdf_fs.html

Pyra, K. (2003). 'Knowledge translation: A review of the literature', Prepared for the Nova Scotia Health Research Foundation: Pyra Management Consulting Services. Available online at: www.nshrf.ca/AbsPage.aspx?id=1280&siteid=1&lang=1

Sackett, D. L., Rosenberg, W. M. C., Gray, J. A. M., Haynes, R. B. & Richardson, W. S. (1996). Evidence based medicine: What it is and what it isn't. *British Medical Journal*, 312, 71–2.

Scott, D. (2001). The practice sensitive researcher. In J. Higgs and A. Titchen (eds), *Professional Practice in Health, Education and the Creative Arts*. Blackwell Science, Oxford, UK.

Scott, D. (2002). Adding meaning to measurement: The value of qualitative methods in practice research. *British Journal of Social Work*, 32, 923–30.

Seethaler, S. (2009). *Lies, Damned Lies and Science: How to Sort through the Noise around Global Warming, the Latest Health Claims, and Other Scientific Controversies*. Pearson Education Inc., Upper Saddle River, NJ.

Shonkoff, J. (2000). Science, policy, and practice: Three cultures in search of a shared mission. *Child Development*, 71 (1), 181–7.

Walshe, K. & Rundall, T. G. (2001). Evidence-based management: From theory to practice in health care. *The Millbank Quarterly*, 79 (3), 429–57.

Spreading promising ideas and innovations in child and family services

Kerry Lewig, Fiona Arney, Mary Salveron, Helen McLaren, Christine Gibson and Dorothy Scott

Learning goals

This chapter will enable you to:
1. Recognise the importance of spreading good ideas in child welfare
2. Understand Diffusion of Innovation Theory and how it can be utilised in the transfer of programs, policies and practice in child and family services
3. Understand why some innovative programs and practices spread and why some fail to be adopted by child and family services
4. Recognise conditions under which good ideas (programs, practices, policies and ways of working) spread
5. Understand the facilitators of and barriers to the wider adoption of successful child and family approaches in Australia.

Introduction

The services provided by the child and family sector are broad and range from addressing the private troubles of families, including family breakdown, drug and alcohol abuse, domestic violence and mental health disorders to public issues faced by communities encompassing poverty, homelessness and unemployment. Within the sector, innovative models, programs, ideas, policies, practices, beliefs, behaviours, approaches and new ways of working continue to emerge to address these issues. A number of such innovative approaches have been described throughout this book. The provision and delivery of child and family services is constantly evolving. There is a long history of innovation in the child welfare field, ranging from the introduction of foster care in South Australia in the 1870s (Spence, 1907), the spread of the kindergarten movement in the early 20th century (Wollons, 2000), to the contemporary social marketing strategies to modify parenting behaviour.

Whether such innovations were developed locally (are home-grown) or have been imported from overseas, there is significant commitment from Commonwealth, state and territory governments and non-government organisations to fund and implement such innovations and initiatives to enhance the safety, protection and well-being of children. Increasingly, funders and service delivery organisations are paying attention to the cost effectiveness of programs and their abilities to deliver outcomes for their target groups (Lewig, Arney & Scott, 2006). With this focus, has come the move towards evidence-based and evidence-informed practice in the field of child and family services as a way of maximising the impact of scarce resource dollars (see the previous chapter for more detail on evidence-informed practice).

Despite a rise in the number of innovations being implemented across Australia to promote child safety and well-being, efforts to replicate, sustain and scale up effective innovations have proven difficult both in Australia and overseas (Schorr, 1997; Scott, 2000). Consequently, child and family practitioners, policy makers and researchers and various funding bodies are interested in obtaining answers to the following questions:

- How and why do innovations spread?
- What makes an innovation effective?
- What conditions are conducive to spreading innovations?
- What are the conditions under which the spread of an innovation are most likely to fail?
- What makes an innovation sustainable?

In an attempt to answer these questions, we have brought together our knowledge about what enhances the spread of promising programs in this chapter, and ideas about what helps and what hinders evidence-based practice and policy in the previous chapter. Others have also closely linked these two objectives (see Sanson-Fisher, 2004; Fixsen et al., 2005).

Millions of dollars are spent in developing new ways of working and evaluating them for their effectiveness. Without considered attention given to how these programs and practices may be communicated, adopted, implemented and then sustained in practice, the initial investments will essentially be wasted and the effects only visible at the local level (Fixsen et al., 2005). Haines and Jones (1994, p. 1488) present the challenge as one of 'promot[ing] the uptake of innovations that have been shown to be effective, delay[ing] the spread of those that have not yet been shown to be effective, and prevent[ing] the uptake of ineffective innovations'.

One body of knowledge that can help answer some of the questions about spreading good ideas and innovations in child protection is the Diffusion of Innovation Theory. Diffusion of Innovation Theory allows us to examine why some ideas, particularly programs and practices, thrive and why some fail to be adopted (Salveron, Arney & Scott, 2006). For example, why is it that the promising Family Group Conferencing Model for children in need of care and/or protection, adopted from New Zealand, is successful in some jurisdictions across Australia but fails to spread in others? Why is it that given the evidence and advantages supporting some innovations, they still fail to spread and be used? Understanding this will hopefully enable those working in child and family welfare to scale up and transfer effective programs and initiatives throughout the field.

Diffusion of Innovation Theory

Innovations are recognised as 'something new' by an individual or group of individuals and include new ideas, products, practices, policies, programs, approaches, behaviours and ways of thinking or doing something that is considered different to the current practice (Osganian, Parcel & Stone, 2003; Rogers, 2003). According to Brown (2003), new ideas or innovations come about in different ways, for example through dissatisfaction or discontentment with existing systems or as part of being seen to be 'doing something' to solve a problem.

Diffusion of Innovations Theory seeks to explain how these new ideas, programs, and products are spread among groups of people over time. The theory is based on the work of Everett Rogers and authors such as Greenhalgh and colleagues in the UK. Diffusion of Innovations Theory originated in the agricultural and rural sociology sector in the 1940s and has since been applied in a wide range of fields and disciplines including sociology, education, and health. For example, in the education sector, the theory has been used to study the factors that influence the process of school improvement (Huberman, 1993), while in the public health arena, diffusion theory has been used to examine the spread of new behaviours such as screening for high blood pressure, mammography, immunisations, smoking cessation, physical activity and eating low fat foods (Rogers, 2003, pp. 44–5). While some preliminary research has been conducted to examine the diffusion of specific interventions within the social services (e.g., Family Group Conferencing in the UK by Brown, 2003), it is not known to what extent the factors influencing the process of diffusion identified by research in other fields are applicable to innovations in child and family services.

The process of diffusion and the factors believed to influence the diffusion of an idea, program or product are illustrated in the model below (see Figure 13.1).

The model is a simplified linear illustration of a process which in reality is non-linear and dynamic. The process of diffusion in reality is influenced by many factors such as complex service, social and political systems, which can make the process haphazard and unpredictable (Nutley, Davies & Walter, 2002). As illustrated by the model, the process of diffusion involves becoming aware of an idea or innovation (*communication*), deciding to use an idea or innovation (*adoption*), implementing the idea or innovation, either in its current form or adapting it to suit personal, organisational or social requirements (*implementation, replication* or *adaptation*) and continuing to use the idea or innovation over time (*sustainability*) (Salveron, Arney & Scott, 2006).

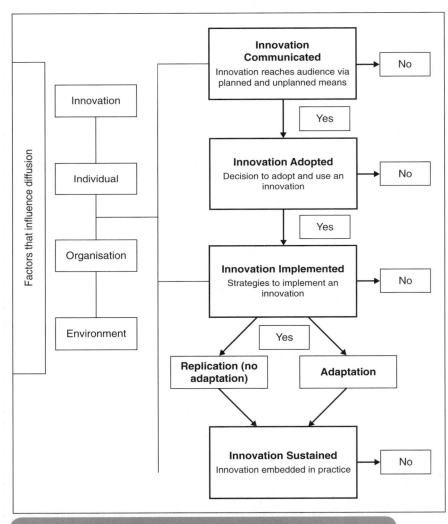

Figure 13.1: Representation of diffusion as a linear process (Salveron, Arney & Scott, 2006)

Similar to the factors that influence the uptake of research described in the previous chapter, Figure 13.1 shows that the process of diffusion is influenced by factors related to the innovation itself, the individuals who adopt an innovation, the organisational context and the wider socio-economic environment (Bowen & Zwi, 2005; Flueren, Wiefferink & Paulussen, 2004; Greenhalgh et al., 2005; Salveron, Arney & Scott, 2006). These factors are outlined below as they pertain to innovative programs and services.

The innovation

Characteristics of the program or service

Research tells us that the characteristics of an innovation contribute to making it more likely to spread and be taken up by others. The characteristics of innovations that result in successful diffusion include: the relative advantage that the innovation offers over an old or current idea or practice (this might include improved efficiency, effectiveness or cost effectiveness); compatibility of the innovation with the needs, values and norms of the user; simplicity of use and the ability to trial the innovation; clearly observable benefits of using the innovation; a low level of risk associated with using the innovation; and the ease with which the knowledge required to use the innovation can be transferred to others. It is also beneficial if the innovation can be supported by current technological and support systems or can be readily implemented to support the innovation (Greenhalgh et al., 2005; Rogers, 2003).

Adaptation versus adoption

There is conflicting evidence about how the degree of adaptation of an innovation affects the extent of its diffusion. For example, the Diffusion of Innovation literature suggests that the more adaptable an innovation is to the needs of the user the more easily it will be diffused (Dusenbury & Hansen, 2004). This can be seen in the successful diffusion of the kindergarten across the world where each country was able to reinvent the kindergarten concept to incorporate cultural and national values and aspirations (Wollons, 2000).

The program implementation literature, however, indicates that the likelihood of successful implementation is increased if the fidelity of the program (the extent to which it resembles the original) is maintained throughout the implementation process and any modifications are made to it only after full implementation has been achieved (Fixsen, Naoom et al., 2005; Rogers, 2003). Adapting a program to a new context may mean that the effective components of the program may be compromised or lost (Schorr & Auspos, 2003). As described in the previous chapter, the implementation of evidence-based practices with fidelity monitoring might also increase staff retention (Aarons et al., 2009).

Reflective questions

Think of a program or practice you know well. Where and when did it start? What modifications have been made to it since it was developed or adopted at this site of practice? Why was it adapted/refined? How might these modifications have improved its effectiveness? How might they have reduced it? Has the program been formally evaluated in its original state and in the form it is now?

The individual

Individuals come with their own skills, beliefs, values and experiences and are not passive recipients of new ideas or innovations. Rather, people actively seek out new ideas, experiment with them, evaluate them, make sense of them, develop positive and/or negative feelings about them, challenge and modify them, and aim to improve them.

Rogers (2003) identified that people play different roles with regards to the introduction and implementation of a new idea or innovation, whom he subsequently categorised as: innovators, early adopters, early majority adopters, late majority adopters and laggards (see Box 13.1).

Box 13.1: Adopter categories

Innovators – venturesome, tolerant of risk, information seeking

---

Early adopters – opinion leaders, socially well respected, have the resources and tolerance of risk to try new things

---

Early majority – learn mainly from people they know, rely more on personal familiarity than science or theory, more risk averse than early adopters, adopt new ideas just before the average members of their social system

---

Late majority – sceptical, will adopt an innovation when it appears to be the status quo, peer pressure is needed to motivate adoption

---

Laggards – traditionalists, pay little attention to the opinions of others

---

Sources: Berwick, 2003; Rogers, 2003

Research indicates that 'early adopters' who are held in high regard and respected by their peers, and who act as 'champions' or 'opinion leaders' for a new idea or innovation, are particularly important to its successful diffusion. The professional roles and networks with which people identify also play an influential role in the spread of new ideas and innovations. For example, research from the health arena shows that 'ideas are more likely to spread naturally between individuals who identify with each other and each other's needs' (Salveron, Arney & Scott, 2006, p. 43). On the other hand, a study of the diffusion of Family Group Conferencing in the UK identified professional resistance as a major barrier to program implementation (Brown, 2005). In particular, professionals perceived Family Group Conferencing as changing their work practices by sharing power with family members – those who could not work with this power shift were far less likely to take up the innovation than those who could see potential benefits in sharing power with families.

Reflective question

Thinking about Rogers' model – how might you encourage the people you work with to adopt an idea that you regard as innovative and useful to your organisation?

The organisation

Innovations take time to spread within and among different organisations just as they do among different individuals. As with individuals, the characteristics of organisations play a significant role in the spread of promising innovations. The ability to identify these characteristics and the role that they play in the diffusion process is especially important for the child and family welfare sector as one of the main reasons cited for the lack of sustainability and replication of successful programs in child and family services is the failure to understand the institutions and systems within which programs are required to operate (Schorr, 1997; Scott, 2000).

It has been shown that programs are more likely to be successfully adopted where a 'learning organisation' culture exists, and there are visionary staff in pivotal positions, good managerial relations and strong proactive leadership with a clear strategic vision focused on sharing new knowledge (Greenhalgh et al., 2004). Staff cohesiveness and autonomy is also important, together with open communication, willingness to change, and a shared understanding of the organisation's vision and goals (Barwick et al., 2005; Fixsen et al., 2005). An organisation must also have the capacity to systematically integrate new knowledge, a process that is influenced by previously established organisational structures and roles, and the existing knowledge and skill base (Greenhalgh et al., 2004). Importantly, sufficient resources such as time, money, equipment, manuals, materials, performance evaluation, on-going training and access to expertise, need to be in place to support the staff delivering the program and to sustain the program over time.

The wider environment

Finally, environmental factors can also impact on the successful diffusion of promising programs and ideas. Health care research has shown that environmental factors related to the socio-economic infrastructure of the community, collaboration among community networks, regulations and legislation, urbanisation, competition among institutions to attract special-ised professionals and acquisition of prestige, competitive performance and legitimacy all impact on an organisation's decision and capacity to adopt new innovations (Bowen, 2005; Dobbins et al., 2002; Greenhalgh et al., 2004; Plsek, 2003; Westphal, Gulati & Shortell, 1997). Sometimes, there are politi-cally imposed constraints, incentives and mandates with which organisa-tions must contend. Furthermore, in times of environmental uncertainty, the uptake of new ideas or innovations may result more from 'peer group pressures associated with fads and fashions than evidence in support of their use' (Nutley, Davies & Walter, 2002, p. 19).

A lack of funding; competing priorities; a lack of advocacy; and the lack of incentive or a link to rewards or outcomes, have been identified as envi-ronmental barriers to the adoption and implementation of 'best practice' interventions in the field of child and family welfare (Chadwick Center, 2004; Lewig, Arney & Scott, 2006). Far less is known about the barriers to program uptake that relate to the characteristics, needs and preferences of potential program recipients – something of key importance when looking to reach vulnerable families who may not find it easy to engage with services (Salveron, Arney & Scott, 2006). Mulgan (2007) has more closely examined the need for strategies that match effective 'pull' (demand) for innovations with effective supply (or 'push') of services, concluding that very little is done to systematically address the gaps between supply and demand for promis-ing programs.

Examining the spread of promising programs in Australian child and family services

The Australian Centre for Child Protection, in partnership with the University of Bath and UnitingCare Burnside (a large, non-government welfare organisation based in New South Wales), conducted an Australian Research Council funded research project to examine the diffusion of seven promising programs within child and family services across Australia. The research used a mixed-method research design to examine the development or adoption and the implementation of the programs within UnitingCare Burnside (Burnside) and in other organisations across Australia. The seven programs were:

- Family Group Conferencing
- New Steps Home Visiting Program
- NEWPIN (New Parent and Infant Network)
- Intensive Family-Based Service
- Family Learning Centre
- Men in Families
- Moving Forward.

See the Appendix at the end of this chapter for a more detailed description of the programs and www.burnside.org.au/organisation for evaluation details of the programs.

Of the seven programs, the first four were 'imported' from overseas and the final three developed locally. They were selected for the research because they met the following criteria: they appeared to address significant issues; to be promising in their original form; others had expressed an interest in implementing them; and there was sufficient evidence to consider their utility (Schorr & Auspos, 2003). Historical case studies of each innovation were developed from archival data, other organisational documents and from semi-structured interviews with relevant persons. The extent of spread of the innovations and the factors seen to help or hinder their spread were examined through a survey completed by 223 child and family services across Australia and through 92 in-depth interviews with individuals from those organisations (McLaren, et al., 2008).

Findings

Context for development and adoption of the innovations within Burnside

Burnside is a learning organisation which enacts an action learning philosophy of program development, piloting, evaluation and refinement. At the time the innovations were adopted or developed (mid 1990s to the early 2000s), Burnside was making a transition from mainly providing out-of-home care services to working across the continuum of care including prevention, early intervention, family preservation and out-of-home care. During this time, Burnside developed a strategic plan which identified geographic areas of New South Wales requiring more concentrated efforts along this continuum of care. Believing that the ability to shift resources is critical for the development of a culture of innovation meant that flexibility was also being promoted so as to be able to continue to meet the shifting needs of children and families. The description used by Burnside was changed from 'client focused' to 'client needs driven' to reinforce this need for program responsiveness and flexibility. Together, these activities provided a fertile time for the development and adoption of innovative practices.

Communication and persuasion about the innovations in organisations across Australia

As part of the nationwide survey we asked respondents from child and family services if they had heard about any of the seven programs, and if so, if they had ever considered adopting the program, or if they had something similar to the program (see Figure 13.2). In follow-up interviews, respondents described a range of ways in which they had come to hear about the programs. Some of the ways included through: conference presentations; staff who had previously been at Burnside talking about or promoting the programs in their new workplaces; involvement in training where the programs were discussed; programs being identified while conducting literature reviews; direct experience from agency involvement with or referral to the programs; membership of networks in which the programs were discussed; and 'osmosis' (some respondents couldn't recall how programs had come to their attention over time).

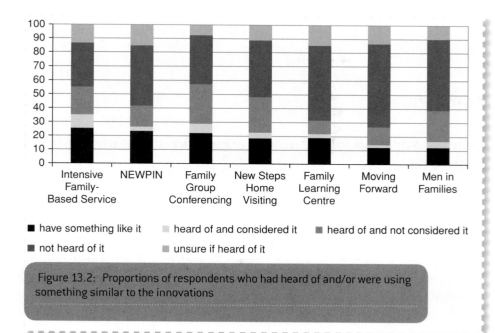

Figure 13.2: Proportions of respondents who had heard of and/or were using something similar to the innovations

An important factor that appeared related to the degree of knowledge about the programs was the origin of the program (e.g., whether it was developed overseas or in Australia), with a tendency for imported programs to be more well-known and in some cases seen as preferred to their domestic counterparts. Those programs which most of the respondents had heard of included the imported programs, with the exception of NEWPIN (see Figure 13.2). Evidence of the effectiveness of programs played some part in this process as well.

> Our organisation is continually looking to support new program models from overseas which have been going for a few years and which have already built an evidence base and a reputation, self-fund them for the first five years and build our own evidence in our own region, then seek external funding to sustain the programs. From our experience, government funders are more likely to fund imported programs and are more likely to take their 'goodness' on face value because they are from the UK or the US. We know we are less likely to win funding for home-grown programs. – Respondent who had heard about NEWPIN

The role of champions both from within and external to Burnside was also seen as playing an important role in communicating about programs and persuading potential adopters of the programs' effectiveness. Such championing included highlighting the programs through mass media, at conferences, in discussions with funding bodies and in new employment contexts.

> A staff member who used to work at Burnside brought the idea for the play, sing and music group to this organisation. Based on her practice wisdom, it was believed that the group could have some therapeutic benefits that might transfer into people's lives. – Respondent who was using something like the Family Learning Centre

Adoption and implementation of the innovations across Australia

Large proportions of the sample had programs similar to the innovations (see Figure 13.2). While these patterns are similar to those who had heard of the innovations, the proportion of respondents who claimed to have something similar to the NEWPIN Program was as high as, if not higher than, those who had something similar to the other innovations. This might suggest that while NEWPIN had not been communicated as widely (or the name of it may be less well-known), the principles and ideas behind it have found currency with a number of organisations across Australia.

For those in the survey component of the study who had heard of each innovation but did not have something like it, the reasons for non-use of the programs are given in Figure 13.3. For all programs, the most frequent

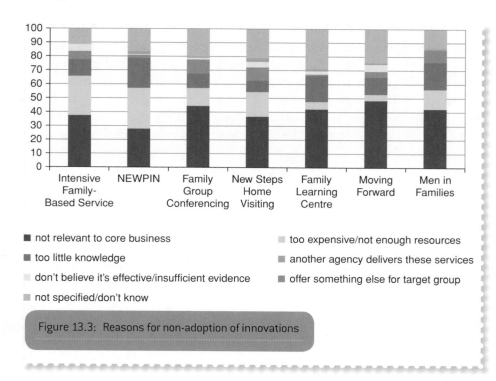

Figure 13.3: Reasons for non-adoption of innovations

reason for not adopting the programs (or something like it) was that they were not seen as relevant to the agencies' core business. The decision about whether to adopt a program or not seemed to be influenced by a number of other factors – not least of which was the availability of resources (human and financial) to be able to implement the program.

> *The problem is that you have to expend the resources to train volunteers and have less guarantee of a stable workforce. The supervision and training costs are high and the service provides a lower level of expertise. – Respondent who had heard of New Steps Home Visiting Program*

Respondents also spoke about already having programs that met the needs targeted by the innovations, and presumably the innovations were not seen as having enough relative advantage to consider replacing the current programs. Related to this, the perceived effectiveness of the programs and the perceived costs and benefits of implementation were also instrumental in decision making about the adoption or non-use of the innovations.

> *We have an advisory committee and a board. The obstacles with the intensive service are that a lot more money, staff and resources are put into clients than in the traditional refuge models. The stress on workers is high, particularly when there are more outreach clients. It takes a lot to argue for a service that costs more than the previous three that the government cut. – Respondent who had something similar to the Intensive Family-Based Service*

As with the perceived lack of organisation–innovation fit described above, the degree to which innovations fit with individual practitioners' current and preferred ways of working was an important factor influencing uptake and effectiveness of innovations within organisations.

> *We were instructed to use it as a process that is embedded in legislation. However before Family Group Meetings were in use, our workers would get the families here and tell them before court what they have to do – 'like it or lump it'. With Family Group Meetings this has shifted. Many workers have learned to let go of the power because they have seen that it is quite positive to family change and ownership of decisions. In fact, workers who have had more difficulty with Family Group Meetings are those who are more authoritarian and who have traditionally used their own power in practice. My observations are that those workers have had the least positive outcomes. – Respondent who was using something like Family Group Conferencing*

Replication or transplantation of the innovations studied

Consistent with the literature, one of the strongest factors that enabled programs to diffuse was their ability to be flexibly adapted to new contexts and to meet local needs and resource levels. For example, versions of Family Group Conferencing, in the most part adapted from the original New Zealand model (see Chapter 10), were seen in a diverse range of contexts including a sibling sexual assault service, long day care, parent–youth conflict resolution, a service for young parents who are homeless, and in statutory child protection services across Australia. However, in some cases this transplantation of programs to adapt them to new contexts was seen to cause dilution to the potential effects of the innovations and was inconsistent with the values and principles of the original innovation.

> *The government's use of it, without the 'family-only time' means that families are not given responsibility and power to be truly engaged in making their decisions and owning them. You know, when people are in crisis the people they can speak to happens privately. The model needs to reflect this. They also don't always bring in Indigenous workers, so that is an issue too. – Respondent who had heard of Family Group Conferencing*

Sustainability of the programs

The sustainability of programs was seen to be supported in part by activities such as evidence building (e.g., developing a sound body of evidence about the effectiveness or promise of programs meant they were less likely to be defunded), the availability of resources, relationships with funding bodies and the political climate. Where there were abundant resources and the programs fitted with the political ethos at the time, programs that had been developed or adopted were able to be sustained in their sites of practice.

All the way through our program, the government has been supportive of our work. We have a high level of credibility in the service sector. We are the only service of this type in [this state] and we are in high demand. However, we put a lot of effort into nurturing our relationship with [the state department responsible for funding]. – Respondent who had something similar to Intensive Family-Based Service

Implications from the research – innovation–evaluation–dissemination–transplantation strategy in child and family services

The findings related above, together with those from other research in the field of diffusion of social innovations highlights the need for rigorous and systematic processes of 'innovation, evaluation, dissemination and transplantation' (Scott, 2006, p. 20).

At the innovation development stage, Hetherington (2008) recommends focusing on four properties of successful social innovations: 1) they focus on a specific unmet social need; 2) they creatively match assets (e.g., resources, skills and technologies) to capabilities of participants; 3) they involve a process of iterative development and refinement, rather than 'big bang' breakthroughs; and 4) they demonstrate flexibility and adaptability.

Our research highlighted the need for positive, on-going relationships with funding bodies (and if possible, having the ability to self-fund programs, at least for piloting) to facilitate this development and innovation process. Other key factors associated with the ability to innovate and/or adopt programs for local contexts included risk taking and perseverance, and having an organisational culture that supports innovation and new ways of working. However, research shows that a cohesive organisational culture does not necessarily produce the 'tension for change' required to modify ways of working (Jaskyte & Dressler, 2005). The role of planning and strategy to meet local community needs, to meet the needs of the organisation and to meet the needs of funding bodies are also important.

The pressure to deliver services to a specific population rather than promote the dissemination of innovation, may limit the spread of promising approaches. Practitioners are concentrating on optimising outcomes for their clients and are dealing with heavy workloads. The results of our research highlighted the important role that evaluation and dissemination of these findings can play. Unless provisions are made for this at the start of programs (or unless it is made a part of someone's role) this phase of the diffusion process is likely to be overlooked or to happen in an ad hoc, haphazard fashion. Our research highlights a need for programs and practices to produce and communicate their evidence base 'to publish or present, or to perish'. Where possible, the evidence base should include details of estimated costs and benefits of the programs – this will greatly enhance the powers of persuasion of the program. Similarly, being able to identify and engage champions within and outside the organisation will greatly enhance the likelihood of program uptake and highlights the credibility of the program. It is also important that practitioners, organisations and researchers are open to the possibility that research will not provide evidence of an innovation's efficacy or effectiveness. Action research methods that include components of consultation, research and program refinement, allow this information to be used as a part of program improvement strategies.

The flexibility of programs has consistently been highlighted as a key factor in diffusion – it is important to consider this in the design and dissemination stages. An entire program might be less likely to spread than some of its components or key principles, as these can be adapted to a wider range of contexts and organisational mandates (Brocklehurst & Liabo, 2004). Having a range of programs, practices and/or principles available to meet the emerging or future needs of funding bodies and service users is a strategy likely to further enhance the chances of uptake.

Conclusion

This chapter has provided an overview of the Diffusion of Innovation Theory that centres on how the adoption or adaptation of a new idea, policy, product or practice can be promoted or hindered. Drawing on our own research and that of other fields such as health and education, diffusion research offers some rich ideas about why some ideas and innovations spread in child and family services and why some do not. The process of adopting innovations is influenced by characteristics related to the individual, organisation, environment and innovation (Dobbins et al., 2002). While there is no prescriptive approach for diffusing innovations in a given population, one needs to pay close attention to the complex interrelationships among the factors and the unpredictable diffusion process, before promoting and spreading new ideas or innovations. It is therefore paramount to consider all aspects of the innovation–evaluation–dissemination–transplantation strategy.

Given the field of child and family welfare abounds with innovation (in terms of programs, policies and practices), diffusion theory helps us learn about program exportability and effectiveness in less controlled conditions. Equally, it is envisaged that the development of such a framework with specific application to child protection and more broadly to the human services sector will increase the capacity of child protection and other service organisations to track the diffusion and sustainability of programs they have developed locally or imported from overseas. In doing this, we believe we can enhance the ability of individuals to take on new ideas and innovations and increase an organisation's capacity to spread promising programs that promote child safety and well-being by developing guidelines for successful diffusion in child and family services.

Activities

Imagine your organisation is interested in trialling a new parenting program (locally developed or imported from overseas) designed for working with families with multiple and complex needs. Using the checklist for spreading good ideas in child protection in Box 13.2, discuss with your colleagues the barriers you may face in implementing or spreading a program that relate to the innovation (program), the individuals concerned, the organisation and the environment.

Think of a program, practice or idea that you have implemented or that has been implemented in your workplace. Draw a time line of the uptake of this innovation and highlight key events along the way. Identify what has helped and what has hindered this process and see if these barriers and facilitators related to the innovation, the individuals implementing the innovation, characteristics of your organisation, or the broader environment. Is there sufficient evidence to justify its spread? If so, what might help to further spread this innovation?

Box 13.2: Spreading Good Ideas and Innovations in Child and Family Services Checklist

Characteristics of the new idea or innovation:

- **Advantage:** Does the new program have advantages over the current program or way of doing things? Has it been evaluated and shown to be effective? Is the program cost effective?
- **Compatibility:** Does the new program fit with the existing values of yourself (as the practitioner), your team and the organisation? What would be the consequences if the program was to be implemented and there are individuals who are not fully convinced of the program?
- **Complexity:** Is it easy and straightforward to implement and deliver?
- **Observability:** Can the program be seen straight away in action? What changes have been seen?
- **Trialability:** Do other people have the opportunity to test the new program on a small scale first?
- **Reinvention/adaptation:** Do others have the ability to change aspects of the program? What are the positives and negatives of changing parts of the program? How are the changes/adaptations documented, assessed and monitored?

- **Potential risks:** What are the risks associated with the program? (e.g., what if it doesn't work?, what if referrals to the program do not come through? what if the recipients of the program don't like the program?)
- **Nature of knowledge:** Are all elements of the program clear? Are there step-by-step instructions available for the implementation of the program from start to finish?
- **Support:** If there are difficulties with using and implementing the program, can the original developers be contacted? Are there people to help/assist?
- **Support and resources:** Does your organisation fully support the program? Are the resources realistic? What plans are there to keep the program operating?
- **Sound knowledge and skill base:** Do you have the right people to run the program? Are there individuals within the organisation that need to be upskilled?
- **Communication:** Are there opportunities for people to regularly get together and discuss the program so that experiences can be shared and discussed?
- **Leadership:** Does the program have full support from management? Does top management provide strong and competent leadership and vision?
- **Risk-taking climate:** Are you more likely to be punished or rewarded for taking risks, such as introducing a program? Have you explored how your organisation is going to embed the program into routine practice, so it is sustainable?
- **System readiness:** Is the organisation ready or prepared for the change?
- **Implementation:** Is the organisation coping with the change as the program is implemented?
- **Reinvention/adaptation:** Does the program need to be customised and adapted to suit the local context?
- **Feedback:** What plans are there for evaluating the program as it is implemented? How will the results of the evaluation be communicated to those within and those outside the organisation?

Useful websites

Nutley, S. Davies, H. & Walter, I. (October 2002). Conceptual synthesis 1: Learning from the Diffusion of Innovations: www.ruru.ac.uk/PDFs/ Learning%20from%20the%20Diffusion%20of%20Innovations.pdf

'Will It Work Here? – A Decision-Maker's Guide to Adopting Innovations'. Agency for Healthcare Research and Quality: www.innovations.ahrq.gov/ resources/InnovationAdoptionGuide.pdf

References

Aarons, G. A., Sommerfield, D. H., Hecht, D. B., Silovsky, J. F. & Chaffin, M. J. (2009). The impact of evidence-based practice implementation and fidelity monitoring on staff turnover: Evidence for a protective effect. *Journal of Consulting and Clinical Psychology*, 77 (2), 270–80.

Barwick, M. A., Boydell, K. M., Stasiulis, E., Ferguson, H. B., Blase, K. & Fixsen, D. (2005). *Knowledge Transfer and Evidence-Based Practice in Children's Mental Health.* Children's Mental Health Ontario, Toronto.

Berwick, D. (2003). Disseminating innovations in health care. *JAMA*, 289, 1969–75.

Bowen, S. & Zwi, A. (2005). Pathways to 'evidence-informed' policy and practice. A framework for action. *Policy Forum*, 2 (7), 600–5.

Brocklehurst, N. & Liabo, K. (2004). Evidence nuggets: Promoting evidence-based practice. *Community Practitioner*, 77 (10), 371–5.

Brown, L. (2003). Mainstream or margin? The current use of family group conferences in child welfare practice in the UK. *Child & Family Social Work*, 8 (4), 331–40.

Brown, L. (2005). 'Innovation in social work: Family Group Conferencing: A case study'. Paper presented at the 2005 European PUBLIN Conference, UCL, Cork.

Chadwick Center (2004). *Closing the Quality Chasm in Child Abuse Treatment: Identifying and Disseminating Best Practices – The Findings of the Kauffman Best Practices Project to Help Children.* Children's Hospital and Health Center for Children and Families, San Diego.

Dobbins, M., Ciliska, D., Cockeril, R., Barnsley, J. & DiCenso, A. (2002). A framework for the dissemination and utilisation of research for health-care policy and practice. *Online Journal of Knowledge Synthesis for Nursing*, 9 (7).

Dusenbury, L. & Hansen, W. B. (2004). Pursuing the course from research to practice. *Prevention Science*, 5 (1), 55–9.

Fixsen, D. L., Naoom, S. F., Blase, K. A., Friedman, R. M. & Wallace, F. (2005). *Implementation Research: A Synthesis of the Literature.* University of Florida, Tampa, FL.

Flueren, M., Wiefferink, K. & Paulussen, T. (2004). Determinants of innovation within health care organisations: Literature review and Delphi study. *International Journal of Quality in Health Care*, 16 (2), 107–23.

Greenhalgh, T., Robert, G., Bate, P., Macfarlane, F. & Kyriakidou, O. (2005). *Diffusion of Innovations in Health Service Organizations: A Systematic Literature Review.* Blackwell Publishing, Malden, MA.

Greenhalgh, T., Robert, G., Macfarlane, F., Bate, P. & Kyriakidou, O. (2004). Diffusion of innovations in health service organisations: Systematic review and recommendations. *Millbank Quarterly*, 82, 581–629.

Haines, A. & Jones, R. (1994). Implementing findings of research. *British Medical Journal*, 308, 1488–92.

Hetherington, D. (2008). Case studies in social innovation: A background paper. *Percapita Research Paper*, 1–13.

Huberman, M. (1993). Linking the practitioner and researcher communities for school improvement. *School Effectiveness and School Improvement*, 4 (1), 1–16.

Jaskyte, K. & Dressler, W. (2005). Organizational culture and innovation in non-profit human services organizations. *Administration in Social Work*, 29 (2), 23–41.

Lewig, K., Arney, F. & Scott, D. (2006). Closing the research-policy, research-practice gaps: Ideas for child and family services. *Family Matters*, 74, 12–19.

McLaren, H., Gibson, C., Arney, F., Brown, L. & Scott, D. (2008). 'Sowing the seeds of innovation: Exploring strategies for sustaining the spread of innovative approaches in child and family work'. Paper presented at the The History and Future of Social Innovation Conference, Adelaide.

Mulgan, G. (2007). 'Ready or not? Taking innovation in the public sector seriously'. Paper presented at the National Empowerment for Science, Technology and the Arts, London.

Nutley, S., Davies, H. & Walter, I. (2002). *Conceptual Synthesis 1: Learning from the Diffusion of Innovations*. Research Unit for Research Utilisation, University of St Andrews, St Andrews, UK.

Osganian, S. K., Parcel. G. S., & Stone, E. J. (2003). Institutionalisation of a school health promotion program: Background and rationale of the CATCH-ON study. *Health Education and Behaviour*, 30 (4), 410–17.

Plsek, P. (2003). 'Complexity and the adoption of innovation in health care'. Paper presented at the Accelerating Quality Improvement in Health Care: Strategies to Speed the Diffusion of Evidence-Based Innovations Conference, Washington, DC.

Rogers, E. (2003). *Diffusion of Innovations* (5th edn). Free Press, New York.

Salveron, M., Arney, F. & Scott, D. (2006). Sowing the seeds of innovation: Ideas for child and family services. *Family Matters*, (73), 38–45.

Sanson-Fisher, R. W. (2004). Diffusion of innovation theory for clinical change. *Medical Journal of Australia*, 180 (6), S55–6.

Schorr, L. (1997). *Common Purpose: Strengthening Families and Neighbourhoods to Rebuild America*. Anchor Books, New York.

Schorr, L. & Auspos, P. (2003). Usable information about what works: Building a broader and deeper knowledge base. *Journal of Policy Analysis and Management*, 22 (4), 669–76.

Scott, D. (2000). Embracing what works: Building communities that strengthen families. *Children Australia*, 25 (2), 4–9.

Scott, D. (2006). 'Sowing the seeds of innovation in child protection'. Paper presented at the Australasian Conference on Child Abuse and Neglect, Wellington, New Zealand.

Spence, C. H. (1907). *State Children in Australia*. Vardon & Sons, Adelaide.

Westphal, J. D., Gulati, R. & Shortell, S. M. (1997). Customization and conformity? An institutional and network perspective on the content and consequences of TQM adoption. *Administrative Services Quarterly*, 42 (2), 366–94.

Wollons, R. (2000). *Kindergartens and Cultures: The Global Diffusion of an Idea*. Yale University Press, New Haven, CT.

Appendix

Program descriptions

1. Family Group Conferencing (Family Decision Making) – aims to engage families (and significant others) in decision making relating to the care and support of children in need of protection. Conferencing is used to identify/agree on suitable means of maintaining the child's safety within the family/kin group. Targets families where concerns for the safety of children exist and where families agree to participate. The family is provided with information, time for private discussion, assisted with action planning to ensure a suitable care plan and follow up. Material assistance and child care is provided to facilitate attendance. Conferences are held at agreed venues and times and may take up to five hours.

2. New Steps Home Visiting Program – aims to support new parents so as to prevent social-emotional isolation and increase parent–child interaction and positive attachment. Targets parents and carers with children aged 0–2 years. Regular visits are used to provide material support, information, linking to other services and modelling of parenting strategies. Employed professionals train and supervise volunteer home visitors who attend parent's home weekly/fortnightly for an average of six months.

3. NEWPIN (New Parent & Infant Network) – aims to prevent child abuse. Targets parents with at least one child under five at risk of abuse. NEWPIN offers a therapeutic environment in which parents are able to develop new emotional skills through the provision of structured personal development, counselling and peer support. The information and support offered is non-judgemental. Parents are required to commit to attend at least two days per week. Education, play and care are provided for children. Parents usually stay for approximately two years, or until their youngest child starts school. Centres are home like environments and use a peer support system where past consumers are trained as 'befrienders' for future consumers.

4. Intensive Family-Based Service – aims to protect children known to be at risk, prevent unnecessary out-of-home placement and improve family functioning. Targets families in crisis, that is, where children are at the point of removal due to protective concerns. An experienced worker enters an intense engagement with a family during a time of crisis. Practitioners have a caseload of two families. A 'contract' is developed and agreed to. A strengths-based approach is used to focus on family skills and to build solutions via behavioural modelling,

linking to supports, counselling, education, information provision and material assistance. Contact is limited to six weeks. Staff are available 24 hours a day. Intervention occurs in the family's chosen environment, that is, home, shopping centre, school.

5. Family Learning Centre – aims to assist children to achieve educational success, to improve their family relationships and facilitate the development of local support networks. Targets disadvantaged families with children and involves individual tutoring (with primary students, parents are present), homework groups, social skills classes and after school groups, breakfast club, parent education groups, family counselling, TAFE adult literacy, playtime, home visiting and a children's program. Some children receive tutoring support for a significant period of time. Most of the activities are centre based, with some student engagement during school classes.

6. Men in Families – aims to assist fathers to acquire the information, skills and supports needed to contribute positively to the well-being of their children. Targets first-time fathers and works in conjunction with a hospital-based antenatal program. Activities promote a 'dad friendly' environment and father inclusiveness in their child's care and development.

7. Moving Forward – aims to assist drug and/or alcohol users to recover from addiction and to attain a stable lifestyle. Other family members are assisted to cope with and assist this process, as well as developing strategies to improve the safety and welfare of any children involved. Targets homeless individuals affected by drugs, drug-affected parents and drug-abusing children, drug-affected young people living with their families and young people at risk. Bilingual workers provide drug counselling, personal and family counselling, intensive support, skill development, group therapy, information provision, practical assistance and community education. Individual work is conducted at the office, through home visits and after hours by arrangement.

Index